To Clint,

Best wishes

Tom Landry

THE DALLAS COWBOYS
WINNING
THE
BIG ONE

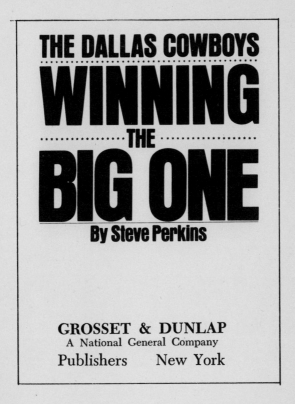

THE DALLAS COWBOYS
WINNING THE BIG ONE

By Steve Perkins

GROSSET & DUNLAP
A National General Company
Publishers   New York

for higher education

Contents

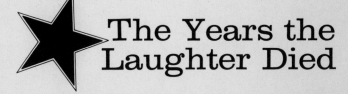 # The Years the Laughter Died

"The whole idea is someday you'll grow up to a point you can beat the Packers."
—TOM LANDRY

It was the kind of lavish party at which the Players' Association believes *their* money is being wasted by the National Football League. It was at the plush Fairmont Hotel in Dallas, January 1, 1972, the night before the National Conference title game between Dallas and San Francisco, the last gateway to the Super Bowl. A groaning buffet table (eight entrees, twelve seafood salads, choice of six desserts) circled three-foot blocks of ice carved into the initials "NFC." Two open bars flanked the entrance to the ballroom, where a strolling trio of banjo and guitar players sang the hit of the moment: "I've got a brand-new pair of roller skates, you got a brand-new key . . ."

And all alone, leaning against a pillar near the bar, stood Dallas Cowboy owner Clint Murchison, without even a Scotch-and-soda to keep him company. Murchison is often discovered like this in a crowd, a man of deceivingly pixyish appearance, who respects his own opinions mightily, frankly because he knows he can back any one of those opinions with millions of dollars. Therefore, he is a big man for *pronouncements,* and I suspected he had an apt one for the moment. He did.

"What is the word, Clint?" I said.

"Two weeks from tomorrow," Murchison said, "we will find out if Somebody Up There believes in justice."

The name of the Lord would not be invoked again this

Super Bowl trip until Miami quarterback Bob Griese explained the theological aspects of defeat: "God didn't want us to win the game, because he wanted to make us better people." If Griese had the correct formula for divine assistance, then the Dallas Cowboys in the previous five years had become good enough people to qualify for instant holy orders. They had certainly become the national joke—a team that waited for the Big Game before snatching defeat from the jaws of victory.

Season after season their dramatic points of frustration became legend, and the true Cowboy fan could capsule each incident with a catch phrase. 1966: Boeke moved. 1967: Starr sneaked. 1968: Kelly escaped. 1969: The punt hit Rayfield on the leg. 1970: Billy Ray Smith conned the refs.

This adversity was easy to take, at first, because those mid-1960s Cowboys had a quality of endearment about them. They were explosive, with Olympic champion Bobby Hayes catching the long bomb enough times to pace the entire NFL over the five-year period as the top touchdown scorer. And they had a certain carefree insouciance, established by their leader, a country boy from Mt. Vernon, Texas, named Joe (Dandy) Don Meredith. Meredith had a way, in dire circumstance, of reminding his teammates that this was only a game, but if they would stick with him things would turn out all right in the end. Two touchdowns behind, he would come into the huddle, snapping his fingers, singing, "I didn't *know* God made honky-tonk angels," or his other favorite, "I been down so long it looks like up to me." Meredith set the tone of the Cowboys from the last half of the 1965 season, when they first became winners, through his last curious defeat at Cleveland in the playoff game of 1968. There was laughter in the locker room. Red Hickey, then end coach for the Cowboys, circulated a story about a hard-luck lover who, when surprised by the husband, explained his presence in a closet with the words "Everybody's gotta be some place," and Meredith used it as a slogan weeks later as Dallas took over leadership in the Eastern Conference.

But Meredith never understood coach Tom Landry, and if Landry ever understood Meredith, it was plain he did not

approve of what he understood. "Roger Staubach," Landry
was to say three years later, "has more dedication and de-
termination than any quarterback we've had here." That
means more than Meredith or Craig Morton? "Each quarterback has his own good qualities," Landry replied.

Meredith had an old East Texas aphorism to cover the
Cowboys' hairbreadth losses in the title games: "If ifs and
buts were candy and nuts, we'd all have a Merry Christmas."
No catch phrase, however, could erase his essential differences with Landry. To the Cowboys' coach, the championship was next to Godliness—and the two were in fact
intertwined. Meredith wanted to win also, but he wanted to
smell the flowers along the way. Meredith finally came to believe that Landry was a football genius. That is, he believed
it intellectually. There is reason to doubt that he ever believed it viscerally, and this essential gap probably cost the
Cowboys a couple of championships.

The Dallas frustration at the two-yard line against Green
Bay in the NFL championship of 1966 has been laid at the
feet of poor Jim Boeke, the offensive left tackle. On second
down at the Packer one, Green Bay linebacker Ray Nitschke
raised an arm and pointed at Dallas tight end Pettis Norman
as Meredith was calling the snap signals. Boeke's eye caught
Nitschke's movement (an uncanny movement, because the
play was indeed to be a pass to Norman), and he moved
prematurely, penalizing the Cowboys back to the six-yard
line. That was not the play that caused Meredith sleepless
nights the next few weeks. Meredith was haunted by a third-
down pass from the six, to Norman on the two. Norman had
to come back from the end zone for the low pass and kneel
as he caught it. The instant before he got his knee off the
ground, Packer safety Tom Brown touched him, killing the
play there, though Norman then dived in for an apparent
six points. "I didn't have faith in my call," Meredith said
months later. "If there's one slogan that Landry pounds into
us again and again, it's 'Never give the defense more credit
than it deserves.' The play is designed on the premise that
the linebacker on that side—Dave Robinson—will not cover
Pettis. I guess I couldn't really believe it. Surely, I thought,

they'll cover him this time. So I came up hesitant when I threw the ball. That's why it was low. I hesitated looking for Robinson. If I'd thrown it chest high, Pettis could have waltzed in with the touchdown." Dallas was only seven points from sending the game into sudden death and stayed that way—seemingly forever.

Meredith's confession about his throw to Norman emphasized his basic trouble and the apparently crippling handicap to Cowboy fortunes: Meredith did not believe what Landry told him. Their lives were following different game plans, and the schism carried fatally to the football field. Meredith was a great natural athlete who performed with a gamesman's instincts, but constant introspection robbed him at crucial times of his native confidence. As the teams "warmed up" for the thirteen-below championship game in Green Bay, 1967, Meredith looked across the field where Bart Starr was going through a passing drill. "Bart was sort of sliding the ball off the palm of his hand," Meredith recalled later, "because the dang thing was too cold to grip like you always do. So I tried it—and threw the ball nine feet high." Meredith never got a touchdown for Dallas that day, and when the game hung in the balance and one first down would have preserved a 17-14 title victory, he turned to make a hand-off and fell down.

One of the team physicians of that era, Dr. John Gunn, worked out a psychological explanation. "In critical moments," Dr. Gunn said, "Meredith is hampered by a death-wish syndrome. Subconsciously, or perhaps at a shallow level of his conscious, he considers himself unworthy of being the best, being a championship quarterback. And when it's all there to grab, he finds a way to fail." Gunn is an intelligent man, and his theory on Meredith is an example of the lengths to which Cowboy fans were driven in those days to find a reason why pro football's number-one offense could not score in four downs from the two-yard line, or gain ten yards when ten yards meant a trip to the Super Bowl.

It escaped no one's notice that the Cowboys seldom, if ever, won a Big Game even during the regular season. As fate and Pete Rozelle would have it, Dallas had Green Bay on its league schedule in 1968. What a moment for sweet revenge! What a moment for showing the world what really would have happened if the Cowboys hadn't had to play on an ice floe the previous December! It was the seventh game of the season, and the Cowboys were unbeaten. The Packers meanwhile had fallen on hard times, with Vince Lombardi a silent step removed into the general manager's office, and one more defeat would eliminate them from their Central Division race. "Wouldn't it be just too damn bad," said Bob Lilly, "if we shoved them over the edge?"

This time Willie Davis broke Meredith's nose by yanking his helmet downward, and when the gutty quarterback returned one series later—unfortunately after Morton had thrown a touchdown bomb to Hayes—he was roundly booed by the Cotton Bowl crowd. Green Bay won the game 28-17.

Landry, ever the positive thinker, said in his locker-room press conference, "Well, this makes us six-and-one, and I would take six-and-one the second half of the season."

"Yes," I said, "but then you'd have to meet Green Bay again."

This was one of the few occasions I have seen Landry angry. He fairly barked his answer: "I'm not making any excuses for this team. The whole idea is someday you'll grow up to a point you can beat the Packers." Some fifteen minutes later Landry had calmed down enough to admit, "The only way we can redeem this loss is to win the championship."

It was during that season, on the team plane home from a road game, that Meredith asked, "What do you think Tom *really* thinks of me?" Meredith was in his ninth—and, as it turned out, his last—year with the team, and I had been covering it for five. But still he wanted to know.

"Don," I said, "I think Landry wishes you had never been born."

Meredith thought it over. "That's a little rough," he said, "but basically I think you are right."

The Cowboys did go 6-1 the rest of the season, as Landry had said, won their division and carried a five-game winning streak into the Eastern Conference title game at Cleveland.

Early in the first quarter Meredith threw for Hayes curling deep over the middle, and the pass was stolen by safety Mike Howell. Cleveland got a field goal out of it. The mistake seemed relatively inconsequential when Dallas went ahead 10-3, but it loomed large in Meredith's mind. "That play confused me," he said in retrospect. "It was a perfect pass and Bobby ran a beautiful route. Howell didn't figure to be anywhere *near* the ball. I knew what coverage they were supposed to be in, for the formation we were in, for the down-and-distance and for our position on the field. And I read my 'key' perfectly, the defensive backs' reactions which told me the area was open for the completion—and then Howell is there to intercept! It didn't jibe with anything we'd counted on going into the game. I started wondering if the whole deal was screwed up."

It was. When Cleveland intercepted two more Meredith passes in the third quarter and took a 24-10 lead, Landry took him out of the game and inserted Morton. The final score was 31-20.

An era had ended. Landry looked ahead to the 1969 training camp and said there would be competition at all positions, "not just at quarterback." Meredith, thirty-one, announced his retirement in July, "because it's just not as much fun as it was."

Things would be different now, the anti-Meredith forces were assured. Morton—the big, beautiful, curly-haired man with the golden arm, 6 foot 4 inches and 220 pounds, strong as a tank and never injury-prone—would take over and lead Dallas to the elusive championship. The Cowboys had chosen him over Joe Namath in the first round of the college draft for 1965, and more than once he had shown a knack for winning a game that seemed lost. As early as 1967, the season Dallas got into the title game with a 9-5 record, Morton had won three of the nine, subbing for an incapacitated Meredith. Now he had come on to be number one—in perfect timing with a Landry dictum that held that five years was the minimum experience to become a championship quarterback. But you do not hand over control of a football team as easily as a baton in a relay race. Along with his peculiar legacy Meredith left Morton a paragraph of advice: "The responsibility as a number one is great. Different people handle it different ways. What he's got to do is say, 'My name's Craig Morton and this is the way I do it. Not the way someone else does it. This is my game and if you want to play it my way, get on the wagon.' That's an important thing to get across."

Morton is surface-friendly, basically aloof. He had to make an effort to do things which flowed naturally for Meredith. That training camp, on the players' Wednesday nights off, Morton would get himself to Orlando's in time for the cocktail hour, and he would mingle with his teammates, buying more than his share of the drinks. The gesture was impressive, especially to a second-string defensive tackle, Ron East. "I know it looks artificial," East said, "but I appreciated it. When do I ever have a chance to talk to the quarterback? I hardly even knew the other guy [Meredith]."

Morton made light of his efforts. "The only way to be a leader is to *perform*," he said. "If I produce on the field, the team will have confidence in me, and leadership comes from there." When Morton led a 31-13 exhibition victory over the Packers, game captain Ralph Neely flipped him the Game Ball and said, "We're all with you." Eight months later Morton was to recall, "I knew I was really accepted after the Green Bay game, when Neely gave me the ball. That was one of the highlights of my athletic career."

Landry was equivocal about the change. "Initially," he said, "there will be some drop-off in our offense, but Craig has the potential to give us the best attack we've ever had." The club's progress through the league season was weirdly parallel to the year before. Six straight victories and then a defeat—by Cleveland—42-10. Dallas won its division with a 11-2-1 record, only a half game off the 1968 record, and again the Browns were waiting in the Eastern Conference championship game.

When the Cowboys went in at halftime, behind 17-0, the catcalls of their Cotton Bowl fans chased them up the ramp. Many times Meredith had been the recipient of boos, but now the crowd was giving the Bronx cheer to the whole team. "In the locker room," said Morton, "you could see the mental effect on everyone." The Cleveland triumph was more emphatic than the previous "upset," by 38-14.

Meredith meanwhile had been goofing off as a stockbroker in Houston and Dallas, having put most of his money into a new firm, forcefully named First of Texas. Upon Meredith's entrance into the market, the Dow-Jones average plummeted like a Green Bay thermometer, and the following spring I teased him about coming out of retirement.

"Why should I play this year when I didn't want to play last year?" he said.

"Because the Cowboys have done it without you," I said. "They blew the Big Game again. Which shows the other ones weren't your fault."

"Nobody but a stupid ass ever thought they were," Meredith said. And then he said, "There is too much pressure on the quarterback in the Cowboy system. He always gets the brunt of the criticism."

"Isn't it that way everywhere?"

"No," Meredith said. "Some places they fire coaches."

Meredith used to tell the newspapermen who covered the ball club, "You fellas are going to miss me when I'm gone." It was one of the truest things he ever said, because—perhaps coincidentally—with Meredith's departure an essential gaiety disappeared from the Cowboy training camp, from the practice-field locker room, from the team plane. At first I discounted most of this because I had too subjective a view; the earliest ramification of the new Cowboy style was a detachment from the press. In the summer of 1969 the press was suddenly barred from visiting in the players' wing of the dorm at Thousand Oaks, even at a player's invitation. On plane rides home from road games, the writers were allotted a thirty-minute period to circulate in the players' section and find out what really happened that afternoon. In previous years on the road the assistant coaches, Landry, the various club officials and the press dined together the night before the game. Since 1969 the coaches have gone their separate ways, and so, for the most part, have the writers. This was in spite of the fact that Dallas had the most benevolent coverage in the league.

The change went deeper than that. At the practice field

fewer players found their shoes filled with talcum, or their dress pants tied in knots and tossed in the shower. The Muzak seemed to have switched from rock to "Begin the Beguine." Didn't anybody here remember "You Got to Have Heart"? Or were they all gutted by defeat?

"Naw, that wasn't it," said veteran linebacker Jackie Burkett, who once had been with a championship Baltimore club. "Landry puts the screws on for the first exhibition game and he keeps tightening 'em. That's why the Cowboys are sick of football about the twelfth week of every season. They're mentally exhausted. I never spent a more tiring season in my life, and I didn't even play much."

Other things had been happening to the Cowboy team while it changed quarterbacks. The great scouting system kept feeding talent into the maturing squad. In 1969, Calvin Hill, Tom Stincic, Claxton Welch, Halvor Hagen, Clarence Williams. In 1970, Duane Thomas, Bob Asher, John Fitzgerald, Pat Toomay, Cliff Harris, Charlie Waters, John Douglas, Steve Kiner, Mark Washington. In 1971, Tody Smith, Bill Gregory, Rodney Wallace, Isaac Thomas, Ron Jessie, James Ford. Of those twenty, six were dealt off to stockpile draft choices (Hagen, Williams, Douglas, Kiner, Jessie, Ford). Trades brought Herb Adderley to solidify the defensive backfield and Lance Alworth and Billy Truax to boost the receiving corps.

The Cowboys were still the Computer Team as the club entered its second decade, and the organization's freewheeling way with a dollar kept pace with the image of their Texas millionaire owner. Office expenses of $100,342 in 1960 had climbed ten years later to $383,335.

The Cowboys lurched upward to achieve their greatest defeat, in Super Bowl V at Miami, and their grimmest days were still ahead. A starting receiver had to be traded, not by choice but because he had been convicted of a felony. A rookie running back saw his $73,000 in salary and bonuses melted away by taxes, by agents' commissions, by domestic troubles, and he became an angry black, a story that would not go away. Then they learned that their quarterback had made it through the previous season with the help of a hypnotist and that their other star receiver had paid extortionists $200 to call off a bombing of Landry's home. The vacillation of their head coach, who proved he could be equally hardheaded about *not* making a decision, kept them playing their first seven league games without a number-one quarterback. When the long victory streak to the Super Bowl championship got rolling, the triumphs were received on the squad with thundering ennui—even the last one.

"How could we get excited about beating Minnesota and San Francisco?" said Cornell Green. "We'd been there. There was only one game that mattered to us, the Super Bowl. Winning it was as great as I dreamed it would be—but it was inside, where you feel deep. I wasn't too excited about playing the game. I'd been in too many big games before."

Cornell had been there the years the laughter died.

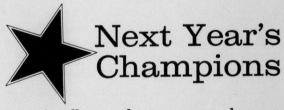 # Next Year's Champions

"I can't tell you what our game plan was. I'm not sure I know."

—CRAIG MORTON

This one had no color to match the four previous Super Bowls. It didn't have a first confrontation between the AFL-NFL. It didn't have the Lombardi Dynasty flavor of Super Bowl II, or the Joe Willie braggadocio of Super Bowl III, or the drama of a Len Dawson implicated in a gambling scandal the week of Super Bowl IV. It had to have something, so the nation's sportswriters stepped into the vacuum with a label: the *worst* Super Bowl. And Morton was the worst quarterback ever to appear in it.

The newsmen would huddle gingerly around Morton at the daily press conference, trying to think of tactful questions about his inefficiency. "It's eerie," Morton said to me after one such session. "They ask me about Tom calling all the plays. They want to know if my arm is sore, because we mostly ran the ball in the playoff games. What they really want to ask me is 'Besides handing off, what the hell do you *do?*' "

The Cowboys were lodged at the Galt Ocean Mile Hotel in Fort Lauderdale, and Tuesday through Thursday buses would deliver the writers from the NFL headquarters in Miami Beach. After bracing Landry en masse for forty-five minutes, they would spread out into an adjacent banquet room. Earlier, before Landry began talking, they had shouted out nominations to an NFL publicist, and now the chosen players were sitting here and there around the room, sur-

14

rounded by a cluster of chairs. Not all of the starters were called down for questioning, and the day's subjects were not always the same. George Andrie would be there on Tuesday, say, and Larry Cole on Wednesday. There was an embarrassment on Thursday, shared by both the writers and the NFL man, because no one had asked for Chuck Howley, the only All-NFL player in the game. Morton was there every day, as were Hayes, Lilly, Adderley, Neely, Thomas, the voluble Hill and center Dave Manders. The writers feel guilty about neglecting centers during the season and make up for it by filing reams of copy on the Super Bowl centers.

This element of Super Bowl week is not to be taken lightly. It is part of the "pressure" that attends this game like none other. The Colts had been through it before. For the Cowboys it was a heady experience. Morton seemed to cope with it well enough. "Tom started calling the plays," he said, "because he thought I'd gotten too conservative. Also, he thought maybe I was being affected by the static we were getting from the fans. And we won that game, so he called them the next week, too. And we kept winning, so you don't change a winning combination. . . . I don't understand your questions about my role as a quarterback on this team. The pass standings just came out and I was fifth out of twenty-six teams, so I must have done better than a lot of other guys. Our philosophy right now on offense is not to make mistakes, control the ball. We have a great running game going, so we stay with it. We've won seven in a row, and I've had two interceptions in those seven games, no fumbles. . . . Ahh, to hell with it."

If the writers were doubtful of Morton, they were fascinated enthusiasts about Thomas, the rookie from West Texas State who had gained one thousand yards through the playoffs, though he never started until the sixth league game. They tested him on the subject of pressure. "I don't believe in pressure," Thomas said.

But this is *it*, they insisted; this is the ultimate game.

"No, it isn't," Thomas said.

How did he figure?

"If this was the ultimate game, they wouldn't be playing it again next year."

There was not much speculation about the pre-game strategies of either team. It was all cut and dried. Dating back to 1965 the Cowboys had always ranked one, two or three in rushing defense—and Baltimore had no outside runners. They had a rookie, Norm Bulaich, a power runner, at halfback and a Detroit reject, slow-stepping Tom Nowatzke, at fullback. Obviously, the Colts would have to score on Dallas with Johnny Unitas' passes to wide receivers Roy Jefferson and Eddie Hinton or tight end John Mackey. It was equally obvious that the Cowboys were not going to rely on Morton's arm. His right elbow had had to be drained every week of the season. Dallas would hope that Thomas could have another one-hundred-yard day and that his ability to break for long runs, outside or inside, would set up fullback Walt Garrison for quick openers and traps through the middle.

"Anyway," Landry said sixty-five times during the week, "the defense will control this game. It always does in the Super Bowl."

At the beginning of the week I had visited the coaches' wing of the hotel to see their private lounge and bar, and I ran into Ermal Allen, the backfield coach. Offhandedly I asked him, "You think Dallas can handle Unitas?"

He crooked a finger at me. "Come down to my room a minute. I want to show you something."

Allen was the staff's statistician, breaking down game films into enough charts to launch an invasion of Normandy. The one he showed me was a diagram of a football field, spotted with circled numbers. They represented the completed passes Unitas had thrown in his last five games. The circles were all clustered in the middle of the page. There were just four on the edges.

"He's not throwing the sideline pass," I said. "Is his arm gone?" On a sideline pass the quarterback really has to have a hummer going, because if he hangs the ball it will be intercepted for six points.

"I don't know anything about his arm," Allen said. "I just know he throws to the middle."

The next day I stopped Mel Renfro as he walked across the swimming-pool patio toward the beach, and I asked him about Allen's statistics.

"That's interesting," Renfro said. "We haven't gone into that yet." Did it mean he would play his man to the inside? Renfro looked shocked. "Hell, no," he said. "I'll cover him wherever he goes, same fundamentals. The other way you can outsmart yourself. The idea scares me to death."

Landry meanwhile was daily fielding The Question: Did he think his team was handicapped by the feeling it had a black cloud hanging perpetually over its head, preventing it from winning the Big Game? "This season," Landry said, "we've laid that one to rest. We won tough games over Green Bay, Cleveland, Detroit and San Francisco when a loss would mean we were out of it. That idea might have been a problem at one time, though I doubt it. But it's certainly not now."

The game, just as Landry had foreseen, was completely dominated by defensive plays and by turns of good and bad fortune. Dallas recovered a muffed punt at the nine and got a field goal out of it. Morton hit his best pass of the day, for forty-one yards to Hayes, to set up another field goal. Then Unitas connected to Mackey for a seventy-five-yard touchdown, the first of two controversial calls by the officials. Unitas had been throwing to Hinton, coming across the middle of the field about fifteen yards deep. The ball hit Hinton's hands and skipped downfield to Mackey like a rock on water. Renfro made a swipe at it as it went over his head. Mackey's role in the play had merely been to clear free safety Charlie Waters out of the area. The ball's deflection found Mackey in the open behind Waters, and he went all the way. But the pass was illegal, coming off one offensive man to another— unless a defensive man had his hands on it in the interim. "Blue touched the ball," ruled field judge Fritz Graf. So the touchdown was allowed. Jim O'Brien's extra-point try was blocked, however, and the game remained 6-6.

When Unitas was chased out of the pocket and ran the middle, Jordan and Howley hit him high and low to cause a fumble. Morton threw seventeen yards to Reeves on the left and on the next play hit Thomas on the right for a seven-yard touchdown. Just before halftime it looked as if the Cowboys had taken the hearts out of the Colts by denying them a touchdown in four tries from the two-yard line. Mc-Cafferty was second-guessed for not taking the field goal on fourth down. When kick-return specialist Jim Duncan fumbled away the second-half kickoff at the Colt thirty-one, it seemed Dallas was destined to wrap up the game. But on first down from the two, Thomas crossed into left tackle and fumbled—the second controversial and fateful call of the day. Colt tackle Billy Ray Smith began screaming, "Colts' ball!" Line judge Jack Fette, whose view was obscured by back judge Hugh Gamber, immediately began signaling that Baltimore had recovered.

Andrie had broken Unitas' ribs, causing an interception in the second quarter, and Earl Morral was running the Colt offense—but not well enough to get a touchdown. In the fourth quarter, a Morton pass for Garrison went off his hands to an interception by safety Rick Volk, who ran the ball thirty-one yards to the Dallas three. Two line smashes got the tying touchdown with 7:35 left.

Both offenses had been so ineffective that everyone immediately began thinking of sudden death. "My God," said a guy in the press box, "if this goes into overtime we'll be here till Monday." But at the two-minute mark, the Colts had to punt from the ten and got the ball out only to their forty-eight. One first down would put Dallas into winning field-goal range. Then Neely was called for holding, a twenty-four-yard penalty, and a Morton pass went off Reeves' hands to an interception by middle linebacker Mike Curtis. After two running plays left nine seconds showing on the clock, O'Brien used four of them to kick a thirty-two-yard field goal.

In the Dallas locker room the players' anguish was driven out by anger. Renfro, Green and Waters all denied touching the ball on Mackey's touchdown. Manders said *he* had recovered Thomas' fumble at the goal line. "It rolled right under me," Manders said, "and I got up and handed it to the ref. I couldn't believe it when he said it was the Colts' ball." Thomas was nowhere to be found; his locker was empty.

Landry seemed to have aged ten years overnight as he told the writers, "We're disappointed but not ashamed. You just can't play defense better than we were playing it. My gosh, three tipped passes gave them all their points. I guess our luck ran out on us when Thomas fumbled at the goal line. We go ahead twenty to six there, and I don't see how they could catch us."

Later, in a calmer moment, Landry analyzed what had happened. "There never was a point where we didn't think we were going to win it—that's what makes it so tough to take. We expected, going in, to win a very close and low-scoring game. We knew we could handle their offense, because we were playing defense so doggone good. But we knew their defense was stronger than anything we'd played against. Their strength was their two safeties—Volk and Logan. They were much stronger force men and better tacklers than we'd seen at safety before. They gave them one more man in a lot of defenses, quicker than we'd worked against. That shut down our wide game." (Thomas was held to a 2.1-yard average on eighteen carries.) "Up until the fumble at the goal, the game was going exactly as we planned. The defense was making the plays for us. Our offensive plan was to run the ball, keep moving it and take advantage of opportunities as we got them. We couldn't change our pattern of the playoffs. We didn't have a passing game, because of Craig's arm trouble. Our plan for throwing the ball was to drop it off short and not go into the deep zones, where the Colts take it away from you. There at the end we were going for the win. I wanted him to throw that one pass and, if it was complete, throw another. If incomplete, we run the ball on third down, punt and take our chances in sudden death."

Usually a losing team's dressing room clears out as if someone had yelled, "Fire!" These Cowboys lingered, with chins high. "Freak plays beat us," said Howley, who had been voted the game's most valuable player. "In fact, I don't feel like we were beat. I feel like we won, but they got the title."

"There's always next year," Morton said. "That's a great line, isn't it? I wasn't the worst quarterback on the field. Look at what happened to Unitas. They were lucky to win or he would have been the goat. I keep thinking about the last two calls, about running the clock out instead of throwing. I did mostly what I wanted to do in the game, throw to the backs, but I couldn't hit Bobby [Hayes] on a couple of turn-ins there when I should have. It would have made a differ-ence, loosening them up. The second pass I threw I took a chunk off my finger"—Morton showed a sliced-up fore-finger on his throwing hand—"on somebody's helmet. And it wouldn't stop bleeding. Then the ball kept sailing. Little stupid things like that happen—why, you never know."

Murchison was standing near an equipment trunk in the center of the room. "At least," he said, "we're closing in on them. We got it down to five seconds from thirteen."

Green, in his customary matter-of-fact way, was fielding the inevitable question about this last in a five-year succes-sion of title losses. "Every year," he said, "there are twenty-five teams who can't win the big one. Only one team wins the big one. If you finish eight-six and don't make the playoffs, you might as well be oh-and-fourteen and get the number-one draft choice."

And at the other end of the room, a fierce-eyed Jordan stood, clad in a sopping T-shirt and a jockstrap, his hands still taped, arms akimbo, fists planted on hips, facing a ring of writers. "I don't have any complex about this game," he said, "and I'm not going to take any lip about it. We're com-ing back. I hate to tell 'em, but we are. We've got a great bunch of people, we're playing defense, and all we need is a passing game. We're coming back."

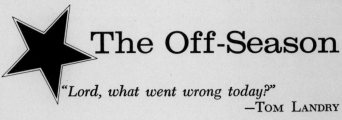

The Off-Season

"Lord, what went wrong today?"
—TOM LANDRY

The Cowboys who live in Dallas during the off-season got back from the Super Bowl on Monday. On Tuesday Staubach was on the practice field alone, throwing the ball at a passing board. On Thursday he was at the club offices wanting to know when they could take films of his workouts so he could study his moves. Ermal Allen was flabbergasted. "For God's sake, Roger," he said, "you've got six months to get ready."

"*I* don't have six months," Staubach said, "and I'm ready now. If I don't start or play this season, it will be my last with the Cowboys."

In the aftermath of the Baltimore loss, Landry had taken pains to spell out his view of the quarterback job. "I'm not going to say the quarterback position is open," he said. "I won't take that approach at all."

But already pressure had begun to build up. Jordan told the Birmingham Quarterback Club, "Morton will have to prove himself next summer in the exhibition games or lose his starting job. I don't believe the coaches will go all season with him again unless he does better." And Howley, in New York to accept the new car which went with his MVP selection, said, "What Craig's problems are I don't know. He's had a lot of injuries, but it's more than that. Something within himself. Possibly it's a mental picture. Something is handicapping him from being the great quarterback he could be.

I think he's been trying too hard not to make mistakes, not to throw the interception, not to get trapped. Anyway, I know *I'll* have to fight to keep my job, and the quarterback will have to fight to keep his."

Morton had not been getting this message. He told a businessman's luncheon group in Abilene: "I accepted the fact Landry called plays because I thought it would help the team, and it did. I don't want to experience it again, though, because I don't think I could go through another year with him sending in the calls." And on Staubach: "He's going to have to do a lot more than he has. You know, he has to beat *me* out. I don't have to beat *him* out."

Morton, about this same time, was a guest contributor for vacationing columnist Blackie Sherrod of the *Times Herald*. "Many people consider me aloof and carefree," he wrote. "Some say I need a wife to settle me down. Still more consider me a playboy. Others have voiced added opinions. Perhaps in other eyes I do touch some part of these typecastings, but when I look at myself I see a sensitive, quiet, dedicated person who enjoys people and has always given as he has received. I've probably become more withdrawn the last two years because of many unpleasant moments in public. I know all this goes with being an athlete, and I accept it as such. I have accepted criticism and blame without comment, and I have been first to praise others where praise was due. I have always done these things and will continue to do so as a part of my real self."

Morton never seemed to comprehend what he was up against in the case of Staubach—Annapolis graduate, Heisman Trophy winner, lieutenant in charge of the port near Da Nang, married man, a father, daily Mass attendant, a year older than Morton and, above all, the fiercest of competitors. "When I'm the quarterback," Staubach said, "and I walk on the field, I know that some way, some*how* we are going to walk off the winner." There were no "ifs" or "buts" in Staubach's lexicon; everything was candy and nuts. Shortly before he took his discharge from the Navy, in 1969, he used some accumulated leave to attend Landry's "quarterback school," a springtime refresher. Staubach had been puzzled by the relationship between Meredith and Morton.

"Are they always like this?" he had asked me.

"Like what?"

"Well, friendly."

"Sure. Why not?"

"I just don't think it's a good idea to be that buddy-buddy with some guy when you're trying to take his job away from him."

This remark was passed on to the coaches, who gleefully repeated it to Landry. "Roger," Landry said, "is an unusual fellow." Calvin Hill had put it another way: "Let's just say I'm glad Roger isn't running third string at my position."

Now Staubach has shaded his version of how he got along with Morton. "We're friendly enough," he said. "His locker's next to mine and we talk a lot, but I never see him away from the field. Let's face it—our life styles are different. I'm a married man, and he's a happy bachelor."

In the space of a few days in March, Morton's "life style" would be compared, in exaggerated fashion, with the straight-and-narrow paths of his coach and his rival. Morton had been in the hospital for an elbow operation, the repair of pinched nerves, an injury he said was caused by repeated falls on the Cotton Bowl AstroTurf. The morning he got out of the hospital he could have read a column by Landry, one of a Lenten Guidepost series in the Fort Worth *Star-Telegram*. It was the most revealing statement Landry had ever made in explaining how religion and football dovetailed in his life.

"After one setback that was especially hard to take last year," Landry wrote, "I drove home with an overwhelming sense of disappointment. Before going to bed that night, I sat down in my bedroom chair to review the whole day. Not a pragmatic review, but a spiritual assessment. 'Lord, what went wrong today?' I asked. As almost always happens during these sessions with Him, I soon found perspective. A crushing setback today, yes, but I've learned that something constructive comes from every defeat. I thought over my relationships that day with the players, coaches, officials, friends, family. Nothing wrong here. No bad injuries, either. 'Thank you, Lord, for being with me out there,' I said. And with that prayer the bitter sting of defeat drained away. Disappointment remained, but I've found that it doesn't sap energy and creativity. One football game after all is quite a small fragment of one's total life.

"When my football playing days were over and I became a fulltime coach on the New York Giants in 1956, I used my college training in industrial engineering to devise a complex and, as it turned out, a highly successful system of defense that had never been tried before in professional football. Another accomplishment, but a sense of dissatisfaction remained. After the 1958 football season, I returned to Dallas where my wife Alicia and I had settled. I was thirty-three years old. I had achieved almost every goal I had aimed for and had every reason to be happy and content. Yet inexplicably there was an emptiness in my life.

"One day a good friend casually invited me to attend a men's breakfast at the Melrose Hotel in Dallas. 'I think you'll like it, Tom,' he said. 'We probe into the Scriptures and have some good fellowship together.' We met at 7:30 on a Wednesday morning. After breakfast the men at each table chose their own moderator, who kicked off the discussion. What happened in the weeks that followed is not easy to explain, but I do know that these informal sessions of probing, questioning and searching the Gospels together began a whole new era in my life.

"In looking back, I find it hard to pick out any one specific turning point, but my early attention was certainly grabbed by this passage: 'Therefore I tell you do not be anxious about your life, what you shall eat or what you shall drink, nor about your body, what you shall put on. Is not life more than food and the body more than clothing?'

" 'Is not life, then, more than football?' I asked myself, uncomfortably. Challenged by this statement, I turned my thoughts to the Challenger. Who was He, this Jesus? Did I accept Him, really? For, I reasoned, if I accepted Him, then I accepted what He said. And if I accepted what He said, then there was something unsatisfying in the way I was living my life.

"I began reading about Jesus. As a football coach, I measure things in terms of results. During each game we keep a chart of the players' efficiency in carrying out their assignments. If most players perform well, we will probably win the game. Therefore, I couldn't help thinking about Jesus also in terms of what He did, of the results of His life. The impact of His life on the lives of countless millions down through the years is impressive, compelling.

"Finally, at some period during the spring of 1959, all my intellectual questions no longer seemed important, and I had a curiously joyous feeling inside. Internally, the decision had been made. Now while the process had been slow and gradual, once made, the decision has been the most important of my life. It was a commitment of my life to Jesus Christ, and a willingness to do what He wanted me to do, as best I could be seeking His will through prayer and reading His word.

"The result was that I learned what He meant when He said, 'I came that they may have life and have it abundantly.' He didn't ask me to give up football, or my ambition to be the best coach in the business, but to bring Him into my daily life, including football. I begin each day now with a person-to-person effort to contact Him. 'Lord, I need Your help today when we make our squad cuts,' or 'Please give me the right words to say to the coaches at our meeting,' or 'Help me to forget football today when I'm with Alicia and the children.' At the end of the day I take inventory. Was my criticism of the quarterback handled right? Did I get across to the squad my moral convictions without preaching? Was I too stern with my daughter Kitty over her last report card? The main evaluation concerns whether I had brought the Lord into these situations, or whether I was barging ahead on my own.

"When I get out of touch with Him, I flounder. Power seems to ebb away, and that restless feeling returns. When God is in control of my life, that gnawing sense of dissatisfaction is gone. And I know for myself what Augustine, that great fifth-century saint, meant when he wrote, 'Our hearts are restless until they find their rest in Thee.' "

That night, or specifically at 3:00 A.M. the next morning,

Morton was arrested by Dallas police and charged with "indecent conduct and using abusive language to the arresting officers." The policemen said they arrested him, "because he was urinating behind a parked car in which a young girl was sitting."

The "young girl," of course, was Morton's date, and he gave a different version. "It's ridiculous," he said, "I never urinated in the street and that's not even on the charge. We pulled into a service station and when I got out of the car I told my date to move it nearer the gas pump. Then these two policemen come up and say I'm under arrest. I say, 'What for?' and they tell me to get in the patrol car. Then one of them grabs my arm and doubles it behind my back. I said, 'Look out, I have to use that thing next season— I just got it operated on.' I admit, that's when I started using abusive language." Morton had to post $50 bond.

The following week, Staubach made the papers. He was addressing a meeting of the Salvation Army. Staubach said: "I personally believe that in life as in football all of us have good field positions. I believe God has given them to us to save our souls, and we must use them to attain our goals."

I was in the Cowboy offices a few days later, and I asked one of the coaches for an opinion on Landry's reaction to Morton's arrest. "It's not what Tom thinks," he said. "It's what Tom thinks the *team* thinks."

For a while there the Cowboys were spending as much time on the police blotter as they were on the sports page. Steve Kiner, the rookie linebacker out of Tennessee, had been arrested at a rock concert in Knoxville, charged with "disorderly conduct and resisting arrest." There had been a dispute with an off-duty policeman about seating and Kiner had finally said, "You want this seat, pal, you can have it," and hit the cop with a folding chair. An allegation that Kiner was under the influence of drugs made the wire services. Kiner was a strange and controversial gentleman of the South who sported a handlebar mustache, shaggy locks and a big lip. In college, when Kiner pretended to take lightly an upcoming game against Ole Miss, a writer reminded him "the Rebels have a lot of horses." And Kiner said, "That's the trouble with you guys—you can't tell horses from mules." Johnny Vaught happily reminded his team of this remark all week, via a brace of mules under the goalposts, and Ole Miss beat the hell out of Tennessee.

When Kiner reported to the Cowboys in 1970, it seemed clear that he had been marking time at Tennessee only until he could get into professional football. He elected to room with a fellow Southerner, Duane Thomas, and made light of the pairing. "So Duane's black. That's not why I roomed with him, or he roomed with me. I found a guy who thinks like I do—we both believe in the individual." When the veterans were delayed reporting to camp by the player union strike, Kiner made so many big plays in scrimmages against the San Diego and San Francisco rookies that there was serious speculation that he might play himself into a starting job. That spring when he came to Dallas after the Knoxville incident, but before the case had been settled, he apologized: "My attorney says don't talk about it, which is a joke. But he's costing me money, so I have sense enough to go along." Kiner did have a few other observations he wanted to unload, particularly about the club's turnaround the past season from a 5-4 record, two games behind St. Louis, to a seven-game winning streak into the Super Bowl.

"There was a definite racial problem accumulated from the past," he said, "and Duane and I helped break it down. There's a player–front-office problem, and we have to break that down as a group. But that didn't have anything to do with the club losing, or starting to win. The older people became the leaders they should have been all along. The older players were trying to achieve things on the basic of past success, sitting back and waiting for good things to happen. When we got five-four, they said, 'Hey, I got to get off my butt and keep my job.' And they started making good things happen. They became leaders and we all got to know one another. To play football you got to know what the guy next to you feels, and what he thinks. In football, you got to have great individuals, but you only move forward as a team. I'd like to see some changes this year, beginning with training camp. Instead of harassing the rookies with all those songs and running to get ice, the veterans ought to start helping the new guys out, getting to know them. This harassment is what made our rookie group close—Harris and Waters and Duane and I and Mark Washington and Toomay, we went along with their little games because it seemed to matter so much to them. We used to sit around and talk about how stupid they were to make us do stupid little things. What this leads into is the idea they carry into the season: a rookie will be okay in a couple seasons when he gets experienced. They're the ones that tried to pattern us into thinking that. We didn't buy it. They should try to fill our knowledge gap. We had a lot to learn, but we felt like we could contribute. If I stay around long enough, that bullshit with the rookies is going to change."

Lance Rentzel came into town in late March and asked me to come out to his house. He said it was important. I couldn't imagine what I could do to help, but I was willing to try. Rentzel, in many ways, had been the most admirable athlete on the Cowboy team. The son of wealthy parents, he was an All-American at a private prep school in Oklahoma City, then went on to become a star running back, and particularly a clutch player, for Oklahoma. He was drafted by Minnesota, but Dutch Van Brocklin didn't know what to do with him except have him return kickoffs and fine him for staying out late. After his second year with the Vikings, the Cowboys got him in a trade, told him he was a flankerback, and he'd been the starter there ever since—1967 through the first ten games of last season, when his world fell in on him. The year before he had led the club with forty-three catches and twelve touchdowns, which means he had outdistanced Hayes. He was a fellow who seemed to have everything going for him— blond good looks, a 6-foot-2-inch, 200-pound physique, a college degree with honors in the field of business computers, professional music talent and a marriage to glamorous, young Joey Heatherton. But occasionally, when talking with Rentzel, I had the sense of facing a Dorian Gray. There was a tragedy lurking behind his facile exterior. The trade with

Minnesota had come about because he'd been convicted of "disorderly conduct" and given a suspended sentence. His parents now lived in Dallas, and the Cowboys hoped the change of scenery and his family's moral support would redeem Rentzel and also provide them with a player whose skills had been underrated on the Vikings. This had seemed to be so until last November when he was arrested the week of the Thanksgiving Day game and charged with "indecent exposure to a minor child," a felony. Rentzel immediately quit the team. The last time I'd seen him had been at the Galt Ocean Mile in Fort Lauderdale. His wife had arranged a booking at the Diplomat on Miami Beach to coincide with the Super Bowl, in case the Cowboys made it. They had, but Rentzel hadn't. There he was, at the hotel desk on the eve of the game, writing brief notes to leave for his teammates. "I'm not going to the game," he said, "because I don't think I could stand it. It'll be tough enough listening on the radio." I'd told him maybe there was some way I could help when his trial came up, to check with his lawyer, then let me know. Rentzel's trouble was a mental aberration, a compulsion, not a willful act. His fault had been in not acknowledging its hold on him. Morton, one of his closest friends on the club, had said at the time, "Maybe this is the best thing that could have happened to Lance. Now he'll admit his problem and cure it." Medical specialists in Dallas were sanguine about Rentzel's future.

Rentzel's parents lived in a chateau-style house, tastefully oriented and elegantly furnished. He looked haggard, and that wasn't my imagination. He'd played down to 195 during the season, then lost another ten pounds in the ensuing months. We sat across from each other at a chess table in the living room, and Mrs. Rentzel brought us Cokes in tall glasses of ice and left. I asked him how he was bearing up.

"Oh, great!" he said. "I'm having the time of my life, the worst. You know, I went to the game after all. I figured I might as be miserable there as miserable listening on the radio. But it was weird. You're with a team four years, you feel like they've got part of you down there. I felt like I was off somewhere watching a part of me with the team, and this

Calvin Hill, the intellectual from Yale, is a triumph of the
Cowboy scouting system. He grew an inch taller
between the 1970 and 1971 seasons.

ALL PHOTOS BY RUSS RUSSELL

George Andrie smothers
NY Giants quarterback
Fran Tarkenton, with help
from Larry Cole (63).

Herb Adderley escapes
with one of his three
interceptions against
Philadelphia, this time in
front of Ben Hawkins.

Duane Thomas (33)
follows John Niland's blocking
on a power sweep around the
49ers' Earl Edwards.

Calvin Hill (at top)
looks for opening behind
phalanx of Blaine Nye (61)
and Niland.

The oldest Cowboy, Chuck
Howley, readies his meat
hooks to stop an end run.

Craig Morton had his first healthy year, and
lost his starting job. The protection is by Blaine Nye.

Tom Landry at the height of
excitement. His hats are supplied
free, by a grateful industry.

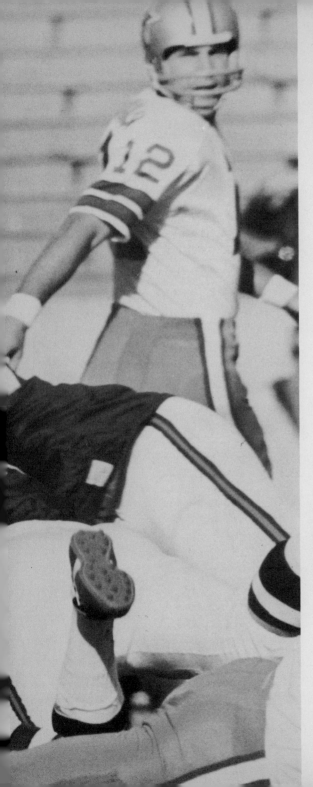

The Bears grab Duane
Thomas in midflight. Roger
Staubach is in the game
fleetingly, on the Landry
quarterback shuttle.

Trainer Larry Gardner
finds that Lance
Alworth is all broken up:
three cracked ribs in
the Cleveland game.

Offensive line coach
Jim Myers lectures
his starters on a switch
in assignments.

Bobby Hayes (22),
who averages ten TDs a year,
waits for a bomb to
drop at Philadelphia.

Right in the eye,
instead of the mouth, is
Dave Manders'
water-bottle formula to
beat the heat.

On Morton's last game as a starter, at Super Bowl Stadium against the Saints, he has Hayes (22) open for a touchdown—and throws an interception to Hugo Hollas (not in picture).

The last man the President
called, Tom Landry in the jammed
Super Bowl locker room.

Mel Renfro (20) listens in as defensive line coach Ernie
Stautner huddles with linebackers Dave Edwards,
Tom Stincic and Lee Roy Jordan (55) on pass coverage.

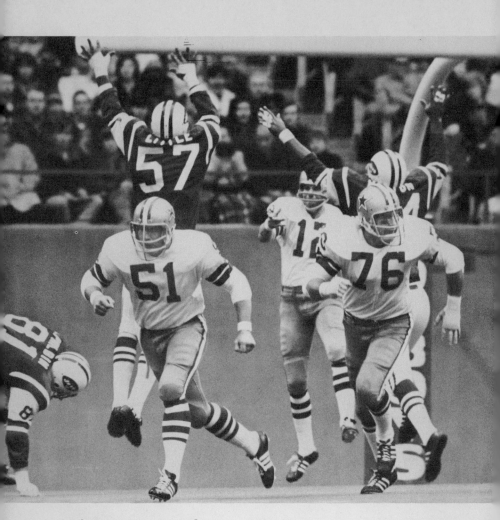

It's a screen pass, and
Manders and Niland let the
Jets through on a leaping
Staubach.

Duane Thomas is outnumbered
nine-to-one by Chicago Bears,
which was the story for the day.

(Below right) Fullback Walt
Garrison gets a block from
Calvin Hill (right) for goal-line
yardage in the Houston
Astrodome.

Bob Lilly and Rayfield Wright boost Landry to his
twelve-year victory ride at the Super Bowl.

other part of me in the stands. . . . I could have come back. I started to, a dozen times."

"Come back?" The Cowboy captains had held a team meeting of their own at the practice field after Rentzel had been indicted, and the sentiment of the meeting was that they wanted him to return to the club. "It's *his* home, too," Hayes had said.

"Sure," Rentzel said now. "I never was suspended. I could have come back and played. The only reason I thought about it was if they needed me. I got about halfway to the practice field one day before turning around. I thought about it some more and realized I'd only be taking the pressure that was on me and spreading it all over them. Listen, this is going to sound crazy, but there's something you can do for me. I want you to tell me every dirty, crappy story, joke, wisecrack you've heard about me since all this happened. Anything, everything. Believe me, it could help."

I saw what he meant. This wasn't an exercise in masochism. There was plenty of evidence of "cruel and unusual punishment" which had already been meted out. "Look at this cartoon," Rentzel said, handing me an eight-by-ten sheet of paper. "The goddam thing was run off on a Xerox machine at the county courthouse." I told him a fellow in the newsroom had been circulating a page and a half of one-liners on the subject, and I'd get him a copy. There was also an issue of a *Confidential*-type magazine which was fairly purple and a syndicated series by Newspaper Enterprise Alliance which quoted a psychiatrist in long-distance diagnosis. Rentzel was delighted and then saw the humor in his own delight.

"That's great," he said. "And isn't it great I can say, 'That's great'? Everything has gone upside down. . . . Do you think I can play for the Cowboys next season? Wait, do you think the Cowboys will want me?"

"I don't know," I said. It was understood that by "Cowboys" he meant the organization, the front office. "Most of the time I can't figure them out."

"What do you think would happen at the Cotton Bowl next summer when we came back and played the first game?"

"If the offense was introduced, you'd get booed. But not

all that much. People have short memories, and more compassion than you'd think. Still, you might be better off someplace else."

"If I got traded," Rentzel said, "there are only three places I'd want to go—New York, Miami or Los Angeles." I didn't tell Rentzel, but a few weeks before, I had called Tommy Prothro, the new coach of the Rams, and asked him if he'd trade for him. Prothro had said, "What do the Cowboys say?" I told him the Cowboys had said they'd cross that bridge when they came to it, after Rentzel's trial. "I'll have to wait for the same bridge," Prothro had said.

"I was going to ask you," I said to Rentzel, "but it seems obvious. *You* want to play next season?"

"Steve," he said, "I just can't end my career this way."

In April, Rentzel pleaded guilty and received a five-year probated sentence, with the stipulation that he "continue to seek medical help." The ball, it turned out, was now in Landry's court. "It's my decision to make," Landry said on the subject of trading Rentzel. "And the decision will be based first on what is best for Lance."

About the time Rentzel was sentenced, Duane Thomas called me at home, from Los Angeles. "Say, I might want you to do something for me in about six weeks. They are screwing me around on my money, and I'm not going to let 'em. But, hey, you know why I'm calling you? I think you understand me when I talk to you. I mean I think you look at me and listen to me like a person. You're not just seeing a player, you know?"

"I know," I said. "If I can help, okay. What you got in mind?"

"They don't want to give me a new contract," he said, "and if they don't, I'm not coming to camp. They've seen the last of me. I want you to write it, put it in the payer out in the open so everybody will know what they're doing to me."

"Duane, they're just going to say you've *got* a contract."

"But I don't have a contract for what I did. I got a rookie's contract. I don't have a thousand-yard contract."

"I'm just telling you what they'll say." He was right, of

course. The Cowboys like to sign their rookies to three-year contracts—in fact, they prefer to sign everybody to at least three-year terms, on the theory that they'll have to negotiate with only a third of the players every season. Ironically, the club had hit long-shot number-one draft picks at running back in successive years, and now they were to have trouble with them over their contracts on successive years. Calvin Hill had claimed to have a verbal promise of a pay increase if he did well as a rookie. He never got a raise in salary last season, and now I reminded Thomas of that.

"Look!" Thomas shouted into the phone. "Don't *you* start telling me about Calvin. That's all *they* tell me. Calvin this and Calvin that. Well, I'm not Calvin Hill. Calvin didn't get any more money last year? Well, maybe that's what was wrong with Calvin. That's their trouble. They look at you and don't see you. They see a number or something but not a real person. Hey, I'm not Jim Brown. I'm Duane Thomas, one only of a kind, and they got to deal with me."

"Why do you want to wait six weeks on this?" I said.

"I'm going off on a trip, to some friends in Bermuda, where I can be alone and think about myself. About what I'm doing in my life. Say, football is only part of it, you know?"

The winter the Cowboys drafted Thomas, the day he came into town to sign his contract, I'd gone to a television station to meet him and get an interview. I had met him once briefly, about fifteen months before, when he was visiting the club offices during his junior year at West Texas State. Gil Brandt, the personnel director, had said, "I want you to meet the Cowboys' rookie of the year in the NFL for 1970." He'd seemed shy. Now I saw that it wasn't shyness but a rigid reserve. He held his chin up so that he seemed to be staring down at me, though I'm two inches taller. His face was carefully expressionless, as if he were waiting for a wrong word so he could pass a negative verdict. This studied pose reminded me of the ominous poise of Jim Brown. That was one of the first questions I asked him: Would he use Jim Brown as his goal?

"All the yards he gained? Yes, I'll aim for that," Thomas said.

"What about the rest of it? You want to emulate Brown there, too?"

"Matter of fact, I would. I'd like to get into something, television, acting maybe, someday."

Certainly Thomas was better looking than Brown. Bobby Hayes, that unerring marksman with a quip, sized up Thomas' brooding composure and called him "Othello."

This would be a big story, his threat not to report to camp, but there was more here than that. I didn't think he knew what he was getting into. "Duane," I said, "they'll never believe you'll hold out until you don't show at training camp. Then they'll let you sit there and sizzle for four or six weeks."

"I'll take that," he said. "I'll go get a job, any job, and at least I'll have peace of mind. They act like all they want is to hassle me. Hey, I'll be getting five hundred dollars *less* this season than I got last season. Don't ask me why—that's just the way my contract reads. I love the game, the playing, but I can't stand the hassle with people who are supposed to be fair to you and they aren't. Let me ask you something else. Who's having trouble getting money from 'em? Does this tell you something—Hayes, Renfro, Pugh, Calvin, me?"

"You do have something in common," I said.

"Yeah. Black. They want to put me down. Nobody in the office cares what happens to the players. They give you the cold straight. It's all business, the dotted line. Then when you get in the season, you're supposed to be one big family, pulling together. How do they figure? People can say that I knew what I was doing when I signed for three years and I should stick by the contract. What did I know? I had an agent, okay, but after I signed and he got his cut I haven't seen him since, 'less he wanted some of my Super Bowl money. I had an obligation to put out my best every minute for the team, and I did. Well, I feel like the club should have been obligated to me, obligated to be honest with me. They've been in the business longer than I have, so they ought to know better than me what's fair in a contract. They can't keep me down. I'm not going to be there, and I won't be there."

This was the first chance I'd had to talk with Thomas since several days before the Super Bowl. I asked him about his disappearance from the locker room.

"I showered," he said. "I dressed like I always do, no faster, no slower. I guessed they missed me because I didn't gain a hundred yards that day. Everybody was down talking to Landry and Morton. What was I going to do—stand in line and wait my turn? I didn't have anything to be ashamed of. Hey, I read later that the fumble was the play that lost the game. I didn't know that *I* was the one who was expected to win it. I hit into the hole and there was no hole. Mike Curtis was right there, so I tried to spin to hit him so he'd take me off balance. I was that close to the end zone. The move didn't work, but you've got to try. Baltimore just had a great defense. That's what got them there, and that's what won it for 'em. Then they had the run and the pass going for them and we just had the run. I gained a lot of knowledge about playing a Super Bowl. We'll be in it again, and I'll have a more intense attitude in preparing myself. I was trying to make it just a game, because all year long I know I play better when I'm relaxed. But I was getting vibrations from people around me, breaking my concentration."

"You had to prepare to play both fullback and running back," I said. "You talking about that kind of concentration?"

"No. That's a bunch of bull, football is supposed to be so complicated, the Cowboy offense is supposed to be hard to get with. I never went for that, from the first day I reported to camp. I never believed you had to wait years before you could participate. Football is common sense. When people explain things to me right, I can take it from there. I have twenty-twenty vision—I can see the hole."

Sure enough, six weeks later Thomas called me again, and he told me to go ahead with the story. "I can't stand the strain any more," he said. "I thought Gil Brandt was trying to help me, but every time Gil went to help me, he curved me, and I wound up worse than before. I don't want to go around four or five years like Hayes and Renfro and Jethro waiting for fair treatment. I don't want to go around smiling in the public's face while I carry around the feeling I've been had."

The club's reaction was predictable. "He has a contract," said Tex Schramm, the club president and general manager. "We expect him to be in training camp."

"Why don't you give him some more money?" I said.

"It's none of your damn business," Schramm said, "but you *know* we never tear up contracts."

"What about Hayes and Andrie and Lilly?" Schramm had torn up their contracts in 1967 and given them raises.

"They had been with the club several years. Hayes had been here two years."

"What about Reggie Rucker?" Rucker, after a year on the taxi squad, had replaced Rentzel at flankerback, and Schramm had just given him a new contract in place of his old one.

"Rucker was a free agent. We do that with a lot of free agents. We've been through all this before, with Calvin Hill."

"Duane says he isn't Calvin Hill."

"Hell, I know he isn't Calvin Hill."

"What we have here is a communication problem," I said. "Duane is not Calvin, but you're still Tex Schramm, is that it?"

"Something like that."

Brandt, in the next office down the hall from Schramm, seemed more hurt than angered by the Thomas outburst. "I like Duane," he said. "I really do. He has a lot of problems and I hope he works them out and plays for us. I don't know what he means about me 'throwing curves' or losing any money for him. If he means money was lost by paying off his debts and bills, then I'm guilty."

The headlines on Kiner and Morton had fizzled out, as they mostly do, to three-paragraph stories on the sports page. Kiner had been fined $50, so evidently he hadn't hit the cop very hard with that chair. Morton's "indecent conduct" charge was dropped. He pleaded "no contest" to the abusive-language error and was fined $15.

It seemed like a good time to check in for a long talk with Landry on his plans for training camp and his anticipation of the season. As always, I was struck by the sameness of the man and his phlegmatic manner. After eight years I was used to it, but it was still notable. Landry never greets anyone with a remark, "What have you been up to?" or "How are things going?" That is small talk and feckless, and he doesn't have time for it. He says, "Hello. Sit down," and then waits for you to get the subject rolling. Pleasantly and patiently, but silently. In many ways he was an exasperating subject. In other ways he was a sportswriter's dream. There were few peaks and valleys on his Richter scale. He had hit one nadir that I knew of, in Pittsburgh in 1965 after a fifth straight loss. I was told he'd cried when he talked to the team in the locker room that day, taking the blame for failure upon himself. Dallas then won five of the last seven games from there and had been a winner ever since. His lighthearted remarks over the years had been so few they could be inscribed on a mashed-out penny, like the Lord's Prayer. The year the Cowboys switched to a prop jet for their team charters, the team hit a mid-season streak of two defeats and a tie, and Landry was asked if he could think of any changes that would snap them out of it. "Well," he said, "we could go back to a DC-7." When one of the writers covering the club kept getting hurt playing basketball in training camp—chipped disk, sprained ankle and finally a broken leg—Landry looked at him solemnly and said, "I'm glad you're not my responsibility." In a press conference he would never answer a flippancy with a quotable remark, but any other question, ill-informed or not, he would answer fully. Over the long haul his constancy was a comfort. He never showed any anger over adverse stories. He once told the squad about newsmen, "Remember, when we're all wrought up and mad about losing a game, so are they, but they're the ones with the typewriters."

Landry and I had been at the University of Texas at the same time, right after the war—in which he had flown thirty missions over Europe as a B-17 pilot. I remembered him as a hard-driving fullback on a team that wasn't good enough to win a conference championship but good enough to win Sugar and Orange Bowl games his junior and senior years.

Landry spent a season with the New York Yankees in the All-America Conference, and when that league was absorbed by the NFL the Giants got him. He was a cornerback of a particular kind. "I wasn't fast enough to play cornerback, even in those days," he says. "I had to make up for it by anticipating plays and outguessing the receiver on his routes." This casually put principle conceals a ton of man-hours spent with a movie projector. Before and after Giant practices, Landry would closet himself with opponents' game films, charting their probabilities according to down-and-distance, field position and score, and also charting the propensities of individual receivers. "Even the best player," he said, "has one thing he does better than anything else. On a crucial down, nine times out of ten, that's what you can expect he'll do."

New York head coach Jim Lee Howell remembered, "The assistants used to gripe about game films—'Where's the Cleveland–Pittsburgh reels?' And another one would say, 'Where the hell else? Landry's got 'em.' He was putting in longer hours than anybody on the staff, so when I took over in 'fifty-four I made him a coach." Dick Nolan, now at San Francisco, was a defensive back with the Giants then. "Tom was already coaching us anyway," he says. "He'd tell me to watch for the pitchout to my side, and here it would come, like he was calling their plays in the huddle."

Vince Lombardi, during his next to last year as both coach and general manager at Green Bay, complained to me one day that the demands of modern pro football were growing excessive. "When I was an assistant with the Giants," he said, "during the off-season we'd spend a couple hours at the office in the morning and spend the rest of the day playing golf. Now everybody gets in at eight and stays to six, and the only real fun all year is the season itself."

While others were playing golf, Landry was playing with a slide rule, which he'd learned to use in getting a degree in industrial engineering from the University of Houston in 1952, to add to his business degree from Texas. And of course there was the ever-present traveling lab of the football scientist, the movie projector. After two seasons as a player-coach,

Landry became a full-time member of Howell's staff in 1956, in charge of the entire defense. That was the year the Giants won their first NFL title since 1938, and they have never won another. Sam Huff, a rookie linebacker in 1956, had an apartment in the building where Landry lived, and several times a week he would get a phone call during the evening hours. "Sam, what are you doing?" Landry would say. Huff, engrossed in a *Playhouse 90*, would say, "Oh, nothing at all," and Landry would say, "Why don't you come up and we'll talk football."

"I'd go up," Huff says, "and he'd have the projector going, and we'd sit there for two hours looking at draw plays, or circle routes in my area, or whatever the hell there was, I didn't care. I learned more in a few hours with Tom than I'd learned playing football all my life."

Landry devised and refined the 4-3 defense to stop the wide-receiver formations which had been introduced by the Rams and the Browns. Along with it he invented what he calls "the coordinated defense," a philosophy which is so complex it has never been used by another team, with the exception of Nolan at San Francisco. Basically, this defense assigns areas of responsibility to each of the eleven players, contradicts their instinctive reaction to the play and holds off pursuit of the ball for several split seconds. "Everybody was 'running to daylight,'" Landry said. "That's what Lombardi took to Green Bay. They'd pull a lineman to get the flow going one way, and the back would take a counter step back into the hole. I wanted to coordinate everybody's assignments so there wouldn't be any daylight." Landry's thoroughness at spelling out "keys" for his defense—"If the guard and tackle do *this*, the play has to go *there*"—was an affront to Ernie Stautner, the Hall of Fame defensive end at Pittsburgh, when he joined the Cowboy staff in 1966. "I opened the defensive playbook," he said, "and there was everything I'd spent fifteen years learning how to play my position. I felt like it was a cheat. The bums ought to find out the hard way, like I did." When the Cowboys were rushed into the NFL in 1960 and Landry became their head coach, he turned his attention to offense. "Now I had to defeat the four-three," he

says, a matter-of-fact acknowledgment that the whole league
had adopted the Giants' defense. The answer was multiple
formations. "You have to put strain on the four-three to make
it adjust, and when it adjusts they are not playing the defense they want to play. Also, you have to create a moment
of doubt—by shifting into formations." By 1962, the Dallas
offense was explosive. "That year," Landry likes to recall now,
"we scored more points than Green Bay or New York, the
two teams that played for the title. And you know we didn't
come close to them in talent."

The players came to believe that everything Landry said
was gospel. Before the 1966 championship game, the offense
ran a play in practice which had fullback Don Perkins coming through the right side of the line and then cutting *inside*
middle linebacker Ray Nitschke, who was to be blocked out
by tight end Frank Clarke. Clarke protested to Landry:
"Tom, how can I take Nitschke outside when I'm lined up
over here and he's in the middle?" Landry said, "Watch,"
and went to Nitschke's area. "He won't be here." Landry,
facing Clarke, took four steps to the left. "He'll be over here,
and you can nail him easy." That was the way it went in the
game, and Perkins ran twenty-three yards for a touchdown.

Between seasons, Landry would refigure his percentages
and add new specialties to an already super-specialized game.
That first run at the title in 1966 had been helped by the
creating of "strong-side" and "weak-side" linebackers. The
language of pro football is complex to the point of childish-
ness, but a fan has no hope at all if he doesn't understand
that the "strong side" of an offense is the side where the tight
end lines up, so that there are three blockers to one side of
center and only two on the other. Landry had long ago
divorced the safeties. The strong-side safety must cover the
tight end man to man on pass routes and he must have the
physical strength to be a sure tackler, because the majority
of running plays are run to the strong side. The weak-side
or "free" safety—"free" because he has no man-to-man coverage—is the speedster, an interceptor, preferably an instinctive
player who can read the action and go to the ball. In Landry's
system he is the only defensive back who looks at the quarter-

back; the others concentrate totally on the man they're covering. Now Landry wanted to take this logic a step farther. He had an outside linebacker of great speed and quickness, Chuck Howley, and another of great strength and toughness, Dave Edwards. Of course Howley was also tough, and Edwards was comparatively fast, but one was more so than the other and vice versa. Percentages show that most passes to running backs are thrown to the weak side; therefore Howley was installed on that side. Edwards' talents would then be used more often to stop a running play. This device, too, was to be adopted generally by the other teams in the league.

If Landry's technological advances were his genius, they were also quite often his undoing. He would move players around as if they were so many knights and bishops and forget that they were flesh and blood. As the Cowboys were coming into the Cleveland playoff game in 1969, Landry's great concern was the Browns' wide receiver, Paul Warfield, considered the best in the league. In the regular season against Dallas, Warfield had caught touchdown passes of forty-eight and twenty-one yards in the first half to turn the game into a rout. Compounding the problem was the trouble Dallas had had all year at right cornerback, where one candidate after another had failed. Landry had finally yielded and moved Renfro there from free safety, though still contending that free safety was *the* vital position in his defensive backfield. Now he worked out another refinement especially for Warfield, who always lined up on the left side of the Browns' formations. When the tight end was to Warfield's side, and Warfield was technically a flankerback, Renfro would be the cornerback and cover him man to man, and a rookie named Otto Brown would be the free safety. But when the tight end was to the other side and Warfield was spread out wider as a split end, Brown would be the cornerback, Renfro the free safety, and they would combine to blanket Warfield with double coverage. On paper it made sense. On the field, Warfield caught eight passes for ninety-nine yards. The uncertainty that existed between Brown and Renfro uncoordinated the Landry defense. "It was a farce," an angry Renfro told me in the locker room. "I didn't know where the hell Otto was half the time, or if he knew where he was supposed to be."

"But hadn't you been working on this all week?" I said.

"I'd been working both positions in practice, and so had Otto, but I thought it would be one or the other."

"When did you find out you were going to switch on War-field?"

"About forty-five minutes before the game," Renfro said.

Landry's celebrated placid exterior had been noted by comedian Don Rickles: "Eighty thousand people in the stands are going bananas, and there's Landry walking up and down trying to keep his hat on straight." Dallas *Times Herald* cartoonist Bob Taylor drew a panel of eleven identical Landry faces, each one expressionless. In the first panel Landry says, "I got to get the boys 'up' for the game, so I better put my game face on." In the eleventh panel Landry says, "Want to see me do it again?"

Landry has always seemed to shrug off these comments as if this were a subject over which he had no control. In fact, his role is deliberate. "Football is an emotional game," he said, "but don't ask me what gets a team 'up' for a game. Every game is important, some more than others. The players are old enough to realize this and react to it. As for me, I've been at this game a long time, and I don't get overly excited. There are points where I get emotionally keyed up inside. I try to keep it down as much as I can, because I think it takes something away from your effectiveness."

Landry had just come through a season in which his apparent refusal to acknowledge the human side of things had brought the team to the brink of disaster. It had started with a new Landry phrase for 1970— "performance level." The phrase grew out of a questionnaire he had sent the players during the winter, an eight-page form listing multiple choices and asking them to rate everything from the qualities of the assistant coaches to the smallest routines in practice procedures. The questionnaires were to be sent unsigned to Lee Roy Jordan, who would then turn them over to Landry, leaving each reply anonymous. Landry took many mandates from these answers. One, in response to players' complaints that

too many teammates had conflicting "outside business inter-
ests," was to rearrange practice-field time so that it stretched
from 9:30 A.M. to 4.00 P.M., Tuesday through Thursday, and
considerably lengthened the Friday and Saturday workouts.
Another mandate was the "performance level," which stipu-
lated that the player who showed more dedication and did
the best job during the week in practice would have the
starting job on Sunday, regardless of the longevity or reputa-
tion or track record of the starter he replaced. As a conse-
quence, the season was five games old before Bob Hayes,
Ralph Neely and Craig Morton were all in the starting offensive lineup at the same time. Hayes had been found wanting
as a blocker, and Dennis Homan of Alabama was starting
in his place. Neely, a former All-NFL tackle making the shift
to guard, had been outperformed by young Blaine Nye.
Staubach had thrown the ball better than Morton, who was
trying to adjust to a radical operation which had transplanted
a tendon from his foot into his damaged shoulder. Finally,
in that Monday-night television game, division leader St.
Louis had dealt Dallas its fourth loss in nine weeks, and
the team came apart in Landry's hands. Then, amazingly, the
team started winning, all the way to the Super Bowl. In the
middle of the streak I had asked Bob Lilly for an explanation
of the reversal.

"When we got to five-four," Lilly said, "we were out of it.
Two games behind with five to play. Hell, you can't even cut
that in baseball. So everybody said to hell with it, and the
pressure was off. Everybody said to hell with it, to hell with
what the coaches have to bitch about when they run the films
on Tuesday. They couldn't put any more pressure on us, because we had nowhere to go. If they thought I was making
mistakes in a game, well, they could trade me. Maybe I'd be
better off someplace else is the way I felt. Everybody else felt
the same. So we started enjoying ourselves, started playing
football and started winning."

Stautner told a group of oilmen in Roswell, New Mexico,
in March: "The players turned it around. The coaches didn't
have anything to do with it."

Now as I went in to keep the appointment with Landry, I

wondered if he had any similarly disruptive ideas for the coming season. I still might not know after talking to him. A major development for the team may come from a Landry idea which at first mention goes as unnoticed as the proverbial cloud no larger than a man's hand. His fifteen-by-twenty-foot office is modern in style, done in black and white and red. The wall to his right is clear glass, floor to ceiling, looking down eleven floors to a clogged expressway stretching north. His desk top balloons outward into a round conference table, where he can hold meetings with his assistants, and I sat down in one of those chairs. There was a difference about his bearing, though it may have taken an expert in Landry nuances to discern it. His chin was a little higher, his eyes not as preoccupied with thought, and when he walked the halls of the office his step was a bit more brisk. I mentioned this to him.

"No question," he said, smiling. "What we accomplished last season has affected me, too. When there's a good feeling on a team, it sort of spreads itself around. I'm enthusiastic about our possibilities this season. Dallas will have the best team it's ever had. I know it already has the best attitude it's ever had, because of the good off-season workouts." Landry two years before had instituted a March-to-July regimen of weight-lifting and running, and though there were no fines involved for missing these workouts, a record was kept by the trainers on who did what and when. "That's something you can measure. You ought to see the way Bob Lilly worked! He got down to two hundred and forty pounds. Now if a player as great as Lilly works that hard, it's bound to affect every other player on the squad, and it did."

"Tom," I said, "have you figured out what happened last season?"

"I think so. We ran a tougher program last year, to begin with. The performance-level requirement was the new factor. I knew it would have a negative reaction on the team. I knew some players who had started for us would be sitting on the bench at first. I told people we'd sink to a lower level than we'd been in several years before it would eventually pay off."

"People? Do you mean you told the players that?"

"I told the coaches," Landry said, shaking his head. "I would never tell the players something like that. I knew this would create confusion on the ball club, but something had to be done if we were going to progress to a real championship contender. It's been eleven years since I've seen this kind of attitude. It's what the Giants used to have, what kept them going all those years they were winning championships." (He meant Eastern Conference championships.) "This team learned something last year down the stretch. They learned how to pull together, to place individual pride second and think only of team pride first. There's no reason why this shouldn't carry over. You don't easily lose that. It's what got them there, and they *know* it."

Landry always had a twist of the dial for a slight change in the team's direction, and though it sometimes didn't work out exactly as planned, it usually worked out. For 1966 he opened up the offense to shift Renfro from defense to running back. Renfro got hurt in the first league game, but second-year-man Danny Reeves took his place and scored sixteen touchdowns. Last season he went in emphasizing the power running game, to take advantage of Hill. Hill got hurt, but Thomas came on to gain one thousand yards. "This year," he said, "we'll be concentrating on the passing game. Mainly because of Craig's arm troubles, it was below par last season, though that wasn't all of it. We have to re-establish a leader at quarterback, like Meredith was on this team. A leader has to be a performer. Craig hung in there tough in a trying situation last season, which is a big plus for him. But he has to deliver, as he's capable of doing. I have to assume he'll be one hundred percent physically, but I know only the throwing demands of training camp will answer that."

"But Morton goes in as number one," I said.

"It's not that clear cut," Landry said. "If Roger is ever going to do it, he'll make a go of it this year. I said three years ago that this is the year he could make his move to take over as starting quarterback, and let me tell you—he dies hard. When he competes, he really competes. The only thing to do is let them prove it on the field. I planned all

winter to alternate them as starters in the pre-season, leading
off with Morton against the Rams. You just hope that somebody will move the other guy out and establish himself as
number one without question."

"What are you going to do with Rentzel?" I said.

"That hasn't worked itself out yet, but I think it will in a
few days, one way or another."

"And Duane Thomas, do you think he means it?"

"Ordinarily, when a player says he's going to hold out, you
sort of expect to see him in training camp anyway. But with
a guy like Duane—well, you just never know."

The days had dwindled down to Mayday, liberation date
for all NFL chattels who would be free—until they read the
small print, not in their contracts but in the league by-laws.
May 1 is the date a player becomes a free agent if he has
played out the option year on his contract the season before.
Theoretically, he can make the rounds of the other twenty-
five teams, seeking the highest bidder—but there is a catch.
The team that signs him must agree on compensation to the
player's former club. If the two clubs can't reach agreement,
then commissioner Pete Rozelle can stipulate the price in
flesh or draft choices, and usually both.

Bobby Hayes had had a three-year contract which expired
with the 1969 season. His negotiations for 1970 broke down
through an ill-timed remark by assistant general manager Al
Ward, former sportswriter and club publicist who was groom-
ing himself to be an NFL executive. Hayes and his attorney,
Steve Falk of Miami, were in Ward's office and Falk was
extolling his client's assets: fifty-three touchdowns scored in
five years, plus the coincidence that Dallas had never had a
winning season before Hayes joined the team and had never
had a losing one since. "Just think for a moment," warned
Falk, "about a Cowboy team going into the season without
Bobby Hayes."

And Ward said, "Oh, we'll have a split end in training
camp."

Whereupon Hayes, the slowest to anger of all the Cowboys, got up and walked out of the office. He had to take a
mandatory 10 percent pay cut for his "freedom season," but

since he made it through without any crippling injury, the sacrifice figured to be worth it. If Dallas did not pay him what he wanted, somebody would have to do so, regardless of Rozelle's views on compensation. The commissioner could not allow Hayes to go unsigned and idle through the coming season, as spectacular evidence that the option clause was in violation of antitrust laws.

"They could have signed me for a lot less last year than they're gonna pay me now," Hayes said. "Because they're gonna pay me back for what I went through." I'd met him for a beer at Gordo's, a pizza place with good draft beer near SMU. Hayes sipped his beer as if it were hot tea. He doesn't drink, but he pretends he does, in the interest of conviviality. I've seen him get high at parties, but not from alcohol or anything else. Hayes gets high on friendship and happiness.

"Besides the ten percent cut," I said.

"Yeah. I played for under thirty-five thousand dollars, and suppose I tear up my knee, or break a leg? How much is Bob Hayes worth when he can only run a ten-flat? If I get hurt so I can't play any more, I get the thirty-something thousand, and the ball club doesn't owe me a dime. Steve, they gonna pay me eighty-five thousand dollars or I'll find somebody who will—Washington, the Jets, Miami, LA. I could take less from the Jets or Miami, because I could make some real money in New York, catching for Joe Willie. And that Griese cat in Miami ain't bad, plus I got friends in Florida right now where a bank will pay me to work for the Chamber of Commerce. But if everybody's too scared of what Rozelle would hit 'em with, then you're gonna see some shit. The Players Association called my lawyer, said we're behind Bobby and if you go to court we'll be right there with you. I don't want that, 'cause I'd end up like Curt Flood, my career over. I want Dallas to pay—for the humiliation I went through last season and for all the crap Measee had to take." Hayes got up to make a phone call, his sixth in the twenty minutes we'd been sitting there. Hayes had married his college sweetheart, Altamease Martin, a well-to-do girl from New Jersey, soon after signing his rookie contract in 1965. An hour after the wedding, Hayes brought his bride to the club offices and a bunch of us gathered around to offer congratulations. "Well, fellas,"

Hayes said, "this is better than Vietnam." Altamease pretended not to hear him. She has turned out to be a jewel in his life.

"What about Measee?" I said when Hayes came back to the table.

"Man, she went through it. She had to leave her checkbook at home. Yeah, everytime she'd write a check, 'Mrs. Bob Hayes,' somebody'd say, 'Why don't your husband put out and get off the bench?' Or 'That honky coach has got his honky 'Bama boy ahead of Bobby, so all the honkies is happy.' Measee would have to figure how much money she was going to spend, then go by the bank and get the cash. And the phone calls! Measee handles all the phone calls, you know that."

"Yeah, and *you* know black didn't have anything to do with Homan starting. But do you think playing out your option had something to do with it?"

"I don't know. I just wouldn't suspect that Tom would pay any attention to that, but maybe he has to work close with the front office when that happens. Sure, I know it wasn't any black-white thing with me and Dennis, but how did it look? It looked bad, especially him being from Alabama. You try to tell people it wasn't so. You'll never know the grief that caused me. Dennis and I are friends. He's a good guy. You know what he told me when he was starting? He said, 'Bobby, I know you ought to be playing, but this is my chance and I got to grab it.' I told him, 'Go get 'em.' It wasn't like that to me, man to man, teammate against teammate. It was me and Tom. Nobody ever told me why I wasn't starting."

"The word was that you weren't blocking, and you weren't running your patterns the way they wanted, whatever that means."

"Bullshit," Hayes said. "Bull . . . shit! I wasn't doing a damn thing different when they put me back in the lineup than I was doing before. You know why they put me back? Because we were losing, Daddy."

Near the end of May the Cowboys figured out what to do with Rentzel—send him to the Los Angeles Rams. This kicked off the biggest trade in the club's history and the only one in which they had ever swapped away a starter. For Rentzel, the Cowboys got tight end Billy Truax. This cleared the way for them to trade Pettis Norman, along with back-up defensive tackle Ron East and offensive tackle Tony Liscio, who had fallen from starter's status due to a sprained back and knee. For that matter, Norman was by now only half a starter at tight end, used as a messenger for Landry's play-calling, splitting playing time with Mike Ditka. All three went to San Diego for Lance Alworth, who was expected to move right into Rentzel's flankerback spot without any drop-off in talent.

"We would only have traded Lance to a contending team," Landry said. "If we couldn't do that, then I would have decided he was better off staying with the Cowboys."

It was a beautiful move for Rentzel. Since his marriage to Joey, Los Angeles had become his home town. The Rams needed a wide receiver to go with their one good one, Jack Snow, and Rentzel would be playing for the most intelligent coach in the league, Prothro. East was happy, but then East always seemed happy, a fellow who went around with a smile on his face, reminding you of a sailor on shore leave. He had asked to be traded. At 6 feet 3 inches, he had given up trying to dislodge Pugh from the "other" tackle job alongside Lilly. The disruption appeared severe for Norman and Liscio. Norman was a loan officer at a savings bank and he had just begun to insert himself, gently, into local politics and civic affairs as a spokesman for the black community. He had signed with the Cowboys as a free agent out of Johnson C. Smith College nine years ago and had seen all the bad and the good. He surprised me. "Heck fire," he said, "maybe I'll finally get with a team that throws to the tight end." Norman had caught six passes in 1970 and Ditka only two more than that. It was an old trauma with Norman. One season, when he complained to an assistant coach about his few opportunities to catch the ball, the coach told him, "Meredith just doesn't have any confidence in you." Norman said he went home that night, sat on the edge of his bed and cried.

"I don't feel very good about leaving Dallas," Norman said, "but one thing happened today that made me feel good. Tom came all the way out to my office, here in Oak Cliff, to tell me I was traded. He called me first and said he wanted to talk to me, and I thought, 'Uh-oh.' I knew what it had to be, and I said I'd come to see him, but no, he said he'd come out here. I tell you, maybe he isn't emotional, like they say, but the man cares."

Liscio, as Norman, is a family man who faced uprooting his brood to go play games in another town. "Maybe after they check my bod," he said, "they'll send me back." I told him the San Diego coach, Sid Gillman, knew all about his "bod" and wanted him anyway. Gillman also knew about his desire, carefully disguised by an easy-going manner and soft talk. After some Cowboy defeats, Liscio was so overcome by depression and self-accusation that he would lock himself in a room in his house and not come out for twenty-four hours. Yet Landry always cited him as the offensive lineman who made fewer mistakes than any other.

It often happens that a departing player makes headlines with comments about his former team. There were no headlines in Liscio, but he could look back with candor on the seasons past. The first subject, as ever, was Landry and the second was the "new team attitude." Liscio said, "Tom is hard to get close to and he was very difficult in the early days. A lot of guys thought he put himself on a high pedestal above everybody. He's not so much that way any more, maybe because he feels he has better players, his kind of people. He's a good coach and he gets your respect, everyone's respect, even the guys who are griping all the time. But he's not the kind of coach to give you a pep talk or motivate you like Lombardi would. Last year he came on with a lot of strictness, fined the hell out of a lot of people and things got tight, stiff. There was a new deal where people with the best grades after camp would play. That may have screwed up a bunch of guys. Tom believes if something goes wrong, even if you're tired of working, you work harder and harder. I guess it would be great if everyone *was* like that. After the second St. Louis game, we had nothing to lose. We didn't even weigh in any more before practice. I don't think any of us figured we'd be in the playoffs. I certainly didn't. I thought we'd beat St. Louis. When we didn't, I started planning a vacation for the first week after the season ended."

I told Liscio that Landry was counting on keeping that late comeback going into this season. Liscio said, "I was just wondering, thinking about not being with the club any more, can they pick up the way they were playing at the end? That was something the players did themselves. Things got loose. There was no pressure on. The coaches changed. Even Landry got a little easier. Even he got in and had fun in practice, joking around some. It was a different attitude. I don't know—I think it's going to be hard to have all that again."

Alworth, the big man in the trade from the Cowboys' standpoint, wasn't saying anything. For three weeks his maid answered the phone at his San Diego apartment and said Mr. Alworth would certainly return the call. On the maid's day off, Alworth made the mistake of answering the call himself. "It's getting complicated," he said. "I don't know if I can get together with Dallas on the money."

Beautiful. Just what the Cowboys needed—another fellow with contract troubles.

Unless you wanted to accompany Staubach to a church meeting, there seemed to be few happy stories on the Cowboy beat. I found myself talking mostly to agents and lawyers. Chuck Dekeado of Los Angeles was now representing Thomas, and he spelled out the dollars and cents of the running back's problem and put the decimal point on a few of his complaints. Thomas's three-year-contract specified salaries of $18,000, $20,000 and $22,000. He got a $25,000 bonus for signing. Bonus clauses in the contract, most of which Thomas reached ($5,000 for becoming a starter "in the eyes of Tom Landry," $2,500 for being named rookie of the year), pushed his first-year take from the club to $31,500. Together with a playoff-game salary and player shares from the NFC title game and the Super Bowl, Thomas had a take-home total of just under $74,000. "Now," Dekeado said, "Duane reads his contract and even with the two-thousand-dollar salary increase, if he did everything he did last year, he'll make five hundred dollars less. I mean, how many times can you be rookie of the year? Once, right?"

Thomas had been represented by Probus Management of New York. Dekeado said they had taken 10 percent of everything. "Including his Super Bowl money," he said. "I never heard of an agent taking part of a guy's playoff money. And the way it was set up, the Cowboys sent Probus Duane's checks and Probus deposited his balance. When Duane wants to get out of the contract with them, Gil Brandt advises him to buy them out. It costs him seventy-five hundred. Why, they'd already failed on so many parts of the contract—for instance, they paid his bills late, costing him money—he could have just walked away from it. That's seventy-five hundred dollars down the drain."

Dekeado said Thomas was upset by some of the phrases in his contract with the Cowboys. "How about having the starter's bonus clause decided 'in the eyes of Tom Landry'?" Dekeado said. "What kind of baloney is that?"

"That's probably the fairest clause in the contract," I said. "If Duane splits time with Hill, Landry will give him the benefit of the doubt."

"Maybe so, but that's not the point. It's a hook on the player by the coach. It's too damn benevolent. It's demeaning. I know it looks like they're going to hold Duane to the contract. I know the owners have got a pact to hold the line on salaries and especially not to tear up contracts, but I want to leave the salary alone and get Duane another ten thousand dollars or fifteen thousand dollars in bonuses—assured bonuses. But Duane won't go for that. He wants a *lot* more money, and I tell you, he's a funny guy. He just won't show if they don't give it to him."

The next day, after what Dekeado had said appeared in my paper, I was at the Cowboy offices on another story and was talking to the linebacker coach, Jerry Tubbs. "They let this Thomas thing get way out of hand," he said. "What they should have done was beat him to the punch, way back in February, say, 'Look, Duane, you did a great job, and we're going to sweeten the pot for you.' Now no telling where it's going to lead, and we stand to lose a great back."

Morton was standing in the shade of the roofed patio outside the back door of the practice-field locker room, taking
a breather. He was wearing a green slicker over a T-shirt,
football pants and cleats. He didn't look like a man who
didn't have a dime in the world; he looked unconcerned.
"You really went bust?" I said.

Morton nodded. "I had a guy keeping my income tax and
supposed to have paid it. Now I hear from the revenue service
I owe them for three years. He never sent in the money."

Morton had just declared corporate and personal bankruptcy, a double-header. He went broke with a bookstore at
the University of California in Berkeley and with another
bookstore at the University of California in Davis, plus two
sporting-goods stores. "Good thing you didn't have time to
make it to the other University of Californias," I said, "or
you'd really be in bad shape."

"Ha!" Morton said. As we talked he first skipped rope,
looking for all the world like a heavyweight contender, then
did a Globetrotter bit, shifting a football from hand to hand
while always keeping his palms down. "It's good to get out
of all of that," he said. "It was running me nuts. I'm going
to make my money in football, just concentrate on that."

"You better concentrate on keeping your starting job.
Staubach will be climbing up your heels. What do you think
of this deal, being even going into training camp?"

"It puzzles the hell out of me," Morton said. "I never had
that shot when Meredith was here. But I don't guess it makes
that much difference. I mean, I'm throwing well enough
now that nobody can take the job away. After this year there
won't be any more of that stuff. I'll settle it once and for all.
I'm tired of it. I earned that spot through a lot of years."

"You better not jack around in the pre-season," I said, "the
way you usually do."

"What do you mean?"

"This year it counts. Two summers ago you hit forty-four
percent in the exhibition games. I just looked it up. Then you
hit seventy percent in the first five league games, till you got
hurt. Last year you hit forty-six percent in the pre-season because your arm was no good."

Morton frowned. "I wasn't concerned about what kind of

completion record I had in those games," he said. "It's a time
when you should work on other things. Try different pass
routes and see if you can throw it by a linebacker, or what
will work. It may seem like a lot of poor passes, but there
are reasons for it. Anyway, what matters is my arm is okay.
For the first time in two years I can really wing the ball and
no pain. The receivers are surprised the way the ball's coming at 'em, I can tell."

In the space of three days in June, both Hayes and Alworth
came into the fold. The terms of the Hayes agreement were
not announced, but he told me in general what they were:
five-year package totaling $425,000, including a base salary
of $55,000, a bonus in payments deferred to the end of his
pro career, plus bonuses each year that he caught as many as
thirty-five passes and scored as many as eight touchdowns.
"Measee," Hayes said, "is now married to the highest-paid
receiver in pro football."

To trumpet the news that Hayes was no longer a free
agent, the club allowed TV cameras and microphones to be
set up in the anteroom of the office. No Cowboy official appeared. Alworth was welcomed to town two days later with
considerably more fanfare—a press conference in the private club on the second floor of the Cowboys' office building,
an open bar and Bloody Marys all around. Tex Schramm
was there to beam upon the assemblage. "I couldn't even
get a ginger ale when Hayes signed," I said to him. "You
really don't like anybody to play out their option, do you?"

"Don't be unpleasant," Schramm said. "This is just good
old Texas hospitality."

Alworth didn't pose for a contract-signing ceremony;
Dallas assumed the one he had in force with the Chargers,
at $55,000 a year, a happily coincidental figure. The day be-
fore, in San Diego, Alworth had filed for personal bankruptcy,
completing a loser's parlay from a previous corporate bankruptcy.

Frank Luksa of the Fort Worth *Star-Telegram* had a
thought: "If Morton and Alworth get going good as a battery, I know what we can call 'em—Cash and Carry."

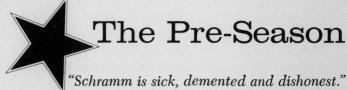# The Pre-Season

"Schramm is sick, demented and dishonest."
—DUANE THOMAS
"That's not bad. He got two out of three."
—TEX SCHRAMM

Every summer's return to Thousand Oaks holds a sense of coming home. It is a forty-mile shot north from Los Angeles on the Ventura Freeway, and there is a comforting familiarity as you top the last big hill, whip past the Malibu Canyon cutoff and enter the Conejo Valley. There is also some apprehension, as a sometime native frowns at what a year has done to his town. The six-lane Moorpark Road, leading from the freeway to Cal Lutheran College, is clogged with traffic, and subdivisions have spilled eastward along it, choked with California stucco and twenty-foot lawns. It is not a town at all but a bedroom community, a suburb unattached to a city, crowded by people chasing the good life and being overtaken by the old life they left behind. But the breezes still funnel their way somehow from the Pacific, you wear a sweater at night in mid-July and in the late evenings a carefree, no-tomorrow attitude prevails—at Los Robles, the restaurant–night club (off limits to the players) tucked into the seaward hills overlooking a golf course, and at Orlando's, the pizza discotheque where someone is always singing "Rolling . . . rolling . . . rolling down the river" (off limits to coaches and club officials until the players' curfew rings). Divorcees, widows, young wives with astonishingly understanding husbands are in the crowd. The ship of life has passed through Thousand Oaks, leaving this flotsam and jetsam behind it, and the Cowboys soar over the scene like seagulls, picking at the spoils. The players call it Peyton Place West.

This is indeed the truest home the team will ever know over the long season, the time when they are forced to live together, work together and, on their off nights, Wednesdays and Saturdays, play together.

In the team's fledgling years it had worked the summers at somnolent Pacific University in Forest Grove, Oregon, just too far north of Portland; next, at St. Olaf's College in Northfield, Michigan; then in a frigid northern Michigan in the tiny hamlet of Marquette. The stay at St. Olaf's led to the solution of training-camp problems, through a house mother who had transferred to California Lutheran, a new school starting out in life a year later than the Cowboys. "You can pick up fifty G's," the lady told the president, "if you get Dallas here between semesters."

The Rams, the Chargers and the 49ers have since tried to outbid the Cowboys for what is recognized by visiting press as the finest summer football facility in the NFL. The club is housed in the men's dormitory—scaled three to a room for collegians and thus just right for double occupancy by pros—an H-shaped structure with two-story wings connected by a one-story link containing the lobby and the meeting rooms. The veterans are on the ground floor of the left wing, rookies on the second, and the right wing contains the coaches, the club officials, the press, and as many college coaches as Gil Brandt can inveigle, expenses-free, for a visit.

These are the weeks when the new and different Cowboy team will be formed, for better or worse. The flaws which can't be erased here will last, fatally, through the league season. The players who will be a bright factor in the immediate future will be known to everyone before the team breaks camp.

Danny Reeves was leaning into Schramm's door, promising a solution to the Duane Thomas disagreement. "All you have to do," Reeves said in his soft Georgia drawl, "is sign a check and leave the figures blank, and I'll take it into LA and come back with Duane." Reeves was still an active half-back on the roster, but he was also backfield coach. Schramm pretended to consider the proposition, then beamed a pearly smile. "Okay," he said, "and we'll take the difference out of your paycheck."

"I knew you'd have an answer I wouldn't like," said Reeves, turning to walk away.

The reporting date for the full squad was three days away, and only the rookies, the centers, the quarterbacks and the receivers were on hand. There had been no indication Thomas would relent on his holdout. Dekeado had given me his client's home phone number, but it hadn't answered for seven days, and as far as I or anyone else knew, Thomas was back in Bermuda. It seemed like a good time to get into an argument with Gil Brandt over the Thomas contract.

Brandt was in his room, sipping a lemonade. He is a tee-totaler but nevertheless has other good qualities. He was wearing the coaches' uniform, ripple-sole shoes, white sweat socks, gray khaki shorts and a nylon shirt with "Dallas Cowboys" stitched freehand across the left breast. "I don't hear a thing from Duane," Brandt said before I could say a word. "Maybe he's in New Zealand."

This crack stemmed from an incident at Fort Lauderdale, when reporters had come across Thomas, his playbook in his lap, staring out into the Atlantic. "I'm thinking about what's out there," he said in response to questions. "I'm thinking about New Zealand . . . because it's a good place to retire. . . . Yeah, I'm a rookie, but that's the best time to think about retiring."

"You people are biting off your nose to spite your face," I said to Brandt. "Why don't you give Thomas some more money and get him here?"

"We offered him more money," Brandt said. "*Last* year, when we signed him. That's right, he's bitching about his low salary. We'd have given him a lot more salary, but he wanted the bonus. That happens every time when you sign guys out of college—they don't believe in themselves. Hell, we believe in 'em, but they want the dough in front, so we give 'em what they want. Only one guy I ever knew turned down the money for salary—Pete Gent, and he was a basketball player. He said if he didn't make our team he didn't want our money, but if he made it, he wanted more money than we were offering him. Fair enough. But he's one out of hundreds."

"Still," I said "for what he did for you Thomas is worth more than what you're paying him, including the bonus."

"What about the guys we sign to three-year contracts who are perfectly happy?" Brandt said. "You never heard Dennis Homan complain." Homan was the club's number-one draft choice for 1968, and a few weeks back he had been traded for another wide receiver, Gloster Richardson of Kansas City, even up.

"That's beautiful," I said. "You got Homan sitting on the bench happy as can be, and you got Hill or Thomas out there starting for you with the red ass. That doesn't make sense. You get a stud tied to a twenty thousand dollar contract and you say, ho-boy, did we put the screws to you."

"What are you going to do?" Brandt shrugged.

"Tie the incentive bonuses to his permanent contract," I said. "Duane gains over eight hundred yards to meet one bonus, he's a starter to meet another, he's rookie of the year—add that to his salary. He comes in the second year making thirty-one thousand five hundred. That's enough raise to keep him from screaming about a lousy contract."

"I'm telling you he wouldn't have taken it," Brandt said. "He would have wanted that extra money in the bonus at the time he signed."

I was partially out of my depth, I'll admit. Brandt was a twelve-year veteran in the field, dealing with draft choices and free agents, and he devoted eighteen hours a day to the job. His is a case of an incurable football buff realizing his wildest dreams. A graduate of Wisconsin in the era of Elroy Hirsch, Brandt had become a baby photographer in Milwaukee, working the hospitals. He solved his man-hour problems in that job by teaching the nurses how to handle a camera and giving them a split of the fee. To while away his spare time he indulged in his love, rating college athletes for pro careers, and sent the results to the Rams, where Hirsch was starring. Schramm, then the general manager at

Los Angeles, used Brandt on several occasions to sign Midwest collegians to contracts. Brandt always got his man, and usually by return mail, so Schramm remembered him when the time came to put together an organization in Dallas. "I told him to sign as many free agents as he could find," Schramm recalls, in the year when Dallas entered the league without a college draft. "He sent me thirty contracts in two days, and I had to tell him to slow down. I also had to hire him full time as our personnel director." The results since have been delightful to Schramm. "Everybody in the league bitches about him," he said. "That's how I know he's doing a great job."

During the bidding wars between the AFL and the NFL, Brandt would get so wrapped up in the competitiveness of it all that he would sign a player for $5,000 or $10,000 more than the limit prescribed by Schramm. Then he would see the business manager and tell him to take the money out of his, Brandt's, pay, at least until he could falsify some expense accounts. Schramm, of course, knew about this too and tacitly approved.

The Cowboy scouting system is famous for its computerized efficiency, but nothing works by machine alone. The thirty-six-year-old Brandt is the human element that greases the wheels. Before the National Collegiate Athletic Association forbade it, Brandt had one and sometimes two coaches at every major college sending in reports, measurements and clockings on their top athletes, in return for a monthly stipend. When this was outlawed, he simply sent his scouts around to wine and dine coaches with their wives, and the ones who were too busy when the scouts came to call were invited out to Thousand Oaks, expense-free, to learn the Cowboy system at Landry's knee. I once met a visitor in camp from tiny Adams (Colorado) State. "How many pro prospects you have?" I said. "One this year," he said, "and maybe one next year." That was enough, and when he asked Ermal Allen, "Coach, will you run over that off-tackle play from the brown formation one more time?" he got an answer. As a result of all this time, effort and money, whenever Brandt wanted to check in depth on a college prospect, he could phone any campus in the country and get the goods: "The kid is flunking out, the draft is on his neck, and I think he's going to defect to Canada."

"What do you think will happen with Duane?" I said.

"I think he'll play with the Cowboys," Brandt said. "It's the best place for him."

The campus at Cal Lutheran was apparently nonexistent. The dining hall was a few steps out the back of the dormitory and chonked into the side of a hill, so that you entered the two-story room at the top, past an ice-cream parlor with juke-box and booths and tables for the coeds. There seemed to be only coeds at this school in the summertime, hurrying to complete their degrees before nuptials caught them. The males passed. To the right from the dining hall were the administration building, a bookstore, library, the Bank of A. Levy, doctors' offices and beyond that nothing but a distant hill where a string of lights spelled out CLC at night. In between was the practice field, where Roger Staubach was dueling Craig Morton and doing a helluva job of it. Staubach's passes fairly whistled to their targets, curving in a low arch. Morton was throwing soft and high.

Staubach was already a phenomenon, a career that couldn't happen. No other academy graduate, forced to take his full four-year hitch, had ever come back and made it in the pros. A gifted three-sport athlete in high school at Cincinnati, Staubach turned down a baseball contract tendered by the Cincinnati Reds to accept a deal from Navy—a year of prepping at New Mexico Military Institute so he could make it scholastically at Annapolis. This preparatory year meant, importantly to the Cowboys, that Staubach's high-school class would graduate a year before he did, the stipulation that made him eligible to be claimed in the college draft of his junior season, when he won the Heisman Trophy. Schramm claims that Brandt had stepped down the hall for a lemonade when the Cowboy turn came that year in the tenth round, and the devil made him say, "Staubach!" After completion of an anticlimactic senior season, Staubach signed an agreement with Dallas, for $5,000 a year, that *if* he would

ever decide to leave the Navy and play pro football he would
play for the Cowboys. This shut off the Kansas City Chiefs,
who had drafted him for the AFL, and also placated the
admirals. Signing Staubach to a 1969 contract, with bonus,
would have been in violation of Navy regulations.

Brandt began to suspect that Dallas had a service-academy
exception on its hands when Staubach sent an SOS from
Vietnam requisitioning a "Duke" football, the official NFL
model. The request was repeated six months later because the
original had been worn through the leather, skidding on
the concrete dockside near Da Nang. Staubach returned to
the States in 1968 to become a supply officer at Pensacola,
and he timed his leave that year to coincide with the Cowboys' rookie portion of training camp. He came in lean as
a whippet, 6 feet 3 inches and 190 pounds, and almost as
fast, for a quarterback—4.8 seconds in the forty-yard dash.
He scrimmaged that year against George Allen's Ram rookies,
which is to say he scrimmaged against veterans and taxi
squadders because Allen never has any rookies—and he made
them look silly. "He's a better scrambler than Tarkenton,"
Allen said, "and he's got an arm." That day I asked Red
Hickey, the Cowboys' chief scout, if he thought Staubach
could help the club the next year, and Hickey barked a
laugh and said, "He could help us in *this* one." Everything
has always seemed to work out for Staubach, but he has a
way of helping fortune along. That fall the admiral at Pensacola decided the air station should be represented by a
football team, and a schedule was arranged against small
Southern colleges. "We had a pass-oriented offense," Staubach said, laughing, "because I was the quarterback *and* the
coach." He took another leave in the spring of 1969 to get
in on the off-season quarterback drills conducted by Landry,
but by the time he reported to training camp in July, as an
ex-sailor, Cowboy back-up quarterback Jerry Rhome had
been traded and Meredith had retired. In the space of a few
weeks, without ever having fired a football in NFL action,
Staubach had moved from number four to number two. He
responded that summer with a show of joyous liberation. He
would stay on the practice field until the last receiver stepped

on a panting tongue, then he would line up for an end-of-day ritual with Bob Belden, the taxi-squad quarterback from Notre Dame. Staubach would run a "fly" pattern, straight down the sidelines, giving a great cry of "Heee-yah!" and leaping with giant strides as Belden launched him a bomb. Catching it on his fingertips, Staubach would keep running at full speed to the locker room, down a hill and up a hill, a half mile away.

After looking at this for a few weeks, Landry revised his famous formula which decreed that a quarterback must have five years of league experience before leading a team to a championship. "In Staubach's case," he said, "three will be about right, because part of that experience factor has always been maturity, and maturity is no problem with Staubach. He's a year older than Morton."

Now he was making that third-year bid to take over the ball club and, as good as he was, I didn't think he would make it. He had started four games the past two seasons for Dallas, the first one in 1969 when Morton had dislocated a finger, the first three in 1970, when Morton was suffering most from shoulder and elbow troubles, and he was 3-1. Staubach lodged a protest about the one defeat, at St. Louis. "I was behind three to nothing in the second quarter when they took me out," he said. "If I'd stayed in there, we would have won with no trouble."

We were walking up from the locker rooms to the dorm. "Physically, I feel great," he said in that soft, reasonable way of his. "Mentally, I'm anxious to see what happens. I wish Coach Landry was a little stronger about my chances. I can't really tell what he's thinking. Here we have the finest team in pro football, and we're trying to settle the quarterback question. It really hurts my pride when I keep reading that the Cowboy weakness is quarterback. I don't like that. I want quarterback to be a strength. Coach Landry has said in my third year I could be ready, but that it's up to me to prove it on the field. I don't believe it will be like last year if I start—starting on a shoestring. But I know he's going to give Morton the inside track. I just wish I had the inside track. I know nobody would get me out of there. I'd love to be in Craig's position." We'd reached the door to the players' wing, and Staubach stopped. "What do you think?" he said. I noted an essential difference in the way Staubach couched the question. He wasn't seeking reassurance. He was just curious for an outside opinion.

"You got everything going for you except time," I said.

"Yeah, and Craig's always going to have four more years in the game than I do. Well, experience isn't everything."

"No," I said, "but it seems to be way ahead of whatever's in second place."

In the cool and quiet afternoons, ghosts walked the halls of the coaches' wing. Dick Nolan striding along, with one knocked-down shoulder lower than the other. Meredith smoking a cigarillo, because he'd bet a hundred dollars he could quit smoking cigarettes. Buddy Dial saying he had just come from "a conference with the Reverend T.L.," and telling me, "Dammit, podnuh, if you want to borry my guitar, borry it at eight o'clock, not two A.M." Dial didn't understand that our guitar player would never play the guitar until the bars closed down. Sometimes the hall rattled with garbage-can lids, the ones the coaches and I ricocheted off the walls the night Landry spent in Los Angeles with his wife, Alicia.

Now there was a real-life apparition on the premises, Lance Alworth, the "Bambi" from the other league, a slender fellow with the eyes of a doe and the grace of a fawn, the lone and unanimous exception when the old establishment looked askance at the AFL. Schramm used to say, "None of their guys can stay in the same ball park with our people—except Alworth. Alworth we'd take."

I stopped Alworth and tugged at the block letters, "Dallas Cowboys," on his T-shirt. "Tell me," I said, "what's a nice guy like you doing in the NFL?"

Alworth grinned. "I guess," he said, "I'd rather switch than starve." He was on his way into the club publicity office to take a call from the Los Angeles *Times*. I followed him in and waited. He was as slender as ever, and nine years in pro football hadn't erased the enthusiasm that goes with youth. Alworth put down the phone and picked up the entry of our conversation. "I used to get so tired of that horse hockey about the AFL being inferior," he said. "Then we played the first two Super Bowls and it looked like we *were* inferior— but that was just Green Bay. Hell, everybody was inferior to Green Bay. When the Jets won the first Super Bowl, I couldn't crow about it. What's one game? And Namath got the credit, a virtuoso. Nobody realized the Jets weren't even the best team in our league. I mean nobody but us. Didn't Namath say three or four other AFL teams could have beaten Baltimore? Then Kansas City put it to Minnesota, and I couldn't wait to get some of mine back. The first banquet I went to that winter, there was Johnny Unitas. Things are never as sweet as you think they're going to be. I just grinned at him and said, 'Hello, John.' We're all in it together now and the rivalry is gone. I wish they'd listened to Lamar [Hunt] and kept the leagues separate."

Then Alworth explained his curious reluctance to accept the trade to the Cowboys. "I had to get one hundred thousand dollars off my back," he said. "I owed the Chargers for a loan. It was actually a deal they reneged on, and it cost me a lot more than that. You're not going to believe this, but when I talked to Schramm about coming to Dallas, he said he would feel obligated to pay off the loan and take the money out of my salary. I guess it was one lodge brother to another. This all goes away back, when Eugene Klein bought the Chargers. He said, 'You ought to make some big money and I don't see any reason you can't.' I thought that was nice. He got me into a one-point-five-million-dollar apartment project, and after I did my part of getting financing nothing ever came of it. Then I went to him with a deal which would take four one-hundred-thousand-dollar investments by the club. Klein okayed it and I got the first one hundred thousand dollars—I never could get the rest, which left me hanging in the middle. That's why I sued the Chargers. You can imagine, this led to a weird season. It got so I was hardly in the game plan. They'd have six or seven patterns to the other side and two patterns for me to run. There wasn't much the quarterback, John Hadl, could do. Out of sight, out of mind. One game I saw we could beat the defense with one of our old routes, and I was telling John about it. [Coach] Charley Weller came over and yelled at me, 'Get away from the quarterback. Don't be talking to the quarterback. If I want him to know something, I'll tell him.' Looking back, it's pretty clear what was happening. I agreed to drop my lawsuit and in return they promised they wouldn't trade me, because I had long-term business plans in San Diego. When my attorney mentioned all the static that went on, how few passes I'd been thrown, Klein told him, 'He was lucky to be on the field at all.'"

As I listened to Alworth it was easy to understand how the kid from Brookhaven, Mississippi, out of the University of Arkansas, had got himself so embroiled in high finances. Alworth's eyes sparkled when he ticked off the big numbers; his whole body became more animated. The subject turned him on. "So," he said, "I had to declare personal bankruptcy before agreeing to terms with Dallas. After all, one hundred thousand dollars deducted from fifty-five thousand dollars doesn't leave you much to live on. There was more to it than the money. I was so stunned for a few weeks after the trade, I thought I was through with football. Then I calmed down and considered all angles, and one thing swayed me, made me realize I had to keep playing. I just couldn't resist having a shot at the Super Bowl. The first thing everybody talks about here is keeping the attitude they had the last part of last season. It's intense. It's great. You can just feel the difference in being with a legitimate contender. What a great break to be on a team that you *know* has got the personnel to win the Super Bowl title."

The due date for all the veterans was July 16, and everyone reported except Chuck Howley and Duane Thomas. Landry made an unannounced trip into Los Angeles with Gil Brandt to talk with Thomas at Dekeado's office. Landry wouldn't repeat how the conversation went, but Brandt told me when Landry came out of the session, he said, "He's not going to play." The no-show of Howley was a surprise, and Landry said there was no contract difficulty involved, that Howley was debating retirement. Of the men who reported, five had not signed contracts—Morton, Blaine Nye, Renfro, Pugh and Kiner.

A story had been bugging me ever since I got to camp. It had actually originated in November when Denne Freeman, the Associated Press sports editor in Texas, told me a friend of his wife's had heard that Morton was seeing a hypnotist, allegedly to cure his football flaws. After a game at the Cotton Bowl, when the other writers had moved on, I'd asked Morton about it, and he said, "It's very complicated. I don't want to get into it with you while the season is on. After it's all over, I'll tell you about it." But Morton had taken so much flak about the Super Bowl, I had put the story on the back burner—until the hypnotist, a retired Dallas furniture designer named Ed Pullman, had started talking to one and all about his "experiments" with the Dallas quarterback. A college kid, Frank Taggart, was working in the *Times Herald* sports department that summer, and he had gotten an earful from Pullman, whereupon the sports editor asked me a good question: "What are you doing, working for the *Herald* or handling PR for Morton?"

I called Morton and arranged to see him in one of the meeting rooms just outside the players' wing. "What's up, big fella?" he said. I told him I wanted to get the straight of this business with the hypnotist. "No, I don't think so. I don't want to talk about it," Morton said. "This is bad timing. I don't want it to come out." I had to tell him it was going to come out whether he wanted it to or not. "Not if I won't comment on it," Morton said. "Then there's no story."

"Except," I said, "Pullman taped all your conversations. Everything is right there, verbatim. If we don't print it, the other paper will. So you might as well let me put the best face on it. What the hell—this isn't the first time an athlete used hypnosis. Sal Maglie, Jackie Jensen, Maury Wills—and I hear John Brodie was into some kind of mind-over-matter deal last year in Frisco."

"It's going to be a controversial subject with a lot of people," Morton said. That was putting it mildly. No matter how nicely I wrote the story, Morton was going to come out looking like a damn fool.

"The thing is," I said, "do you think it helped?"

"I'm not sure," Morton said. "How can you measure it? It's supposed to work on the subconscious, which is unmeasurable. It might have helped when I got hit, but that's an automatic reflex. It seemed to help me keep from throwing interceptions or losing the ball on a fumble. I looked on it with an open mind, and I couldn't see how it would hurt. Any educated man would acknowledge that experiment with the subconscious is a fascinating field. Every day you read about advancements of hypnosis in medicine. But you really have to believe in it for it to work."

Pullman, fifty-eight, had established what he called the Southwest Hypnosis Research Center in his home, not far from the SMU campus, and one of his first subjects was an artist, Lois Shawgo, who wanted to stop smoking and stop biting her fingernails. Morton and a girl friend bought some paintings from Mrs. Shawgo, heard an earful about Pullman, and went to the hypnotist's house one night with the artist and her husband. And so it came to be that the morning of the Dallas game in Kansas City, the sixth league game of the season, Morton was in his hotel room with a telephone to his ear, saying, "Okay, Ed, let me turn off the television and get set."

Then Pullman said, "Now you're perfectly relaxed and comfortable, your mind is completely clear and in a few moments you are going into a deep sleep. Now I'm going to give you your 'post'—*black salt*." This was the code phrase which Pullman had programmed Morton during the week to receive post-hypnotic suggestions. Pullman's voice droned on: "You're in a deep sleep, but you can hold the phone. You feel fine. You must remember everything I told you, all the suggestions I gave you. You must be perfectly relaxed and calm and have all the ability to work the game today. Everything that I gave you must come through today, and you're going to be amazed at the results. You will experience no pain. You're going to fall and not get hurt."

Pullman had picked a good game to get on the Morton bandwagon, or vice versa. The Cowboys beat the Chiefs 27-16, and Morton hit seven of fourteen passes, including an eighty-nine-yard touchdown to Hayes. Pullman had provided me with a copy of his tapes, and in my room at training camp I could listen to Morton's excited voice after the game, in another phone call from Kansas City. "I'm kinda excited," he said. "None of the fluid has come back in my elbow, which is kind of amazing because it usually balloons right up. I had my knee twisted a bit, but it went right away. I got hit a lot harder than I have been in a long time today."

For the rest of the season, right through the Super Bowl, Pullman and Morton continued the hypnosis. "The object," said Pullman, "was to relieve Craig of game pressures, boost his confidence, free him from further injury by conditioning him to relax on the instant of body contact, to keep his elbow from being a conscious hindrance and just generally open up the full potential of his abilities. We also worked on the time he got a pass away. He had been bothered by hesitation. He was taking over four seconds to get off a pass and was getting thrown for losses. I worked to get this down to a flat three seconds, but I had to watch the technical things. I knew I was dealing with one million dollars' worth of ballplayer, and I'm no coach.

"Hypnosis is mostly misunderstood by people who don't know its limitations. Most everyone knows that you can't get someone to do something they wouldn't want to do. Also, you can't take an average person and through hypnosis get him to throw a football accurately or powerfully. But you can clear away distractions that may be preventing an athlete from performing to his full potential—as much as his physical ability will permit. It's like a file drawer in which all the papers are filed out of order. Hypnosis can put all the papers back in order."

Pullman and Morton agreed there were no further sessions planned for this season. "I'd like to get a group thing going," Pullman said on the phone from Dallas, "with Morton and Hayes and Alworth, get them reacting subconsciously to one another."

Landry had been through so much the last few months that I could have told him Morton planned to jump off the Golden Gate Bridge and it wouldn't have lifted one of his eyebrows. "I don't know much about hypnosis," he said, "but I can see how it might help a particular set of problems. Craig was under a lot of strain last season, financial troubles, arm troubles, and we were losing, so I can see it on a short term."

"Well," I said, "this guy Pullman wants to work with Morton and Hayes and Alworth and get them all on the same page."

That did get a rise out of Landry. "Wait a minute," he said. "I didn't say I had no objection. I just said I had no opinion, but when my receivers start getting into it, that makes a different case."

Four days into camp, Blaine Nye decided to walk out, ripping a 6-foot-4-inch, 250-pound hole in the offensive line at right guard. Nye was the fellow who put Neely on the bench last season, then kept the job all the way when Neely moved to left tackle for the injured Liscio. I heard about his imminent departure about 9:00 P.M., but I had no clue to his motive, since the ball club said it wasn't money. When there was no answer in Nye's room, I walked out to the parking lot and saw a taxicab parked near the player's wing. Nye came out of the door and tossed two suitcases in the back seat before I stopped him. "Are you gone for good, or just taking a little holiday?" I said.

"I'm going down to see my folks at Santa Ana," he said, "and do some thinking. Maybe I'll get together with the Cowboys in a couple of days—and maybe I won't."

"Are you sick of the game?" I said. Nye was a graduate of the Ivy League West, Stanford, where students are sometimes educated to believe that pro football isn't everything.

"That's part of it. I don't want to go into it any more than that. I set a goal for myself four years ago what I'd be making after four years or I'd be through. I haven't made it. I don't want to say what the figure is, but it's not a great deal."

When the cab pulled away, I wondered what the fare was

to Santa Ana. Landry had taken a break from his coaches' meetings to go over to the ice-cream parlor for a double-dip vanilla cone. "I don't think Nye wants to play that much," he said. "A lot of people go through high school and college not caring very much about the game. Up here in the NFL the pressures are bigger. Heck, you have to pay quite a price to play in this league. Some people don't want to pay it. I don't get the idea that money was the problem with Nye. If a fellow tells you he's been made a fair offer and in the next breath says he wants another figure, I think he went in expecting not to get it. I think he would have been shocked to get it. We'll put Hagen at Nye's spot tomorrow and see what happens."

Halvor Hagen, 6 feet 5 inches and 250 pounds, was a second-year man, so the Cowboys gained an inch and lost two years' experience.

Two days later Duane Thomas held a press conference at the Press Club in Dallas, and in the course of explaining his holdout he called Landry "a plastic man, actually no man at all," Brandt "a liar," and Schramm "sick, demented and completely dishonest." I pressed Schramm for his personal reaction, and he laughed. "That's not bad," he said. "He got two out of three." Schramm had one of his assistants call a Dallas radio station which had taped the press conference and make a copy-tape over the long-distance phone, about forty-five minutes' worth. A bunch of us crowded into the publicity office for the playback. Landry skipped the beginning of afternoon practice and sat on the edge of a desk, swinging his legs to and fro. When Thomas got to the "plastic man" bit, he looked up and grinned sheepishly. The tape drew a laugh from Schramm when Thomas referred to him as "an ex-sportswriter. You can look at him and tell he never played in the NFL."

Thomas was saying, "I want a new contract for eighty thousand dollars base pay, and I don't want any incentive clauses in it. I think, everything considered, eighty thousand dollars is pretty cheap. We are about fifty thousand dollars apart. I proved myself last year and I think I'm entitled to a new contract. After all, the Cowboys never made it to the Super Bowl without me, and they will never make it again unless I play for them. They were completely dishonest with me in our contract negotiations prior to last season, and therefore I feel no moral obligation to hold up my end of that contract. On my three-year contract I was misinformed, just like all black players are misinformed. I don't doubt for a minute that the Cowboy organization paid off my agent, or rather my ex-agent.

"The problem in general is that I'm black. Had I been a white player, they would have not done me such an injustice. They have done this to all black players and have exploited black players all along. They stereotype black players, but, hey, I'm not Jim Brown or Calvin Hill. I'm Duane Thomas and I want to be treated as an individual. I wouldn't mind being traded. I'm tired of being treated like a stupid animal, and I think these people have been trying to crook me.

"They don't want to pay me what I deserve. Well, they actually aren't paying me at all. Hey, the public is paying me. It's the public that pays the bill."

Schramm refused to comment on the Thomas speech, but Landry didn't mind. Had Thomas just burned all his bridges behind him? "You mean what would I do if he reported to camp?" Landry said. "I'd talk to him." On the exploitation of blacks, Landry replied, "There's not a bit of difference in my eyes between a white athlete and a black athlete. I don't know whether they're black or white when I'm talking to them."

In the wake of the bad news, Chuck Howley reported to camp the next day, ending his "retirement." He said he'd seen the Thomas interview on television. "I was watching it with a few other people," he said, "and I was embarrassed for Duane. But I don't have time to talk about that. I've got enough troubles of my own. I have to see Landry." Howley had a profitable uniform-rental and dry-cleaning business in Dallas, and for the last few months it looked as though he faced a choice: either the business would go down the drain or his pro-football career would. This week he'd worked out a new deal with his partners and was free to keep playing, at age thirty-five.

All of the defensive linemen were sporting mustaches, and so were four of the linebackers. Stautner had started it, growing a straight black job that circled dourly beyond the corners of his mouth. "Hey, Ernie!" Larry Cole said. "You look like a gunfighter of the Old West."

"You really think so?" Stautner said.

"Yeah—West Bavaria," Cole said. The number-two defense was on the field, working against the number-one offense, half speed, which meant no tackling and above all do not zap the quarterback. Cole and Lilly and the rest were standing along the sidelines. "You really think it looks all right?" Andrie said, fingering his scraggly growth. "I'm going to shave it off before we go back to Dallas."

"Don't do that," I said. "If the front four keep the mustaches, I'll make you famous for hairying the passer."

"Now I know I'll shave it off," Andrie said.

Howley was the lone holdout among the linebackers. "I just gave up my crewcut last year," he said. "I ain't going to a mustache."

"I had a great big handlebar back in Dallas," Charley Waters said. "A real beauty. But I'm fighting to keep my job, and anything might make a difference, so I whacked it off." Waters' duel with Cliff Harris at free safety was so far the highlight of the two-a-day drills. Both were rookies last season, and Harris, a free agent from Ouachita (Arkansas) College, started the first five games until called up by the National Guard. Waters took over from there through the Super Bowl. Dallas thus had twelve returning starters on defense, and the shakeout was noticeable. "Don't go across the middle with your eyes closed," Hayes told his pal Margene Adkins, "or those cats will kill you. Harris and Waters are acting like this is mid-season."

Other than Harris versus Waters and the sparks that were flying off Staubach, the competition was quiet. Billy Truax was limping around on a strained Achilles tendon, leaving Mike Ditka all alone at tight end. In the absence of Thomas, there was no squeeze in the offensive backfield, where Hill and Garrison were comfortable. Nor was the rookie crop as much of a factor as it had been all the years up to this one. It used to be that a flurry of movement would catch the corner of your eye, some graceful burst of class, and those of us on the sidelines would ask, "Who was that?" And another would answer, "Oh, that's Renfro." There were starting jobs awaiting rookies in those days, when Landry would say, "If your number-one pick isn't capable of starting for you his first year, you've made a bad choice." This season's number one, defensive end Tody Smith of USC, had apparently received some inflated advice from brother Bubba in Baltimore, and he was still a holdout. Two other top rookies, cornerback Ike Thomas and defensive tackle Bill Gregory, were with the College All-Star squad in Chicago.

There were few places where first-year men could crowd onto the Cowboy roster, deep as it was with youth and talent. Cole, Pugh, Lilly and Andrie were entrenched as the front four, with second-year man Pat Toomay pressing for playing time at end. Jordan, Howley and Edwards were already backed up across the board by Tom Stincic, Kiner and D.D. Lewis. Another gifted sophomore, Mark Washington, was behind cornerbacks Renfro and Adderley. Cornell Green, a former All-NFL cornerback, had found a home at strong safety. Beyond the Harris-Waters battle was third-year veteran Richmond Flowers. The offense was similarly packed. "We are going to have the damnedest dogfight you've ever seen at wide receiver," said end coach Ray Renfro. At split end were Hayes and Adkins and Wendell Tucker, a veteran who came from the Rams with Truax. If he could make the club, Dallas would give LA a draft choice. At flankerback were Alworth, Super Bowl starter Reggie Rucker and Gloster Richardson. The offensive line was solid, left to right, with Neely, Niland, Manders, Nye or Hagen, and Rayfield Wright. Two second-year men, guard-center John Fitzgerald and tackle Bob Asher, were highly rated, especially Asher. Backfield coach Danny Reeves, partly because of his clutch value and partly because he could serve as an emergency quarterback, would claim one of the five running-back jobs, and second-year men Claxton Welch and Joe Williams would pick up what was left.

Clearly, for most of the eighty rookies this camp was an exercise in futility. Why did they come? I'd tried this tactless question on a few of them, with predictable results. "Whaddya mean? I'm going to *make* this club," said a linebacker from Lane College. A 5-foot-11-inch running back from Missouri said, "Somebody must have thought I had a chance, or I wouldn't be here."

"Most of them," said Danny Reeves, "are just not ready to give up football. I was like that when I came in as a free agent in 'sixty-five. I sweated out every cutdown date. I was going to make them tell me I couldn't cut it. I wasn't going to give up on myself. That way, when you're finally out of football, you can live with it. You can tell your buddies at the beer hall, 'I had it made, but there was two sonsabitches ahead of me with no-cut contracts.' Nobody gets no-cuts any more, but who knows that? With the people we've got, it's tough to break in, but that works two ways. It isn't exactly a disgrace to get cut by the Cowboys right now. There are twenty-four teams in the league who didn't get as far as we did, and some of them might take our spillover."

There has to be a single story emerging from the early days of training camp. There always is—and it was Calvin Hill, the articulate black bulldog from Yale, moving with the same abandon he had as a rookie two years ago, and moving with far more power. "You look bigger," I told him, walking back to the locker room at the end of practice. Hill had just run a penalty lap for being overweight, and his high voice was higher than usual.

"Maybe that's because I am," he said. "I grew an inch since last season."

"At age twenty-four?" I said. "Boy, marriage must have really agreed with you. I take it you mean you grew an inch in height, not elsewhere." Hill had become a benedict in January.

"All right, don't get vulgar," Hill said. "I went from six-three to six-four. Your body cells either create more than is lost or they don't. When they start to create fewer cells than you use up, that's when you start to die. I guess I just created more cells the past year than I lost. I came in here at two hundred forty, but I ran a four-sixty-five in the forty. You think I'm not a big train?"

We were at his locker by this time, and I helped him pull the back of his soaked jersey over his shoulder pads. "Until Thomas gets here," I said, "you're the biggest train Dallas has got."

The remark sobered Hill, who usually wants to laugh and joke lightly about everything. "It feels so strange Duane isn't here, after I've been thinking about going against him all the off-season. Now I know what Hubert Humphrey felt like when LBJ decided not to run. I never thought he'd carry it this far. I thought he'd be here when camp started. Last year I felt just like he does because of my contract. I guess the deal I got with Dr. Pepper is what saved me." (After being rookie of the year in the NFL in 1969, the soft-drink company signed Hill to a five-figure contract for a series of public appearances across the country.) "I was ready to go back to Yale and work on my masters."

"Duane wasn't going to be shooting at you alone," I said. "Landry had it planned he'd work at both fullback and half-back."

"Yeah, well, it's occurred to me," Hill said, "that this club is like a mighty river. You can scoop a pail or two out of it, and it still keeps rolling along."

Lee Roy Jordan was "weighing out," at 222 pounds, on the scale near Hill's locker, and he'd eavesdropped. "That's the kind of philosophy Calvin learned at Yale," he said, "but, you know, I think he hit the thing right on the head."

"Nobody can say that we wouldn't have made it to the Super Bowl without him," Hill said. "This is too much a team sport, and especially on this team where there is so much talent. We may not make it to the Super Bowl this year, but it won't be because Duane isn't here."

That night after supper I ran into Kiner in the hall of the coaches' wing. He was wearing Dutch clodhoppers, with wooden soles and white leather tops, blue jeans and a tattered T-shirt. That is, he looked in tune with the times. "Goodbye," he said.

It was a Wednesday, the players' night off, and I said, "You going to a movie?"

"No," he said, "I'm going to Boston. I been traded to the Patriots, and, man, am I happy!"

"You're going from a winner to a loser, and you're happy?"

"You better believe it. I don't want to ride the bench for four years like D.D. Lewis and run down on kickoffs. Boston isn't going to be down forever."

In a few minutes I caught Landry between coaches' meetings and he filled in the Kiner trade. The Cowboys would get a draft choice. I wondered if the trade had anything to do with Kiner's reaction to Thomas' press conference, when he'd said for publication, "Duane is beautiful, because he's only telling the truth."

"No," Landry said. "I didn't even know about that, and it wouldn't make any difference if I did. I told Steve in the off-season it looked like Howley would retire, and he had a shot at the open spot, along with D.D. He worked hard and came into camp ready to be a starter. When Howley came back, that killed everything for him, and the next minute he was in to see me. He's just one of those guys you can't keep on the bench, so I traded him."

There was a foreigner in camp—Toni Fritsch of Austria, the product of a typically wild Cowboy scheme. Tex Schramm had looked at the field-goal records in the NFL for 1970 and noticed that four of the top six were soccer-style kickers, but none of the four had ever been "first division" professionals in that sport. How good would a *real* soccer player be? Schramm wondered. He hired Bob Kap, the former coach of the Dallas Tornado, Lamar Hunt's team in the North American Soccer League, and sent him to Europe. Kap found Fritsch on Mallorca, where his Vienna Rapid team was taking a December holiday. There then began a comedy of tourism, in which Gil Brandt and his wife, Ermal Allen and even Tom Landry all made trips across the pond, at a total expenditure of about $30,000. Brandt had been a little sullen about the project, because he felt Kap was usurping his talent-hunting prerogatives. Three kickers were brought back to Texas, but Fritsch was the one who stayed. He was a legitimate soccer star, the right-winger on Austria's national team. The year that England was to win the World Cup, 1966, Austria had beaten them 3-2 at Wembley Stadium in London on two goals by Fritsch. That made him forever famous in his homeland as "Wembley Toni." The day he kicked twenty-nine out of thirty American-style field goals from forty yards at Vienna Stadium, the Cowboys signed him for a guaranteed $15,000, which was about the same take-home pay Fritsch was drawing from the Rapid F.C. "I have only three, maybe four good years left in soccer," Fritsch said. "This udder business I can kick till I am old man." This line, however, was about the extent of Fritsch's English vocabulary, and the communications gap widened when he joined the Cowboy squad.

Trainer Larry Gardner reported on a loud scene between Fritsch and his roommate, Reeves. "Danny has to come in after curfew from the coaches' meetings," Gardner said, "so he wants to claim the bed by the door. But he can't get Fritsch out of it. You should have heard him: 'Toni, this is Toni's bed, and this, this is Danny's bed, *jawohl?*' And Fritsch would grin and say, 'Yess, yess, vurry goot bed.' Pretty soon Danny was yelling, 'Goddamit, Toni, this is Toni's bed, and this is goddamit Danny's bed.' He just wasn't getting through."

"I know what my trouble is," Reeves told me. "The poor guy has to figure out three languages. First he has to translate my Americus, Georgia, into English, and then get the German." Reeves sought help from Stautner, who had come to the U.S. from Bavaria at age eight. They made quite a scene on the practice field, Stautner laboring with his homespun jargon, Fritsch wearing a Cowboy helmet which on top of his 5-foot-9-inch form in T-shirt and shorts made him seem an invader from outer space. At the end, Fritsch said to Stautner, "I never see Reeves. When I go to sleep, he is not there. When I wake up, he is there, but not long." Stautner went to Reeves and said, "I think you better just sleep in the empty bed."

Blaine Nye returned to camp after an absence of five days.

"It really took a lot to sign him," Brandt said. "We promised to lease him a new car when we get back to Dallas."

Nye seemed content enough. "The words I say," he said, "you can't carve in marble."

The Cowboys scrimmage only a half hour a week in training camp, during the season not at all, and a three-quarter-speed workout is no fun to watch. The pass-skeleton drill is the exception because it is the essence of what has made the pro game popular—one man throws the ball to another, and there are other men trying to bat it down. It's all out in the open where a simpleton can tell what is happening. The pass-skeleton is the reason the bleacher stands along the sidelines are packed every day at Thousand Oaks, despite a sign at the entry road noting that the practice is closed to visitors. (When the crowds start overflowing the bleachers, Landry has off-duty police block the roadway.) The drill is called a skeleton because it includes no linemen, just receivers and running backs versus linebackers, cornerbacks and safetymen. The defenders make no tackles, but they will cream the living daylights out of a receiver when the ball arrives at its destination. This day two rookies were dominating the action: eighth-round choice Ron Jessie of Kansas and Honor Jackson, a ninth-round selection from Pacific U. Jessie kept breaking for long bombs. Jackson caught everything over the middle. "Isn't that wonderful?" said Frank Luksa, the Fort Worth writer. "Just what this club needs, another couple of wide receivers. Let's walk back to the dorm and visit with Hayes."

The pass-skeleton had ended, and the full squad was gathering in the middle of the field to work on the running game. "You don't want to stay and watch the guards pull?" I said.

"No," Luksa said. So we went to see Hayes, who had bruised a knee diving for a pass and was taking the afternoon off. When we went through the swinging doors into the players' wing, Luksa said, "I feel like an enlisted man entering officer's country." Hayes was awake and dressed, in Bermuda shorts and a golf shirt, not listening to the radio, not reading, just sitting there counting his fingers. His left knee was propped up on the bed by a pillow and an ice pack. "Tom sent you over to check on me," Hayes said. Luksa said that was true. I had smuggled in three cans of cold beer wrapped in a towel, but Hayes declined. "So what else is happening?" he said. Luksa said he wanted to get his reaction to Duane Thomas. "I respect Duane for what he feels as a man," Hayes said, "but if it was me, I'd do it differently. Certain things he said I wouldn't say."

"What about being exploited?" Luksa said. "You feel you've been exploited?"

"No, not really. We've had our ups and downs. If the blacks had been exploited, how could the Cowboys have had so much success on the field? You don't win as many games as we have if part of your team thinks it's been put down. Duane can't speak for me. Bobby Hayes will do the talking for Bobby Hayes. He never knew what I got from the club. He may know about the others because they have the same agent."

"Do you think Duane can come back to this team now?" Luksa said.

"Some things would have to happen first," Hayes said. "The players feel he has to apologize to a lot of people. He has to face reality. He's under contract. You got to have certain rules, and you got to abide by them. I signed a three-year contract with the Cowboys and I had a bigger rookie year than Duane did—thirteen touchdowns, a thousand yards, and I made All-NFL. I played the next year on that contract. I had football on my mind. Maybe the value of the dollar means more to Duane than me then. Maybe he's way ahead of me. Before my third year Tex called me in and gave me a new contract. I'd like to help Duane, but I don't know where to begin. Where's first base? I'd go to the airport and pick him up. Some pride may have to be swallowed, but that hasn't killed anyone yet. Look what he said about Tom. I don't think anyone on this team has had more differences with Tom Landry than me, but I respect him. I don't give a damn, black or white. That cat is a good coach and a good man. I had to pay off some people who wanted to bomb his house last year. That's how deep this kind of talk can get—which I don't think Duane understands."

"Hold on," Luksa said. "What's this about . . . bombing . . . Landry's . . . *house?*" It had been Luksa's interview, but at this point I began making mental notes.

"Yeah," Hayes said. "They were wild, like they were on something. I never saw 'em, but I could recognize their voices when they called, two or three of them would get on the line. They started calling last October when I wasn't playing and Dennis was. They said, 'What's Homan doing playing and you're not? You're our brother and we gonna fix Landry. We gonna bomb that mother's house . . . and his car . . . and we gonna get Schramm, too.' I tried to laugh them along, like it was a joke, but after a couple of calls they started to sound serious, like working themselves up to something. I told them that was ridiculous, over a contract, over what was just a game. Then they said, 'You're either with us or against us. You with them? Maybe we bomb your house first. Guess you don't need more money. Suppose we grab your baby, then maybe we get some money.' I don't know they're going to do anything, but when they start talking about my two-year-old baby girl, I start sweating. I told 'em I had two hundred dollars and if I gave it to 'em would they leave me alone? They told me to take it over to the playground at school, the Miller grammar school, and where to put it in the doorway at the back. This was in the middle of the night. I took it over there, and I never heard from them again."

"Did you ever tell Tom about this, or anyone on the club?" I said.

"Tom doesn't know it to this day. No, I never told anybody. I was scared they'd do something. But if I had it to do over, I would call the FBI."

The Cowboys' intrasquad scrimmage, staged in game-style panoply once each training camp, was a big event of the summer in Thousand Oaks, whose natives paid two dollars apiece to see it, and to Cal Lutheran, whose athletic department got to keep the money. Since camp began, a chart had been kept on every practice pass thrown by Morton and Staubach, and Landry's rules for the scrimmage showed how scrupulously he would keep the two on even footing. Each quarterback would work one series against the first defense and one against the second platoon, starting the ball in play seventy yards from the goal line. The Saturday-afternoon crowd—men in beach wear and girls in hot pants—jammed the tiny permanent wooden stands along the west side of the field. I saw Tody Smith in their midst and climbed up to sit beside him. "Naw, I'm not reporting in," Smith said. "We just came out to talk a little." He introduced me to his attorney. Morton had failed to take the offense down the field on the first series, and now the ball was back at the thirty, with Staubach at quarterback. "Who is that sixty-seven?" Smith said. Sixty-seven had just knifed through from defensive end on a sweep and spilled the runner for a three-yard loss.

"That's Pat Toomay," I said. "He moves pretty good, doesn't he?"

"So do I," Smith said, and he wasn't kidding.

In one strike, an eighty-yard pass play to Jessie behind a rookie cornerback, Staubach got the first touchdown. Staubach seemed keyed up. His snap signals came out in a bark, loud and clear. You felt that every pass had his heart riding on it. I mentioned the Morton-Staubach contest to Smith.

"What they do out here doesn't matter," he said. "It's what they do in the first game, against the Rams, then it begins to count."

"Did Bubba tell you that?"

"Some things," Smith said, with exaggerated comic haughtiness, "I figure out for myself."

If Smith was right, it would be a good thing for Morton. He completed three of eleven, one touchdown. Staubach hit fourteen of twenty, two touchdowns. "We gave the fifth series to the quarterback who had done the best up to then," Landry said. "That was clearly Staubach. He was sharp, but he mostly stays sharp. Hard work is paying off. He sets up quicker this year than he did last year. And he steps up into the pocket like he should, which he didn't do very often last year. He's looking like a quarterback."

Landry singled out Toomay for his other compliment of the day. "He caught a few plays from behind, sweeps moving away from him, like that skinny kid at New York."

"Fred Dryer."

"Yeah, like Dryer and like Deacon [Jones] does."

"Tody Smith was in the stands and he wanted to know who sixty-seven was."

"He'd better start worrying about what Bill Gregory is doing with the All-Stars," Landry said, and he wasn't kidding, either. "They tell us he's the best defensive lineman they've got."

Dick Nolan and the San Francisco 49ers came down from their camp in Santa Barbara at mid-week for a "three-ring circus." It was a workout devised originally by Landry and George Allen when he first took over the Rams. The teams would follow their regular practice schedules, but they would be working against strangers. On the main field, Morton or Staubach were throwing against the 49ers in a pass-skeleton drill. John Brodie or Steve Spurrier were backed up to them at mid-field throwing toward the other goal line against the Cowboy defense. The sequence of throws was staggered so that all the action could be captured by a movie camera on a scaffold tower high above the sidelines. Behind the tower, in the outfield of the adjacent baseball diamond, the squads were paired off for an all-out scrimmage of rushing plays. It was brutal. When every lineman and every linebacker knew a run was coming, the ball carrier never had a chance. Once when the Rams were visiting and Deacon Jones was making a travesty of any Cowboy off-tackle play, it had been too much for Meredith. In the huddle he said, "To hell with this." Meredith faked a hand-off into tackle, then raised up and hit Don Perkins with a pass over the middle. The Rams were outraged for a moment before they started laughing.

The big show this day was Brodie passing to Gene Washington, over Renfro. Brodie, with that fluid three-quarter sidearm motion of his, found Washington three times in eight plays for touchdowns. It reminded me of the big fourth-quarter play in the conference playoff game, when Washington tried to beat Renfro deep and Renfro had made the interception. Renfro came over to the sidelines to take a break and I said, "I don't notice you stealing many from Washington today."

Renfro shrugged. "I can't get interested in this deal," he said, "nobody rushing the passer. Besides, I got other things on my mind. I still don't have a contract and nobody's said anything about it. If something don't happen soon, I'm going to start screaming."

The rookie contingent was thinning down toward the maximum squad of sixty by August 1. Thirty of the eighty candidates had gone the first week, five of their own accord. Some can depart with their heads high, as did Ron Jessie, with an airline ticket to Bloomfield Hills, Michigan. Jessie was traded to Detroit for a draft choice.

Late one afternoon at the end of July Thomas came to talk to Schramm and demanded to be traded. He and the fellow with him wore African dashikis, and there was no handshaking. "They tried to stare holes through me," Schramm said. "The other guy introduced himself as Ali Khabir. Believe me, I was a lot happier when Landry got to the room." Schramm told Thomas he would trade him "only if I can find a deal I think is a benefit to this ball club."

I called Chuck Dekeado to ask him what was going on and who was Ali Khabir. Dekeado laughed. "That's Mansfield Collins, one of Duane's many friends and advisers," he said. "Of which I think he might have too many. Mansfield was putting them on, like he was a Muslim." Dekeado gave me a new phone number for Thomas. "If a girl answers," he said, "don't hang up." Nobody answered, just as no one had been answering any of the Thomas phone numbers for the past three months.

That night, after Orlando's closed, Luksa and I came back to the "5:30 Club" to down a few additional beers and solve all the Cowboy problems—such as who should play quarterback and what to do about Duane Thomas. The 5:30 Club is an old Cowboy institution and an even older one with the New York Giants, from whence Landry transplanted it.

Ideally, it was a meeting place for the press and coaches, between the end of practice and the onset of the dinner hour, a stopping time when you could hear off-the-record remarks about the progress of players and anecdotes about the good old days when NFL squads numbered thirty-two and men were men. This was where Nolan kidded Stautner about playing against Pudge Heffelfinger and sticking his helmet in his back pocket, where Glenn Davis told about the time he caught a touchdown over Landry and Landry was so mad he chased him out of the back of the end zone, where Red Hickey told the one about a lover hanging out a window and the punchline, "No, that wasn't the maddest I ever been. The maddest I ever been was when I looked down and saw I was only two feet off the ground." But for the last several years the 5:30 Club had become merely a press-and-visitors lounge. The closets between two rooms had been knocked out to form a connecting arch and double the space, one side dominated by a color TV set and the other by the refrigerator, kept crammed with whisky, beer and soft drinks. Landry would sit for five minutes, then bounce up, saying, "Well, got to get back to work." His assistants hardly tarried longer, and it became a notable event when one would have a beer. Can there be a sadder sight than Ernie Stautner popping a cap on a Diet Pepsi?

Luksa was saying he had bet another writer five dollars that Thomas would play for the Cowboys this season. I said, "Let's call him and find out. If he's ever home, he'll be home now." It was 4:00 A.M.

Thomas came on the line, fighting his way out of sleep. "Wait a minute," he said. "I'm so dead."

"I'm sorry I had to wake you up, but you've got me working night and day."

"That's all right. What's happening?"

"You tell me. You shook things up a little bit coming out here yesterday. Schramm said you intimidated him."

"I wish I could do more than that. That man is trying to ruin my life. I went out to talk to them because *I* was the victim, and Tex Schramm had made me out to be the culprit. I was telling him to take his foot off my neck."

"Do you believe they'll trade you?"

"I don't know, and right now I don't care. I just want the whole thing done and over, one way or another. What do you think?"

"Duane, I think they've got you by the ying-yang. Schramm acts like this is a test case for the whole league, like if he gives in on you he'll be letting all the other owners down. They'll let you rot before they come up with more money. That press conference you had is part of it."

"I was trying to get back at them with words," Thomas said, "and I only scratched the surface."

"Yeah, well, look, you can say what you want about Schramm and Brandt—they're the front office—or even about Landry. But when you said they couldn't get to the Super Bowl without you, or they ain't going back, you lost a lot of people on this team—including me."

"I thought the black players would be wise to what I was saying, that the black players weren't getting the credit they deserved, to the amount that they had contributed. Yeah, I want to retract that about the Super Bowl. You tell 'em I take that back. It wasn't what I meant to say anyway. I realize as well as anybody the unity it takes to do anything."

"Duane," I said, "I think you ought to come out and report to camp and get the thing settled. It won't ever be settled as long as you stay away."

"I've been thinking about that," he said.

"Once you're out here, Schramm might come up with a new deal—especially if nobody ever finds out he's done it."

"The only reason I would come back is for my people, the black people," Thomas said. There was a long pause, and just as I started to say something else, Thomas said, "I'm going to be out there today. Tell them I'll be there by noon."

"Are you sure?"

"Yes. Whatever happens to me after I report is up to the Cowboys. This way I'm going to be putting the pressure on them."

We had talked a half hour. It took me another half hour to write the story and beat the first-edition deadline back in Dallas. Five hours later the phone brought *me* out of a dead sleep, and it was Thomas. "I'm not going to report like I told you I was," he said.

"Why not?"

"My people tell me I can't give in now."

"What people?"

"My friends. I feel spiritual about this. I'd rather sacrifice my career so other black players would have a fair shake—not only at Dallas but other places in the league. I have to stay the same about this, because where I display strength on the field I have to display the same strength off the field."

That night the coaches, minus Landry, got together with the writers and the scouts and their college guests for dinner and drinks in a private room at Los Robles to watch the College All-Star game, and word was passed that a Thomas trade was imminent. At six o'clock the next morning, my phone woke me up again and the operator said, "Long distance calling Mr. Al Ward." Ward's number was one digit different from mine. I said, "May I ask who's calling, Operator?" and she said, "Mr. Upton Bell."

Upton Bell is the general manager of the New England Patriots. Thomas' destination—along with Halvor Hagen and rookie Honor Jackson, in return for halfback Carl Garrett and a first-round draft choice. Garrett had been the AFL rookie of the year in 1969, but he is two inches shorter than Thomas, and Hagen has always been rated a future starter at guard. It seemed like a bad trade, particularly since the first-round choice was not low-ranked New England's but the one the Patriots had gotten from the Rams, who figured to be a contender and whose turn in the draft would be way down the line. The Cowboys had, in effect, paid for Thomas' intransigence.

The same afternoon, Landry announced he had acquired Don Talbert as a back-up offensive tackle from the New Orleans Saints, giving up taxi-squad defensive tackle Doug Mooers and a draft choice. This move was dictated by an injury to young Bob Asher, facing knee surgery to repair torn cartilage.

"Oh, man," said Carl Garrett, "am I glad to be with a

winner. That losing was wearing me out. You know the first thing I thought about when I heard I was traded? I thought about the Cowboys' offensive line. This year I'll have some people blocking for me."

Hardly were the words out of Garrett's mouth than the trade was partly nullified, and Garrett was once again New England property. The story came out piecemeal, and it was impossible to put it all together. Thomas reported to the Patriots' camp at Amherst, Massachusetts, within twenty-four hours of the trade. At the first practice session, New England coach Johnny Mazur corrected Thomas' backfield technique. "We use a three-point stance," Mazur said, meaning that the backs squat down so that one set of knuckles is touching the ground and the other forearm is resting on the knee.

"At Dallas," Thomas told Mazur, "we keep our hands on our knees so we can see what the linebackers are doing."

"Yeah, well, here it's a three-point," Mazur said.

"I'm still doing it my way," Thomas said.

"The hell you are," Mazur said. "You're getting to hell off the field and into the locker room." Or at least so went the dialogue as reported by the Associated Press.

Thomas went into the locker room all the way to the airport and back to Los Angeles, halting long enough at the terminal to tell newspapermen, "They don't want me here. They told me to leave."

Upton Bell said, "On the advice of my lawyer, I cannot say more about the situation at this time." Then the Patriots announced that their team doctor, Burton Nault, had had "certain doubts about Thomas' general condition and these doubts seemed to be confirmed in the brief workout which followed his physical examination." The club said Thomas "had declined to complete a physical examination." Nault said, "The portion of the examination Thomas refused to undergo included a urinalysis and a blood test." By now, of course, everything was laid out clearly between the lines, but it remained for that wonderful old Hearst paper, the Los Angeles *Herald Examiner,* to put it in black and white: "Was Thomas under the influence of drugs?"

Schramm, in one of his frequent imitations of a Supreme Court justice, issued a statement that would allow no cross-examination. He had canceled the trade "for moral and ethical reasons." Hagen and Jackson remained in New England, and Dallas would get the Patriots' second- and third-round choices. What was going on? Neither Schramm nor Bell would say, and Thomas' phone was off the hook.

Schramm did have one comment, off the record: "I hope when Garrett gets back there he doesn't have any trouble with his offensive line."

The plane ride home from Los Angeles is the longest drag of the season, because you are giving away two hours to the clock, but this night was a lark. The aisle of the players' section was choked with standees, reliving the 45-21 beating they had given the Rams. The last touchdown was a 102-yard interception return by Mark Washington, and Cornell Green kidded Jethro Pugh about trying to run interference for the cornerback.

"What you doing, Buzz, trying to catch Mark when he is ten, fifteen yards ahead of you? You're going to get in front and be his convoy? Nobody else could get him either." Washington's steal had come in the flat, and he raced right down the sidelines.

"No, no," Pugh said. "The guy across from me had been holding me all night. *Him* I was trying to catch, so I could blind-side him."

Morton was at the back of the plane, in a card game with Reeves and Garrison and Ditka. I reminded him that his ten completions in fourteen attempts was the same 70 percent he was hitting in 1969 before he tore up his shoulder. "I'll take this one for openers," Morton said. "I feel like I've had a good camp, because my arm was good. I took care of it—heat before practice and ice afterwards. It's going to be a very good year, you watch and see."

Chuck Howley was in the aisle jawing with Dave Edwards. "It took me a little while to get warmed up," Howley was saying. "I said, 'They're trying to pick on the Old Man.' Then I got with it."

"You sure got with that screen pass," Edwards said. "I thought you were going to catch the ball. When Josephson turned around, you said, 'Hello dere.' Whomp!"

Herb Adderley squeezed by us, saying, "And he got clipped on the play."

"Talk about retirement," Howley said. "That 'Y' end almost retired me with a crackback." (In the Cowboy vernacular, "X" is the tight end, "Y" is the split end and "wing" is the flankerback.) "Darn right I was clipped—and my chin strap got knocked over my mouth." Howley started laughing. "I wanted to bitch at the ref, and all I could do was sputter. He said, 'Okay, I got it,' reaching for his flag. I finally got my mouth unstuffed and I yelled at him, 'It's about time you got one.'"

"When I saw him hit you," Edwards said, "I thought, 'Well, Ol' Dad's through for sure now.'"

"When I got up to stand on it," Howley said, "it quivered like jelly. If my cleats had caught, that'd been all she wrote."

Adderley motioned me with his head and I followed him a few steps away. "Listen," he said, "I played with some great linebackers—I mean the outside men, Dan Currie, Dave Robinson, Bill Forester—but Howley's in a class with any of 'em, and believe me, that's saying a lot."

Adderley had been burned twice that night by the Rams' Jack Snow, once for a sixty-seven-yard touchdown. If it had been a league game, I would have asked him about it, and he knew it. Instead, I said, "And how is the great cornerback?"

"Everything," Adderley said, "is going to get better and better."

The roller-coaster ride has started, and from here the exhibition games will zip by like so many telephone poles past a Pullman-car window. The pace was quickened by the shortened California stand. For eight years the Cowboys had opened with at least two games on the Coast, but this season the 49ers were dropped. The rookies were lodged at a Holiday Inn on the expressway which led to the practice field, and their number had been increased by one, Tody Smith. "Not every ballplayer gets what he wants in a contract," Smith said, "but I'm satisfied with mine. Besides, I didn't like sitting in the stands watching them beat the Rams without me."

The Cowboys were coming up to the Saints game, a 73,000 advance sellout in the Cotton Bowl, followed by Cleveland at home, Houston and Baltimore on the road, ending with the Kansas City Chiefs back in Dallas.

"Maybe that's how they pay my salary," said Cornell Green, "but it's all the same to me if they started playing the ones that count right now. I've been ready since February."

Green had been the Cowboys' cornerback for seven seasons through 1969, and then strong safety Mike Gaechter tore an Achilles tendon that ended his career and the club got Adderley from Green Bay. Green thus became the strong safety. Since he signed as a free agent in 1962, the Cowboys have offered him in evidence of their superior scouting system. Green never played football at Utah State; he was an All-American in basketball. When he first reported he didn't know how to put on the equipment. Hip pads come with a long, narrow section to protect the coccyx bone, but Green thought it was designed for another safety. Equipment manager Jack Eskridge was dumbfounded when Green complained that the pads chafed him. Eskridge took a look and said, "You dumb rook, you got 'em on backwards."

From that early confusion, Green had become a master of cornerback technique. He would lecture young Mark Washington: "Say your man is going to run a square-out on you, to the sidelines? Okay, you're with him, closing fast. But then he breaks it into a square-out-and-go, and you're coming up and he's got you beat deep. So how you going to tell when he's running just a square-out or when that's just part of the pattern? Easy. If he's *really* running a square-out, when he makes his cut he'll look back for the ball. If he's faking the square-out, he won't look back."

Green was at his locker stall going through some mail just before the beginning of afternoon practice. It was a roomy, comfortable place, carpeted in dark blue, with meeting rooms at one end, equipment room at the other, shower stalls and trainer's room down one side, wide lockers down the other, with an island of lockers down the middle. "The letters I like," he said, "are when they ask me to get 'em an autographed picture of Bob Hayes."

"They got the right man. You're his roomie," I said.

"The kids don't know that."

"How many years you think you got, Cornell, moving to strong safety?" I meant, added onto his career.

"At least four," he said. "I was getting to be an old man at cornerback. You see any tight ends can move like flanker-backs? I love it at safety. I got somebody to talk to—the other safety. When I was at cornerback, only body I had to talk to was the wide receiver, and sometimes he wouldn't talk to me."

Staubach and Morton were lodged side by side a few rows down from Green, and now that a few days had passed from the opening game, I wanted to sound out their nerves. Both were edgy. "The thought of being graded for a starting job," Staubach said, "puts a little more pressure on you. It makes the game very important. Personally, I kind of enjoy pressure. I only hope I react the way I should."

"You think you fell behind in one game?" I said. "You hit nine of eighteen and threw a touchdown."

"It wasn't that I did bad," Staubach said. "I just didn't gain any ground on Craig. He looked great. But that was his turn. Now I get mine, and I have to do something with it."

Morton had seemed to steer clear of his locker while I was talking with Staubach, but now he came up to slip into his Number 14. "It's ridiculous that people put so much stock in the pre-season performance of a passer," he said. "Do they rate other positions like that in exhibition games? That's what pre-season is for, to get your timing down and get your arm in condition so you'll be ready when it counts."

"Well, it's counting now," I said.

"I'm not worried. Let 'em count."

In a post-game locker room, Staubach is the most coopera-tive Cowboy quarterback the writers have ever known. He will stand and answer questions while unhurriedly getting out of his pads, excuse himself for a shower, then return and wait the last questioner out before departing. Maybe it's because he isn't number one yet, but I don't think so. I think this is just Staubach's style. He will even volunteer information that will make your story.

"Did you notice," he said, "both those long touchdowns came on third-and-long?"

Landry had split up the Ram game the week before, first and third quarters for Morton, second and fourth for Staubach. This one he chopped down the middle, first half for Staubach and the rest for Morton. Staubach ended his stint with a 27-0 lead, then Morton found out what Staubach had experienced in LA, that you couldn't get much done on offense when Landry was subbing rookies in and out of the game. It ended 36-21.

Two of Staubach's touchdowns were to Hayes for sixty-nine yards and to Adkins for eighty-one, both times when he faced a third-and-ten. Two different cornerbacks had been victimized on the plays. "We went in expecting to hit the bomb on 'em like that," Staubach said. "They played New England last week and we saw in the films, their cornerbacks were looking for the sideline pass, the fourteen-yard gain for the first down. They would freeze when the receiver made his first cut. Bobby and Margene just went right by them."

Staubach had completed seven of seventeen, but he was well aware that four of his passes were dropped. Morton hit four of ten. Staubach said, "I wasn't completely satisfied, but overall I'm fairly happy with the way things went. It's very important to get off to a good start when you know the other guy is coming in behind you. I believe very strongly I'm capable of winning with the Cowboys, of taking this team to a championship."

After all the other writers had left and Staubach was knotting his tie, he winked at me. "I'd like to have those touchdowns in New Orleans," he said.

"That's right," I said. "You get them again in the season."

"I'm talking about next January," he said. "Isn't that when they play the Super Bowl?"

The club was beginning to shake out to its final form. Wendell Tucker, the little receiver from Los Angeles, was put on waivers and claimed by Denver. A field-goal kicker, David Conway, went the same way to Green Bay.

I asked Brandt why the club couldn't get a draft choice for Tucker, or even Conway, who had hit field goals from the forty-eight and forty-nine in two games. "At least two clubs have got to claim a guy before you can start dealing," he said. "These guys went one by one. By the way, your buddy Duane has got himself a new agent in LA, an attorney name of Al Ross. I guess he got into Dekeado for as much money as he could get. Now it's Ross's turn."

"You sound bitter, Gil," I said.

"No, I'm not bitter. The guy called me a liar and said I cheated him out of money. Why should I be bitter?"

All I knew about Ross was that he had made a lot of money for Spencer Haywood, jumping him from Denver in one pro basketball league to Seattle in the other. I got Ross on the phone and asked him what he had in mind as the next step for Thomas.

"I'm going right to the commissioner with this," Ross said. "And if he doesn't take any action, I'm going to put it on the President's desk."

I had to take that one in a minute. "You mean Nixon?"

"I don't mean Herbert Hoover," Ross said. "Wait a minute. I got another call." When Ross came back on the line, he'd switched his phone to one of those speaker arrangements. Ross is the kind of guy who thinks the fellow on the other end is too dumb to notice the difference.

"What kind of deal are you asking for Duane?" I said.

"What does Leroy Kelly get?"

"About eighty thousand," I said.

"Then that's what Duane should get. Duane's a thousand-yard runner, like Kelly."

"But Kelly's been doing it for years. Duane's done it once."

"I don't know who I'm talking to," Ross said. "Whose side are you on?"

"Don't you think you're getting to a point where you're fooling with a guy's career? The cards are stacked, but they're the only cards you've got."

"All right, what do you think he should do?"

"I think the boy should report to the Cowboys," I said.

Ross began shouting into the phone: "That's the trouble with you people in Dallas. 'The boy should report!' A white guy is a man to you, a black guy is a 'boy.' "

"He *is* a boy," I said. "I've got two kids as old as him. I don't have to bandy words with you. You ask Duane Thomas how I stand on black and white. Whatever he tells you, that's the truth." I had the feeling Thomas was in Ross's office listening to all this on the speaker phone.

I rang off thinking Ross was a hotdog. But that was the day Vida Blue visited the White House and Nixon hailed him as "the most underpaid player in baseball." The President said he wouldn't mind being his lawyer when the pitcher negotiated his next contract. Maybe Ross could get Thomas into the Oval Room next.

I really couldn't blame Ross for taking my "boy" remark in an Ol' Massa context, except that it was too cliché, and it showed a lack of understanding on his part. I grew up in the Deep South, Mississippi and New Orleans, and I had grown up professionally around black athletes. I knew better than Ross the nuances of racial slurs. From time to time I had been on the scene when race hatred, the kind that is so silent you can't grab a handle on it, had filled the atmosphere with a nameless dread. One night my wife and I were at Cornell and Betty Green's apartment during the season, and he began telling us about the great high school he'd attended in Richmond, California. "You had to watch out for the principal," Green said. "He had a trick of waiting just to one side of a door, and when you came through he'd whap you over the head with a rolled-up newspaper. 'Gotcha!' he'd say. 'You gotta be more alert around here, Cornell.' I mean, it was friendly. I always liked to go to school.

"The basketball coach, he was another case. Every Wednesday he'd have us all up to his house for a crap game. He had a white rug and we'd all get down on the floor and shoot craps on the rug—and *never lose*. Every one of us would walk out of there about three or four dollars to the good. I thought it was funny at the time, but I never thought about it much. It wasn't till years later I figured it out. Coach knew there was a bunch of us on the team didn't have spending money at all—but we did after we got through shooting craps with *him.*"

A couple of Green's friends, a young preacher and his brother, dropped into the apartment about 1:00 in the morning, and somehow they got to talking about how their daddy always made them do the dishes. "We had to wash 'em in a washtub in the back yard," the preacher said, "and the glasses were the hard part, wiping 'em clean so they'd sparkle. There was a railroad track running along the back of our yard, and when we got tired we'd throw the glasses out on the track."

"We must have broken three dozen glasses," his brother said.

"And got three dozen whippings," the preacher said.

We were all laughing so hard we had tears in our eyes, and Green announced that we had run out of ice. He and I would make a fast trip to an all-night grocery in the neighborhood and remedy that situation. Green had a nice apartment in an all-black apartment house in an all-black neighborhood, and when we walked into the small grocery, part of a chain of such stores all over Dallas, I was the only white in the place. Except for the man behind the counter. He wore a three-dollar white shirt from Grant's, the kind whose collar points are guaranteed to curl upward. His shirt sleeves were rolled tight, high above his biceps. He didn't look happy.

"I'd like to get some ice," Green said.

"Just a minute," the guy said, looking at me. He turned to wait on another customer who had just walked up to the counter. Finally, he turned back to me and said, "What is it?"

Green said, "How much is the ice?"

"Sixty-five cents a bag," the man said, never looking at Green. Green handed him two ones, got his change, and we went outside to the icebox. The bags were huge.

"That's too much ice, Cornell," I said. "We only need one of those."

"It's okay," he said, heaving both bags onto the floorboard

in the back seat. When we got back to the apartment house, Green said, "Wait a second." He took one of the bags over to a huge garbage bin, the kind that are handled by mechanized private collection, and dumped it in. Then he came back and grabbed the other sack and we walked upstairs to rejoin the party.

Lance Alworth was on the sidelines in street clothes when I came down from the press box in the middle of the fourth quarter. I thought he would have been in the hospital. Alworth had caught, momentarily, a pass coming deep across the middle, and Cleveland safety Ernie Kellerman dug a shoulder pad into his middle just as the ball got there. This was a national telecast, and the collision was so spectacular that the TV monitors upstairs carried three repeats of the play. Alworth was standing with his shoulders cupped forward slightly, but he didn't seem to be in pain.

"You should have seen it on instant replay," I said.

"Never mind," he said softly. "I saw it in living color. I can hardly breathe."

The Cowboy team doctor, Marvin Knight, passed the word along the bench that at least three of Alworth's ribs were broken, and I noticed several of the players looking down his way.

On the field, Mike Clark missed a nineteen-yard field goal that would have put Dallas ahead 16-15 with 1:53 to play. When he came to the sidelines, no one said a word to him. Clark was "a good old boy" type of Texan, an Aggie, and he had been kicking in the NFL for nine years, mostly with Pittsburgh, but he had never known the pressure he was going through this time around. The little Viennese, Fritsch, debuted the week before against New Orleans by kicking fifty-one and forty-six-yard field goals, and now Clark missed a gimme game winner. The Dallas defense forced the Browns to punt, Morton hit three passes, and Clark was back on the field again. This time his twenty-six-yarder was good, with twenty-three seconds to spare. "It's not often you get a reprieve like that," said Landry. It was also a reprieve for Morton, who had been allowed to go all the way and hit only five of his first fifteen passes. But in the last five minutes he connected on seven of ten and got the victory. "I left Morton in because he was competing, and it was his game to win," Landry said. He preferred to talk about Hill, who broke an eighty-nine-yard touchdown on a trap up the middle and totaled 167 yards for the night. "Calvin is the same as he was in 'sixty-nine, only he may have more power now," Landry said. "I don't think our running game is going to be hurting with him at halfback."

Only in the peculiar circumstances of an NFL exhibition season could the Cowboys breed both victory and dissatisfaction. After beating Houston in the Astrodome, 28-20, the offensive line coach, Jim Myers, said, "If we can play this bad and win, we might not lose a game all season."

Danny Reeves put his mind to the proposition and decided, "We have been getting by on individual plays. We've got enough talent on this club to do that for a while. But if we don't get everything together pretty soon, we're going to have trouble in the season."

Mentioning what Reeves had said, I told Cornell Green that his game-clinching interception against the Oilers must be a good example. Houston rookie Lynn Dickey had been hit by a safety blitz as he tried to throw, and the ball fluttered to Green near the line of scrimmage. "Sure," Green said. "I was outstanding. I was supposed to cover the tight end and when he didn't come off the line, I *knew* the play was a run. I was in the right place at the right time for the wrong reason. That's experience, right?"

Landry put his finger on the source of uneasiness. "We're four-and-oh," he said, "but we haven't played against any experienced quarterbacks." Prothro used Carl Sweetan for half of the Ram game, the Saints split duties between young Edd Hargett and rookie Archie Manning, rookie Mike Phipps went the first half for Cleveland, and the Oilers used Dickey all the way. "Our alertness is going to pick up against Baltimore and Kansas City," Landry said, "against Earl Morrall and Len Dawson."

About his own quarterbacks, Landry was becoming testy. "I'm not going to rate Morton and Staubach for you," he said. "Maybe when the season starts we'll go with both of them. If they weren't performing well, I might have a problem. I don't see any problem now." They would have to be separated by a Solomon, which is right down Landry's line. Morton hit eleven of nineteen in the first half at Baltimore, but put only ten points on the scoreboard. Staubach was given the second half and threw two touchdowns to Hayes. The Cowboys won, 27-14, but the game had no relation to the one last January. Both teams had so many receivers out with injuries that the Colts used field-goal kicker Jim O'Brien as a split end, and Dallas had Reeves at flankerback. Baltimore assistant Dick Bielski made a proposal to Ermal Allen before the game: "Keep Reeves at wing and we'll put a linebacker at cornerback and promise not to bump-and-run him." The 44,000 Baltimore fans who stayed *away* from the contest knew what they were doing. Landry thought the whole thing was worth it for one play, a scrambling rollout by Staubach in which he stopped and threw an eleven-yard touchdown to Hayes. "I'm glad to see his name out of the rushing totals," Landry said. "He had open space in front of him when he threw to Hayes—so he's learning."

Landry was wrong about Morrall but right about Dawson. The Chiefs' quarterback hit ten of twelve, and Kansas City held a 17-14 lead when he retired at halftime to be replaced by back-up man Mike Livingston. The final victory, 24-17, was therefore a bit hollow, but not for the man who hauled in the seventy-yard game-winning pass from Morton. Gloster Richardson, traded away by the Chiefs, was exultant: "It's beautiful when you can beat a team that sits you on the bench for four years, tells you you aren't good enough." A story went with the play, on which Richardson beat a young cornerback, Dave Hadley. "Hadley got bumped around pretty hard covering their punt," Richardson said. "He looked to me like he was winded, so I told Craig I could beat him deep." It was a saving strike for Morton, only his third completion in nine throws.

On looking back it was clear the Cowboys had made it through six games as the only unbeaten, untied team in pro football because their two quarterbacks were superior to any

pair their opponents could field. Landry, in his meticulous
way, had split their work exactly down the middle, and
this was the result:

	Att	Comp	Yds	Pct.	Int	TD
Staubach	83	44	714	53.0	2	6
Morton	81	41	618	50.6	5	2

In the locker room after the Kansas City game, I asked
George Andrie what he thought Landry would do about his
quarterback. "I don't know if he's decided yet," Andrie said.
"You'd think he would, since we start the season next week,
but maybe some things you can decide later on in the year.
At every position, you got to have a number one, a starter.
If you don't, both guys are confused; they don't know where
they stand. You can't play good football like that."

"Who do you think he'll go with?"

"You're not going to get me to vote. Keep me out of it.
I got my own troubles."

"Okay, but a private opinion."

"I think Craig. He's still got the edge in experience, don't
he?"

That's the way I was thinking, but I wondered if I was
too close to the subject. Evidently I knew a side of Morton
that never got across to Cowboy fans, because a citywide
poll would have awarded the job to Staubach by a landslide.
This was brought home to me when a promoter of a lakeside development near Dallas asked which would be a con-
venient day of the week for him to hire Staubach. The
appearance would be three weeks into the season. I told him
Monday was the team's off day. "But he might not be the
number-one quarterback then," I said. The guy thought a
moment and said, "That's all right. If he isn't, we'd still want
him."

Staubach was chairman of the Leukemia Fund Drive, and
Morton was supposedly gamboling every night at the Loser's
Club, a discotheque of ill repute. In this connection, it was
ironical what Morton was doing the next morning, a Sunday,
after the Kansas City game. There was a nine-year-old in

Santa Rosa Hospital in San Antonio, fighting the withering end of a four-year battle against leukemia, and he was a pro-football fan. John Elliott, the New York Jets tackle, had been visiting a niece at the hospital during the summer and stopped in to visit with little Bill Miller.

"Someday," the kid had told Elliott, "I sure would like to meet Craig Morton," The boy's father had passed this wish on to Dan Cook, the sports editor of the San Antonio *Express,* and Cook had called the quarterback. Morton agreed to make the trip south, with one proviso: that there would be no publicity. So there was Morton, finally, in the crowded hospital room and asking the parents and the nurses if they would mind leaving so he could have a private word with Bill. A few minutes later Morton came out and asked, "Where's Margaret? Where's a nurse named Margaret?" A startled nurse, among the crowd that had gathered outside the room, held up her hand, and Morton addressed her sternly: "Margaret, we got to get one thing settled—we got to get more gravy on those mashed potatoes." On the way back to the airport, Cook asked Morton what he and the kid had talked about, and Morton said, "It was kind of personal."

Later, the father told Cook, "Craig said he was proud Bill wanted to meet him, that he promised to write him, and they said a prayer together."

If Cook hadn't been such a blabbermouth, and told all to his readers, breaking the promise to Morton, none of us would have ever known about it.

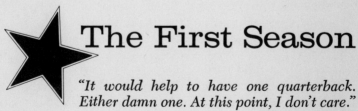 # The First Season

"It would help to have one quarterback. Either damn one. At this point, I don't care."
—RALPH NEELY

The Wednesday before the league opener at Buffalo was a pivotal day in the Cowboy season. At noon, Landry explained why he was going with "two number-one quarterbacks" and why he had named Staubach to lead off the rotation. At 6:15 P.M. Duane Thomas walked into Schramm's office and said he was ready to play football for Dallas. In Thomas' case, it was not that simple. The ball club had placed him on the retired list, and now NFL commissioner Pete Rozelle would have to approve his return to active status. Also—either by the league's demand or the club's, it was never made clear—Thomas would have to pass an extraordinarily thorough physical examination. At any rate, he *wouldn't* be making the trip to Buffalo.

Landry's announcement was not that simple, either. At his weekly press conference—a buffet with beer, in the private club in the Cowboy office building—he chose to make a speech explaining it all. And this is what he said:

"Now, let me talk now about the quarterback situation a little bit. Maybe I can explain the situation where I feel you are all capable of understanding it. Whether I am capable of explaining it is the real problem we have got here.

"The reason there is a real difficulty is because what has taken place in the past in pro football. No precedent has been set to have *two* quarterbacks. Therefore, there is a big misunderstanding of even my statement that we're going with two quarterbacks. Even the quarterbacks don't quite understand it.

"Opening this summer camp there were certain things that had to be accomplished about the quarterbacks. Craig Morton, who has been hurt for two seasons, has been our starting quarterback, and he has received a lot of criticism because he couldn't throw well the end of last year. Naturally, his confidence is something that he had to re-establish himself, that he could do the job. The thing that I have talked about all summer is that I've been very satisfied with his progress. I think he has made great strides coming back. He has thrown the ball as good as he has ever thrown it. Right now he has a lot of confidence in himself and his production has been good—good enough for us to win with. So I think he has accomplished something. A lot of people have felt that this is a letdown for him, or that I've done—by naming Roger the starting quarterback, that I have in some way shoved him down. This is not true, and I could not be more satisfied with Morton at this point of the season.

"Now on the other side of the coin with Roger—Roger came into this summer knowing he had to make great strides in experience and know-how in order to offset some of the inexperience that he has, which is where Morton has the advantage. I think he has made great strides. I think he has an understanding of what we are doing, not as much as Morton does, but he isn't supposed to, because Morton has been at it four more years than he has. But he has enough for us to win with. You watch him work, and he demonstrates poise, he doesn't scramble much, he reads defenses and he hits people, all of which he couldn't do last year.

"So therefore we came into the beginning of the season with two quarterbacks whose performance throughout the summer had been very satisfactory. We played them almost equal in quarters through the games. Roger had a slight edge in some important categories of scoring and passing. It wasn't much, really. I have been on record with performance level. I have said that a back-up man could not replace a starter without superiority over him, a clear-cut superiority. Roger does not possess that over Morton at this time. Therefore, Morton does not lose his starting status with us and this is the reason I have gone to the two-quarterback situation.

"It's new, and it hasn't been done to my knowledge other than at Los Angeles with Waterfield and Van Brocklin, and how they used those two when they were winning the championship, I am not really sure. The Rams had so much talent during those times, it really didn't make much difference. I don't know that we possess that type of talent. But I think it is the best thing for the Cowboys at this point. I do everything based on what I think is best for the team. I believe that here are two fellows who were in the All-Star game at the same time; they are exactly the same age, twenty-eight years old, twenty-nine, whatever they are. Morton has a little bit more experience at this time, but they are both competing in winning style. I think it is important that we establish a quarterback for the Cowboys' future and at this point I cannot make that decision, because if I make it we will go with that quarterback in the years to come. Now we must go with the two of them on a pretty equal basis. It is not what I like because I know that I am going to be second-guessed every decision that I make. I am going to be second-guessed if it brings any defeats or anything else. But I am willing to do that, take that responsibility, in order to establish one or the other as our number-one quarterback in the future, and I think that this is important. I don't know that I have explained it well, but I have done the best I can."

I had been out to the practice field that morning to see Staubach and Morton. Morton said, "This is the most ridiculous shit I've ever heard. But just say I have no comment."

Staubach said, "I guess I couldn't have hoped for anything better. It gives me a chance. I'm not crazy about the two-quarterback thing, but it's a step up from where I was. I got a feeling things are breaking right for me."

Staubach was in the middle of changing clothes, and I asked him what the hell was that bruise on his leg, high on the inside of his right thigh. It was about the size and color of an eggplant, yellow and green around the edges. "A pulled muscle," Staubach said, "but that isn't going to keep me from playing Sunday, I guarantee you that, not after I've come this far."

Now Landry, at the tail end of his press conference, was saying, "I am going to revert back to Morton as starting quarterback for the Buffalo game, because Roger is not ready to play. If we take a chance on him playing Sunday, and he tears the muscle in his groin again, he could be out anywhere from six to eight weeks. If he can throw well next Wednesday, I would say he'd start against Philadelphia. Course I probably would have started Morton the Philadelphia game anyway, regardless of what happened this Sunday."

When Landry runs something up a flagpole, he does not expect everyone to salute. But when they do not, he is saddened by their lack of understanding. Reeves, who will be a head coach himself someday, felt secure enough to say, "I'm glad I didn't have to make that decision. The drawback is them playing when they realize they might be taken out any minute. That's a lot of pressure. That's where a passer starts trying to point the ball."

Don Meredith, passing through town between Monday-night telecasts, could afford to be considerably more blunt: "It's a disappointment, but not as much as it is to Morton and Staubach, not to mention the thirty-eight other players involved in that wishy-washy decision. . . . If I were trying to put myself in Craig's place going into this first game, I can just imagine what kind of enthusiasm I might have slipping in there. I also can imagine the reaction of the ten guys who have bent down with their hands on their knees and their heads slightly bowed, waiting on me to get in my goddam huddle. I can imagine what kind of feeling they're going to have waiting: 'But don't worry, guys, our number-one guy is going to be in here next week, so says our leader.' That's bullshit. He can do what he wants, but that's still bullshit. . . . I would go with Morton the whole way, or until he stunk up the place so bad that he couldn't cut it. . . . It's Landry's responsibility as a head coach to pick a quarterback. After he picks him, it's his responsibility to go with him. Now after he's spent this long with them and he doesn't have any idea which one is best, then get another goddam coach."

But the lakeside developer was happy.

Many National Football League rules are designed to equalize the competition, such as the college draft. The same reverse order of the previous year's standing is honored when teams cut down their rosters leading into the regular season. But, as if the right hand must not know what the left hand is doing, the owners are constantly passing new rules to circumvent the old ones. In theory, when the Cowboys put a player on waivers the twenty-four other clubs below them in the standings, beginning with the worst (New England), had a right to claim him for one hundred dollars. At one of the exhibition games in Dallas, scouts from eight NFL teams had crowded the press box to look over the spoils. In practice, however, there were precious few spoils, because the owners had also created a "move list." A player can be moved from the active roster to the "reserve list" without being subject to claim by other clubs. He can be left there for five weeks, when the club must either activate him, put him on waivers or use another "move" to keep him there. Twelve such moves are allowed through the season.

The "reserve list" must never number more than seven. This group goes by various names across the league. The Cowboys call their seven the taxi squad, dating back to an owner who circumvented league rules by placing his extra players on the payroll of his cab company.

Within the rules there are several gentlemen's agreements which make things easier. One is that you do not claim a player who has been placed on waivers with a parenthetical notation alongside his name: "(injured)." Thus, for example, the Cowboys were able to get Margene Adkins (foot), Lance Alworth (ribs) and Mark Washington (knee) onto their reserve list.

So heading up to Buffalo, this was the Dallas squad:

Offensive line: Neely, Niland, Manders, Nye, Wright, John Fitzgerald, Talbert, rookie Rodney Wallace and Forrest Gregg.

Receivers: Hayes, Richardson, Reggie Rucker, Ditka and Truax.

Quarterbacks: Morton and Staubach.

Running backs: Hill, Garrison, Reeves, Joe Williams, Claxton Welch.

Defensive line: Andrie, Lilly, Pugh, Cole, Pat Toomay and Bill Gregory.

Linebackers: Edwards, Jordan, Howley, D.D. Lewis and Tom Stincic.

Defensive backs: Renfro, Adderley, Waters, Harris, Green and Richmond Flowers.

Kickers: Widby and Clark.

On the taxi squad were the two top draft choices, Tody Smith and Ike Thomas (moves), Toni Fritsch (move), Washington, Adkins and Alworth (all waived injured) and Forrest Gregg.

Gregg, the great seven-time all-pro with Green Bay, was a late addition. He had retired after fourteen years with the Packers and was working in Dallas when Landry saw his name on the waiver list and talked him into giving it one more shot.

The Cowboys got down from forty-three to forty by trading rookie halfback Jim Ford to New Orleans for a draft choice and by waiving rookie free-agent linebacker Kenny Price and veteran tight end Pat Richter. They had picked Richter up three weeks before for just this occasion.

All in all, it was a beautifully successful evasion of the equalization of talent. Schramm has an apologia about this process and the essential hopelessness of really spreading the wealth. "You cannot," he says, "legislate intelligence."

The first half of the Buffalo game looked like a highlight film of somebody's crazy season. Dallas went bing-bang-bing, with Hill and Garrison and Hill scoring first; then the Bills' young quarterback, Dennis Shaw, threw a seventy-three-yard touchdown to Haven Moses. Moses cut inside Renfro, going deep, and free safety Charley Waters drifted over as if he had the play well in hand. But he went for the ball, clobbered Renfro, and Moses escaped with the touchdown. A Garrison fumble set up a six-yard score by O.J. Simpson through the middle, and Morton countered with a seventy-six-yard bomb to Hayes. Howley's fifty-three-yard interception return led to the next Dallas touchdown, and Shaw came back with a seventy-five-yard throw to Marlin Briscoe. On this one, it was Jordan moving over to take Adderley out of the play, as beautiful a block as Waters had thrown on Renfro.

Buffalo actually led, 30-28, in the second half before the Cowboys pulled away on Morton's pinpoint passes to a 49-37 victory. The players looked punch-drunk in the locker room. "Did it seem like as long an afternoon to you," Morton said, "as it did to me?" He had hit ten of his fourteen passes, and you had to wonder if Dallas would ever have another number-one quarterback. "Don't push it," Morton said. "Everything will work itself out."

Waters, who had kept the free safety job in a dead heat with Cliff Harris, was slamming his gear into an equipment bag. "I had the damn ball all the way," he said, not bothering to explain what the hell he was talking about, because it was clear: the touchdown by Moses. "And then, wham, we're on our ass. But I'm the rookie, so I'll probably get the blame for it."

"You're not a rookie," I said. "You're a Super Bowl veteran."

"Hey, you know, you're right," Waters said.

"So tell me what happened when O.J. ran over you coming up the middle."

"Oh, go to hell," Waters said.

Duane Thomas had been cleared by Pete Rozelle, cleared by the lab technicians at the Southwest Medical School, and now he had to be cleared by the Cowboys. When Thomas finally showed up at the practice field, the Wednesday before the second game, I was reminded of a conversation I'd had with Chuck Howley on the plane ride home from training camp. I'd told Howley that Thomas would eventually rejoin the team, and he'd said, "Yeah, well, I don't know if a lot of 'em would want him back. He's got to get straight with a few people about the things he's said." I looked around and didn't see Howley this afternoon, but I saw Hayes and remembered a similar remark he had made about the apologies Thomas would owe the team. What did Hayes think now? "I think he'll be accepted by the Cowboys the same as he's always been," Hayes said. "If the man wants to come back and play football, why should we hassle him? We want him here. He's a teammate."

What did "plastic man" Landry have to say? "If he comes back and helps us win the Super Bowl," Landry said, "I imagine he'll be very welcome."

Thomas was sitting on a plastic chair facing into his locker, lacing up the high-topped cleats he always wears at practice. He glanced up at me when I said hello, nodded and ducked his head again. Thomas had been the most phlegmatic of the Cowboys in his rookie year. The year before, when Calvin Hill had been stringing together one-hundred-yard games, it was difficult *not* to write a story quoting the voluble Yale graduate. When Thomas did the same, his achievements appeared to be accepted without fanfare—because it was so hard to get him to say something interesting. If he could have verbalized, I imagine he would have given us the line from Flip Wilson's Geraldine: "What you see is what you get." I sat in the chair at the next locker and said, "Duane, what was it made you decide to come back? Was it because the season was starting?"

Thomas shook his head, not in answer.

"Wait a minute," I said. "Is there something crossways between you and me? If there is, let's get it out."

Thomas looked at me, full-on, for the first time. "No," he said, "why should there be? Why do you say that?"

"Because you're not talking."

"Haven't you ever felt like not talking?" he said.

"No, I haven't. Are you in shape? How long before you think you can play?"

"I don't want to talk about it," Thomas said, and he turned and headed for the door to the practice field.

The first pass Staubach threw at Philadelphia was intercepted by Bill Bradley, and Staubach didn't get up. He hadn't moved from where he'd thrown the ball, and I didn't remember him being pressed as he got the pass away, but there he was, cold-cocked. Morton came in and completed fifteen of twenty-two attempts for 188 yards and two touchdowns. The Dallas defense did the rest, intercepting six passes thrown by the Eagles' Canadian League veteran, Pete Liske. "I admire the way Liske throws the ball," Charley Waters said. "He points with his left hand to let you know where he's gonna go with it. That's damned considerate." Four of the Cowboy interceptions set up touchdowns, and it was a breeze, 42-7. Philly's touchdown came on Al Nelson's 101-yard return of a field-goal attempt, when I had noticed Ralph Neely trailing the play down the sideline trying to attract the referee's attention. I found Neely first in the locker room to ask him what that was all about.

"I had a complaint," Neely said. "This guy Tom [Mel Tom, the Eagles' right defensive end] hit me in the mouth when the ball was snapped. Then he grabbed my face mask. Then he punched me in the gut—and that's just the good part. When I saw Nelson running the ball back, he grabbed my jersey. The ref was standing there looking at all this until he saw Nelson go by. You know what he said when I caught up with him? He said, 'Quit your bitchin'—they needed a touchdown.'"

Nobody knew what had happened to Staubach, particularly Staubach. "Oh, I've got a little headache," he said, "but at least I know I'm in New Orleans." This was a considerable wisecrack in Staubach's state of mind. He had labored all summer to get a shot at starting, and now Morton was 2-0 with twenty-five completions in thirty-six attempts. "Disappointed?" Staubach said. "That's putting it mildly. If I keep going the way I am, I'll solve that two-quarterback problem."

The last radio man had just finished an interview when I found Landry's coaching cubicle. "Good defense and so-so offense" was his capsule of the game. I said that Morton's two-game statistics would probably place him first in the NFL pass standings. Landry said, "I guess that's so."

"Well, how can Morton be number one in the NFL and

number one-and-a-half on the Cowboys?"

"But he is number one on the Cowboys," Landry said.

"Since when?"

"We've got *two* number ones," he said, and he wasn't smiling.

On the bus ride from the stadium to the airport, I was telling Dave Edwards and Ralph Neely about this bit of repartee. "Am I crazy?" I said. "He's got to start Morton next Sunday against Washington, right?"

"Yep," Neely said, "and if he starts Craig and we roll through 'em, how can he go with Roger the next game? You have to go with the hot hand in football, no matter what system you're using."

"Maybe we'll stick to the two-quarterback system," Edwards said. "Only thing is, Morton will do all the playing."

The big news on Tuesday was that the game films had solved the mystery of what happened to Staubach at Philadelphia. Mel Tom had clobbered the unholy hell out of him with a forearm. League rules prevent a club from showing writers the game films when a rule infraction is involved, but I got an earful from the players. Tom had been spun around behind Staubach as he threw, and for a moment they both stood there watching the flight of the ball. When Bradley intercepted it, Tom pulled Staubach around with his left hand and slammed him on the jaw with his right forearm.

At the end of the morning meeting the players milled around a bit, talking about the kayo and working themselves into a fine rage. "If we'd seen the son-bitch," Mike Ditka said, "we'd taken care of Mr. Tom, you bet your ass."

Staubach's attitude was one of disbelief. "Nothing like that has ever happened to me in football," he said.

"I talked to Mark Duncan, the guy in the league office who's in charge of officials," I said. "He said the commissioner is aware of the play and he wouldn't be surprised if Tom is fined." Duncan and his staff go over the thirteen game films every week and several times had marked players for fines when no infraction had been called in the game itself.

"When they see what happened," Staubach said, "they've

got to fine him. Then they ought to give the money to *me*."

Bobby Hayes said, "I like that. Make a note of that for the Players Association. New rule—victim gets the money. It could have been worse—he could have broken your face mask, and your jaw . . . and knocked out all your teeth . . ."

"I'd just like to get him alone for a few minutes in a back alley somewhere," Staubach said.

"Look out, now; look out, now," Hayes said, and I started laughing.

"Roger," I said, "Mel Tom is six-four and weighs two-fifty. What would you do with him in a back alley?"

"Listen, I've got four years of hand-to-hand combat I never got to use," Staubach said. This is the seldom seen side of Staubach that keeps him from being an unbelievable Goody Two Shoes. It's a quality of toughness you instinctively know is in him. Lee Roy Jordan, an authority on this subject, commented once: "You *know* Roger's tough. You don't go running all over the place like he does if you're scared of getting your fanny bruised. He don't head for the sidelines like you see a lot of quarterbacks, but he better learn—or we *will* have a one-quarterback system."

Staubach had an errand to run during the lunch break and I followed him out to his car. "Whatever this costs the other guy," I said, "it might turn out to cost you a lot more."

He nodded pensively. "You know Marianne and I were talking about that last night. Getting hit like that hurt, but in a couple of hours I was okay. It's what it could mean in the long run. It might mean the end of me here. I know he's got to go with Craig Sunday, and we figure to beat Washington, then he's more or less got to stick with him. That guy hitting me like that could cost me the whole season." Staubach shook his head and shrugged. "I mean, I'm not all that crushed about it—the important thing is we're winning. I mean that. My personal ambitions will work themselves out eventually. I just don't feel like I have time for many more delays."

The next day at the office I found a note that Staubach wanted me to call him at home. "The way you put that hand-to-hand combat in the paper," he said, "you made it sound as though I was serious."

Lance Alworth gets free for his first Cowboy touchdown,
in St. Louis, where the streak began.

Staubach scrambles at Baltimore,
but not too often, and gets back
in the quarterback race.

Calvin Hill roams with a
game-busting catch in the
opening exhibition at
Los Angeles.

Morton wants to pass, Landry calls a
run, and sets up a summertime win
over Cleveland.

Staubach in flight against the Giants. "I'm not a scrambling quarterback," he says. "But sometimes I run." This time, Staubach was yanked at the half.

Lee Roy Jordan
congratulates rookie Joe
Williams on his touchdown
run against New England.

"Once in a coach's lifetime,
if he's lucky, comes along
a player like Bob Lilly."—
Tom Landry

Lance Alworth tells
Roger Staubach, "If you'd
only throw more
to your flankerback . . ."

All-NFL guard John Niland
was asked to put on his
Game Face.

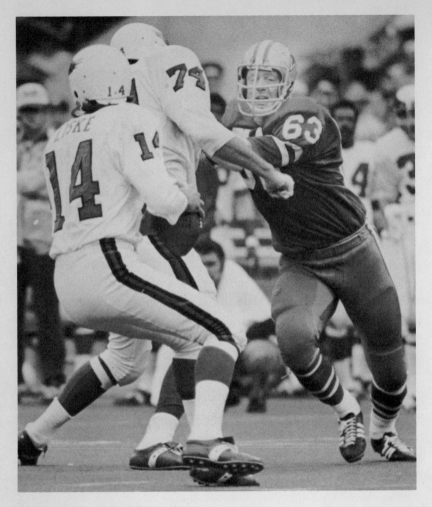

Larry Cole, veteran from the
Granite Falls Kilowatts, crowds in on
Philadelphia quarterback Pete Liske.

Staubach carries out a
fake, with hand behind hip, but
everyone in the park knows
Calvin Hill has the ball.

Left to right, the Cowboy front
four: Lilly, Cole, Pugh and Andrie,
considerably muddy but unbowed.

Landry in rain cap
sends in a play at
Buffalo via Calvin Hill.

Jethro Pugh demonstrates
double-forearm technique on
Buffalo quarterback
Dennis Shaw.

It's the fourth quarter, and
Niland is too pooped to put
his tongue out.

Rookie Isaac Thomas gets underway with his 89-yard opening kickoff return against the Rams. The next game he went 101 with the opening kick against the Jets.

American royalty in the Murchison box at Texas Stadium.
Second from left, Murchison; fourth from left, Mrs.
Dwight D. Eisenhower; fifth, Lyndon B. Johnson;
seventh in row, Lady Bird.

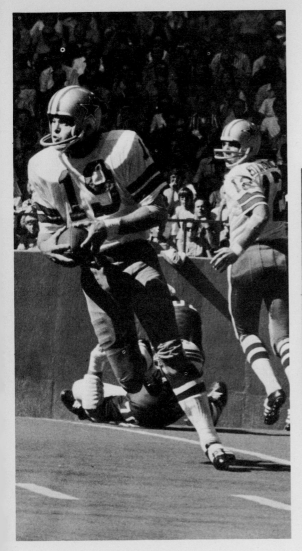

For a quarterback, Staubach spends a lot of time off the ground—after handoff to Alworth on end around. . . .

And here he is really airborne, getting a pass away over the onrushing Curley Culp of Kansas City.

The Silent One speaks at last. With the help of interpreter
Jim Brown (right), Duane Thomas is interviewed
after the Super Bowl by Tom Brookshier, almost.

"So?"

"I was kidding. Didn't you know I was kidding? My friends have been calling the house to tell me, 'Roger, that isn't like you, that doesn't sound like you.'"

"Yeah, well, they're wrong, aren't they?" I said. "That *is* you."

Staubach laughed. "No, really, it sounds as if I'd go teach a Boy Scout troop how to kill people with their bare hands."

"Okay, Roger," I said. "I'll use a note that it was a joke." But he and I know differently.

The Cowboys had now won eight in a row, though only the last two counted. The record was enough to make you take stock of their fortunes. The offense, the questionable half of the team, had just exploded for ninety-one points in two games. Calvin Hill had more than filled the vacuum left by Thomas, and now Thomas was back. What would happen when both of them began running out of the same backfield? The defense was intact from last year's seven-game drive to the Super Bowl, all eleven men. They had endured a funky afternoon at Buffalo, then completely shut down the poor Eagles a week later.

But Dallas had not yet been tested by a good team in a league game, and you wondered if they ever would be. Jimmy "The Greek" Snyder, the Las Vegas oddsmaker, had the Cowboys an eight-point favorite over Washington, though the Redskins were also unbeaten and seemed suddenly to be the only real competition in the East Division of the National Conference. How good were the Cowboys? Was this a great team coming together? The scope of the question was just the kind Clint Murchison likes to handle, and he had an answer: "I worked that out long ago," he said. "I told a luncheon club last April that this Cowboy team would not only be the best in the NFL this year; it would be the best in history. I said I fully expect it will score points like the 1951 Rams and play defense like the 1963 Chicago Bears. And I really believe it. We haven't seen any of their potential yet."

This was not a very timely story, because Washington came into town and showed that the Cowboys could score like the Bears and play defense like the Rams. Fullback Charley Harraway broke inside Howley on a sweep, kept going inside Renfro and fifty-seven yards to a touchdown. He got 118 for the day, and Washington got 200 rushing altogether—against a defense traditionally embarrassed when it gave up 100. Billy Kilmer threw a down-and-in to Roy Jefferson that went fifty yards for another touchdown, splitting between Adderley and Waters, and Curt Knight kicked two field goals: Washington 20, Dallas 16. It was the first inkling that George Allen's "Over the Hill Gang" was for real. Allen had traded away all his draft choices and acquired so many of his former players from Los Angeles that the team became known as the Ramskins. "I like to see a few bald heads on my squad," Allen said. He got linebackers Myron Pottios and Jack Pardee, safety Richie Petitbon, halfback Tommy Mason and flanker Boyd Dowler all from the Rams and all over thirty. He also got Diron Talbert and John Wilbur from Los Angeles, Ron McDole from Buffalo, Kilmer from New Orleans, Jimmie Jones and Verlon Biggs from the New York Jets and Roy Jefferson from Baltimore. "George's formula is simple," said a Cowboy assistant. "He'll take any veteran you want to get rid of, and then he'll take any badass that's giving you trouble." Holdouts Jefferson and Biggs fitted into the second category. "I never saw a lousier defense in my life," Allen said when he took over last winter, but the Redskins held Dallas to eighty-two yards on the ground and only one touchdown.

Morton hit eleven of twenty-six passes and was replaced by Staubach in the fourth quarter. Staubach threw to Ditka three times to set up a one-yard score by Hill and come within four points with three minutes left, then gathered the offensive unit on the sidelines to call the first two plays of the next series when the defense got the ball back. But Larry Brown, Harraway and old creaky-kneed Mason went up the middle for twenty-five yards, and the defense never got the ball back.

Landry was surprisingly ungracious about the defeat. "They're a guessing defense and today they guessed right," he said. "The league's young, and Washington won't be hard to catch. They're not going to play good football every week themselves."

Across the ramp in the other locker room, Allen was telling newspapermen, "I can't remember when I've ever lost to a Landry team," a point of view that explains some of Landry's churlishness. Allen was entitled to be boastful. When Sonny Jurgensen broke a shoulder during the exhibition season, it appeared that Allen's maiden season at Washington went to the sidelines with him. Instead, with Kilmer at quarterback, the Redskins had knocked off the three top teams in the East and enjoyed at least a one-game lead over the field. It fitted with Allen's slogan for the year: "The future is *now*."

Pardee, one of the balding linebackers, was shaving the red stubble off his face when I reached the Washington locker room. Pardee had been an assistant coach for a year at Texas A&M, his old school, when Allen had talked him into returning to the Rams five years ago. I congratulated him on the game, and he said, "Yup, it looks like us old fellows might make it after all." Then he pointed with his razor in the direction of the Cowboy locker room. "That's what Murchison says is the greatest team in history. I wonder what that makes us?"

"It still makes you the oldest," I said.

"That reminds me," Pardee said. "You tell Howley something for me. You tell him at his age he's an inspiration to us all."

A loud yell came from the shower room behind Pardee. "Fuck Jimmy the Greek!" It was Kilmer, showering in the big stall all alone because he'd been delayed by interviews, his red face split by a huge grin. "Fuck Jimmy the Greek," he yelled again.

Pardee turned and said, "You leave Jimmy the Greek alone. He's doing okay by us."

Ron Widby and Mike Clark were using Toni Fritsch's soccer ball for a game of one-bounce into the wastebasket, from a sitting-chair position. They were hitting one out of four. This is the way kickers kill time during team meetings at the practice field. The winner got to play trainer Larry Gardner. After a miss, Gardner tossed the ball at Fritsch's feet, saying, "Here, Toni, you try it." Fritsch flicked the ball with his foot and it went into the basket on the fly. Gardner, laughing, dug the ball out and handed it to Widby. "Okay," he said, "now you clowns try it again with your hands." Fritsch tugged at my sleeve and said, "Come, we must talk." I followed him down to the big leather couches at one end of the locker room.

"I ask Coach Landry for my release," he said, "so I can go back to Vienna. Nothing is happening for me here."

"And what did he say?"

"He said he wanted to talk, so we talked. I don't know if I buy a home here or buy a home in Vienna, and I am not getting in the games. But he promised me—he say, 'Toni, you stay, and you get full share of money when we get to other games.'"

"The playoffs, you mean?"

"The playoffs. So I think—I am better off staying here and getting fifteen thousand dollars from the Super Bowl than if I go with some other team and no Super Bowl."

"It'll be more like twenty-five thousand," I said, "but what makes you so sure this team can win the Super Bowl?"

"I always think winning the Super Bowl," Fritsch said, raising his eyebrows in surprise. "If people don't think we win the Super Bowl, they should get off the team. They should not even go on the field."

All I could tell Fritsch was what I tell every bench rider or taxi squadder, that it is a long season and you never know what will happen. Landry could promise him a full team share because shares are no longer voted by players. Since the Super Bowl came into existence, the commissioner's office has regulated the payoffs. Fritsch had never played in a league game, but he had never been put on waivers, either. If he stayed in this limbo (the "move list," remember?) for seven weeks, he was in for the money.

The team meetings had broken, and I moved through the players to grab Landry before he started a separate session with his quarterbacks. He had an additional thought on the

Washington loss, and he had a remedy. "They didn't respect the Redskins as much as I did," Landry said. "They thought, 'Well, Jurgensen isn't playing, so this ought to be easy.' Nothing's easy in this league when you aren't playing up to your game."

The remedy: "We'll go with Alworth and Truax this week, and we'll use Cliff Harris at free safety."

Alworth and Truax were just recovered from injuries, so it wasn't an upset that they'd go in for Gloster Richardson and Mike Ditka. Landry had made it clear he expected Truax and Ditka to split time at tight end. But the benching of Charlie Waters cut his string of eleven games as a starter. "We have given up four big plays in three weeks," Landry explained. "The long passes to Briscoe and that kid Hill at Buffalo, then Harraway's run and Jefferson's touchdown. Once a defense starts giving up big plays it will constantly be in trouble. The free safety is responsible for stopping the big play."

That put it squarely on Waters' shoulders. He said he would get blamed for everything. "What about your quarterback?" I said.

"Oh, Staubach," Landry said. "It's his turn to start."

I sought out Harris at his locker. Landry had announced to the team the same things he'd told me, so I wasn't bringing him any news. "This has really been weird," Harris said. "I wanted to pull for Charlie. I wanted him to do good because it would help us win, which is the main thing. But if he did too good, that would mean I would never get in there. That's the competitive angle. I didn't know how to act."

"Be careful how you break the news to Linda," I said. "Better make sure she has her swim suit on." Last year when Harris learned he was going to start the opening game, he and his wife were on their way to a party and stopped in their apartment patio to tell some neighbors about it. Then Linda turned around and fell into the swimming pool.

"That'll never happen this year," Harris said. "Last year she was a rookie."

Fran Tarkenton has a refreshing approach to football, especially refreshing in Dallas, where it is well known that it takes any Cowboy player a full two years to learn the Landry system. A few seasons ago, before the club got so success-ful that it could stop holding downtown Quarterback Club luncheons, a fan sent a question to the podium for Landry: "Why is the Cowboy offense so complicated that only the op-posing defense can understand it?" Tarkenton is using the multiple offense with the Giants, but he flies it by the seat of his pants. Two games before, he sent rookie halfback Rocky Thompson in motion, and Thompson went right instead of left. Tarkenton, leaning over center, did not call time out or risk a delay penalty. He just yelled, "Hey, Rocky! The other way!" Thompson made a U-turn and Tarkenton went on with the snap signals.

Tarkenton, then with the N. Y. Giants, was through Dal-las last spring on a public-relations tour for Delta Airlines, and we had a chance to talk about his offensive theories. "The game is not that complicated," he said. "If the line-backers drop off to help the cornerbacks cover my wide re-ceivers, I throw to my backs. If the linebackers stay up to cover my backs, I throw to my wide receivers."

"That takes care of the passing game," I said. "What about the run?"

"Oh, I let Greg Larson call the running plays," he said, naming the Giants' center. "Sure, why not? He knows how the blocking is going up front better than I do, better than the coaches in the press box for that matter. He knows what will work."

Tarkenton had never been allowed to play with a full deck, either at Minnesota in the expansion years or with the Giants, who gave up so many draft choices for him that they couldn't build a team, especially a defense. Former Giants publicist Don Smith described it: "You've heard about the Rubber Band Defense that bends but never breaks? Ours doesn't break either, but it stretches one hundred and one yards."

Tarkenton's system worked fine this time against Dallas, except that his people kept dropping the ball. The Cowboys held the game close by dropping it back again. The Giants fumbled six times and lost five; the Cowboys seven times

and lost five. The difference was that Morton took over from
Staubach and hit Hayes with a forty-eight-yard touchdown,
so Dallas won 20-13.

Morton came into the game at the start of the second half,
with Duane Thomas at fullback in place of Walt Garrison.
On the first play, an end sweep by Hill, Thomas hit the
Giants' defensive end, Fred Dryer, and stood him on his ear,
literally. The first thing that hit the ground was Dryer's
helmet. In three running plays Hill gained nine and five and
eleven—but on the third one safety Spider Lockhart hit him
when his leg was planted and all but wrecked his knee.
Reeves came in for Hill, and Thomas stayed at fullback,
looking as though he'd never been away. He averaged 6.6
yards on nine carries. It was an amazing performance for
a runner who had never been in a live scrimmage since the
Super Bowl.

"Well, he is just an amazing fellow," Landry said as writers
and radio men crowded into his little cubicle in the Cotton
Bowl locker room. "He's a great natural runner and he just
doesn't make many mistakes. We'll work him at halfback this
week, because we don't know how bad Calvin's knee is."

When I found Hill at his locker he was easing his pants
down over his sore knee, grunting a little bit. A bead of
sweat ran off his nose. He looked up and smiled with just
one side of his mouth. "If I didn't have bad luck," he said,
"I wouldn't have any luck at all." When an injury sidelined
Hill last season, Thomas came on, and he never got his job
back. I told him now that Thomas would be working at halfback this week.

"Who said?" Hill plainly suspected I was only needling
him.

"Tom," I said.

Hill slammed a shoe into the floor. "I'm not going to go
through the same shit I went through last year," he said.
"I'll be back, and I'm going to have my *job*."

Thomas' return was stirring up the whole backfield. I
found Garrison outside the shower room combing his hair.
He looked at me with a resigned expression, knowing what
was coming. "How do you feel, Walt?"

"Okay. Why?"

"All right. I mean how did you feel when you sat on the bench the second half?"

"You really want to know?" I nodded. "I felt like a bastard at a family reunion."

Every starter, injured or not, experienced the same reaction when sent to the bench, a sense of estrangement from the team. There is hardly a player on the Cowboy squad who was not a star in high school, a star in college and a celebrity every step of the way—a background that accounts for a lot of strange behavior by grown men in the National Football League. Garrison had had all of that, but he is unique on this team, the only real cowboy. When he signed out of Oklahoma State, the club offered him a Pontiac Grand Prix as part of his bonus. He said that if it was all the same to them he would take a two-horse trailer and a new Stetson hat. On Garrison's first date with his wife, Pam, he made a great impression by tipping over the spittoon he carried on the floorboard of his car. His idea of off-season relaxation is to bulldog steers at a county rodeo. The club forbids him to ride Brahma bulls. He had put in three long years on the bench until Don Perkins retired and now he was back there again, replaced by a guy who had skipped training camp and the exhibition season.

"There's only one way to look at it," Garrison said. "Tom's running the team the way he thinks best. If he feels like we'll get more running with the other two in there, that's what it's got to be. But I know one thing—it'll take all three of us to get to the Super Bowl."

Thomas had come out of the shower while I was talking to Garrison, and he was dressing hurriedly. Our exchange of words was less than classic. How did it feel, getting into action for the first time? "It felt like what it was—football," Thomas said. How come he wasn't rusty or off-timing? "I've been practicing enough." Did he expect to do as well as he'd done? "I always expect good things to happen." Didn't he get tired? "No, but I got a little winded." He would be switching to halfback this week, and did that make any difference to him? "I don't want to think about anything to do with football. I'm just thinking about getting out of here and going home." And he left.

Reeves, across the locker room aisle, had heard part of the dialogue. "He said he wasn't tired," Reeves said, "and that's the amazing part about the whole deal—he *wasn't*. You take me, I haven't worked as hard as everybody else, coaching and all, but at least I did something and I been at it since July. I like to died out there, having to play that much. And Duane wasn't even breathing hard. I don't know how he does it."

"This tell you anything about next July?" I said.

"Yeah," Reeves said. "It tells me I ought to spend it in New Zealand."

At his mid-week press luncheon Landry said he had yanked Staubach at the half "because I very definitely felt we should have been ahead by more than thirteen-six. We got down there four times and scored once." Then he announced that Morton would start at New Orleans and Staubach would start the following week in Dallas against New England.

"Aren't you taking a chance, naming your quarterback two games ahead?" I said.

Landry gave me his blank stare, what Ermal Allen is fond of calling "the brook-trout look." "No," said Landry, "I don't think so. I'm naming Staubach for New England because I want him to know where he stands, that we still have a two-quarterback system."

"If Morton completes twenty-one of twenty-one Sunday," I said, "will Staubach still start the next game?"

"Probably," Landry said.

That afternoon Landry had his secretary call me at the office with a message: "An exceptional performance by Morton *could* change his decision on the next week's starter."

The ball floated high against the wind and kept drifting back toward the line of scrimmage. This was just what the Cowboys needed, a short punt by the Saints in the fourth quarter. Landry was screaming, "Let it go! Let it go!" but the New Orleans fans were screaming louder than he was. They always are. The only thing you can hear in that stadium is Al Hirt playing "When the Saints Go Marching In." Any-

way, Charlie Waters was not about to let it go. "How can
I let it go?" he said. "You can't let a punt hit the ground.
It costs you too many yards. I never have any trouble catch-
ing a punt, but then somebody hit me."

It was John Fitzgerald, the rookie center. "The man I was
blocking said, 'Hold up . . . fair catch,'" Fitzgerald said,
"and I thought, 'Oh, oh, where's Charlie?' And then I
bumped into his leg."

"He caught it right in a crowd," Landry said, "and anytime you do that, you take a chance on losing it. That was
the ball game. Roger had just got us the two touchdowns
and we were all set to take it in for the win."

Well, Landry is sometimes as human as the rest of us. He
has three views of every road game—one in the locker room
immediately after it's over, another on the team plane going home, and another after he has seen the films. Each is
progressively milder. He doesn't really blame everything on
Charlie Waters.

The Cowboys made enough mistakes to lose three football games before they could lose this one to the Saints.
Morton threw an interception into the New Orleans end
zone and threw another that was returned sixty yards. A
short Mike Clark field goal was run back seventy-seven yards.
Adderley tried to intercept a pass that went by him for a
touchdown—and the Saints led at halftime, 17-0. Landry
stayed with Morton for two series in the third quarter, then
came in with Staubach. He hit seven of his first ten passes.
One went forty-one yards for a touchdown to Gloster Richardson, sent in with the call by Landry, who was now calling all the plays. Another went eighteen to Hayes, and the
Cowboys trailed by three with ten minutes left in the game,
when Waters fumbled away the fair catch. There was still
plenty of time for a title-contending team to beat a team
that didn't figure to win half its games. At the two-minute
mark the Saints punted and Harris fumbled it at the three-
yard line. The final was 24-14, and at that moment the
rookie New Orleans quarterback, Archie Manning, could have
been named Rex of the next Mardi Gras.

A motorcycle escort—the specialty of police in New Orleans and Chicago and two or three other cities around the league—hurried the two team buses to the airport, sirens blaring. George Andrie was fidgeting in his seat, rapping his knuckles idly against the window. "You know you're not going to win *all* your games," he said, "so nobody gets upset when Washington comes in and has a good day and we're having a bad one. But you just ain't supposed to lose to teams like the Saints. This is when you know you're in trouble. Hey, what did Washington do?"

Reeves turned from the seat in front of Andrie and said, "They won."

"That makes us what? Two games out?"

"Yeah," Reeves said, "and nine to play. We're in the same spot we were last year, only we got there four games quicker."

The team plane, a Braniff 727, splits the coaches and the press and the club officials into the first-class section and the players into tourist. The middle seats in the rows of three back there are kept vacant so the big men can spread out. At the top of the boarding ramp a stewardess hands out two cans of cold beer apiece. That's supposed to be it for the players, and it usually is. Very few of them bootleg any whisky in the attaché cases they use for luggage. When the plane gets airborne, a curtain is pulled between the sections and a stewardess wheels out a folding cart to set up a bar in the forward entryway. The rule is, you can roam into the players' section with a can of beer in your hand, but you don't tote any of the hard stuff back there.

Once airborne, the players break into the same groups every trip. They have a way of smashing the chairbacks forward to open up two pairs of seats for a card game. There's no poker, only gin, whist, pitch, cribbage, hearts and a game called Tonk, which is a mystery to me though I have been trying to kibbitz it for eight years. Green and Hayes are always in the same seats on the port side, facing Pugh and Wright in what must be the longest-running Tonk game in history. Wright is the come-lately, filling out the fourth when Don Perkins retired three years ago. Further aft and on the opposite side of the aisle, Morton and Edwards and Ditka and Alworth or Garrison are in another one. At training camp these games are played for stakes that would make a sportswriter blanch, but I have never seen any money change hands on a plane. Finally, on the stewardesses' low bench seat between the rear johns sits Ralph Neely. I think Neely got in the habit of sitting there when he and Meredith used to sip Scotch on the long rides home from losing games. It was a vantage point that provided maximum alert when Landry started his tour of the section. Now Meredith is gone and so is the Scotch, and Neely likes the bench because it allows him to stretch his legs down the aisle. I sat down beside him. "I was wondering," I said, "if you heard your name on the PA system."

Neely grimaced. "Yeah, I heard it. The sonsabitches." The league had instituted a new policy this season of announcing the guilty party on a rule infraction. Neely was called for two holding penalties almost back to back, and offensive line coach Jim Myers pulled him out of the game for two series. "I'd like to get ahold of the guy who decided to start that crap," Neely said. "The thing about it, do you ever hear 'em announce, 'Blocking on that touchdown, Ralph Neely'? No, all you ever hear is he cost you fifteen yards. These refs must pass the word around, I swear. They must have an underground wireless, or something. I'm playing the same game I've been playing since I came in the league, and I bet I've had more holding calls in five games than I had in the last five years. I can see one ref meeting another at an airport: *'Pass the word—Neely's holding.'* "

I talked Neely out of one of his spare beers. There are enough nondrinkers on the club to make a mockery of the two-beer limit. "You think this team is going to get turned around again?" I said.

"Oh, yeah," Neely said, "if the coaches ever get off our ass."

"How do you mean?"

"Maybe I put that backwards. We can get straightened out as soon as we stop worrying about the coaches being on our ass. My personal opinion, we're too conscious of what the coaches are going to think of a mistake. When you make a

mistake in a game—and remember, this is *during* a game—
there are two things that hit your mind. The *first* thing you
think is 'Oh, God, that's going to look great on Tuesday
when we look at the films.' The next thing you think is what
the fans are going to think and what's going to be in the
paper."

"I hardly ever mention it," I said, "unless a touchdown is
called back on the play or—"

"But the fans get it, and for road games they get it on
instant replay."

"—or unless it figures in losing a Super Bowl."

"Yeah, Well, you ought to go back and take a look at
that play," Neely said, "and tell me how they could call
holding."

"Are things really that rough when you go over the films?"

"They're shitty," Neely said. "Shitty and childish."

"That's crazy," I said. "This is the same thing all over
again. You remember what Lilly said last year?"

"Yeah, I remember, and he was right."

Almost a year later Neely was repeating the same theme.
"The players have to start playing for themselves," he said,
"and remember the main thing—winning the damn game.
Maybe I shouldn't be saying this, but I think it's time somebody laid it on the line. We're all gonna have to decide to
take our lumps on Tuesday, take 'em as individuals and as
a team—and forget 'em! This is easier said than done. When
you got somebody on your butt, it's hard to ignore. This
isn't a young club any more. It's not old yet, either, but
we've got enough experience now that we shouldn't have to
worry about what the coaches say on Tuesday."

"You think that would do it, huh?"

"That and a quarterback. It would help to have just one
quarterback."

"Which one?"

"Either damn one," Neely said. "At this point I don't
care."

The flight time from New Orleans is only one hour, and
we had almost entered our landing pattern when Landry

began exchanging questions and answers with the writers. "I'm not going to talk about what I'm going to do," he said. "I'll do something. You'll just have to watch and observe." He made it clear the "something" wouldn't be the naming of a number-one quarterback. "We'll go with Roger against New England," he said, "and see how it works from there."

The next night I spoke at a meeting of the St. Rita's Men's Club and gave them an expert, insider's view of what would happen on the Cowboys: Morton would eventually take over at quarterback and take the team to the Super Bowl.

The Reverend Sidney Lange, S.J., a young priest who was born and raised in New Orleans, gave the closing benediction: "We thank you, Father, for the intercession of the saints in heaven and the victories of the Saints on earth."

The whole town seemed to be divided 70-30 on the quarterback question, with Staubach on the front end—or, as Sonny Jurgensen put it, "They sure love those number-two quarterbacks." It was hard to end a conversation at the practice field without touching on the subject. "Hey," said Calvin Hill, "don't you think Tom is just waiting for one of them to take charge?" Bobby Hayes said, "We better settle on one quarterback pretty soon so we can go for the title." Morton essayed his usual cool: "It looks pretty screwed up now, but the thing will straighten itself out. Until it does, I don't want to go into it."

But Staubach, of all people, was showing jangled nerves. "I have to play more than a half, more than a game or two to get things going," he said. Morton was sitting at his locker, a bare four feet away, but Staubach plainly didn't give a damn. "If Coach Landry doesn't want to take that chance with me, someone else will. If things don't work out here, I think there's someone who'll throw me out there and say, 'Hey, *win* for us.' But I think I'll stay here. I believe I'll get my chance to determine what happens here. Whenever I've wanted to accomplish something very badly, I've done it. The problem is, I think Craig and I have both lost a real understanding of where we stand."

But Landry wasn't nervous. He sees his role as described

by Rudyard Kipling: "If you can keep your head while all about you are losing theirs . . ." He was alone in the coaches' tiny locker room when I asked him if he ever second-guessed himself. "Gosh, no," he said. "I've got enough problems ahead of me. I don't need to worry about the ones behind me. I'd go nuts if I second-guessed myself as much as you guys do."

"What if you hadn't gone with two quarterbacks?" I said.

"I believe the results would have been the same," he said, "but everybody would have been blaming the one quarterback instead of me . . . and asking why I picked him."

"Are you going to call plays for Staubach Sunday?"

"It's a good possibility. I'm going to help him every way I can."

Texas Stadium, opening for the New England game ten weeks late, was the House That Clint Built to thumb his nose at the Dallas Establishment. Outsiders are always amazed to learn that a Murchison could be aligned opposite the City Fathers. It happened by degrees. The Cowboys had always played at the Cotton Bowl, which had been enlarged to 80,000 capacity when everybody in town wanted to see Doak Walker. For decades the structure has been the centerpiece of the State Fair, on a 200-acre site which was once surrounded by stately homes. Over the years the area had become a black ghetto. The betting line on night games included the odds on getting mugged. When Cowboy attendance jumped from 38,000 a game in 1964 to 58,000 the following year, Murchison suggested that half of the resultant increase in rent payments be used to refurbish the old place. Not a dime was spent. The landlord, the city park board, had the logic of all landlords on its side: where else could the Cowboys play? "It was fairly obvious," Murchison says, "that they weren't going to do a thing—they weren't going to put in water fountains, clean up the toilets, build new dressing rooms, fix the press-box elevator—hell, we couldn't even get them to water the field when the players complained it was hard as concrete. It occurred to me that we shouldn't be playing out there at all. Without the Cowboy rent, the State Fair and the whole Fair Park operation is a losing proposition.

Why should football be expected to make up the difference?" Murchison at length proposed a downtown stadium to be financed by revenue bonds, on the theory that the stadium parking lot could be used by businessmen during the week and the whole mordant area would be revived by the games on weekends. Mayor Erik Jonsson, a millionaire himself, said there would always be a Fair Park and Murchison should go pump up some footballs. Instead, Murchison bought acreage just outside the city limits, in Irving, and announced that Cowboy fans were going to provide the money for a 65,000-seat stadium. They would buy $250 bonds and get $300 back in thirty-five years or less. For a seat between the thirty-yard lines, they'd buy $1,000 worth. The bonds would be backed by the city of Irving, and Cowboy rent would pay them off. No bond, no season ticket. Between the lower and upper decks would be 170 "inner circle suites," sixteen by twenty feet, at fifty thousand dollars apiece plus an annual outlay for twelve season tickets. Mayor Jonsson responded by pushing through a bond program allocating $12 million for Fair Park improvements, including a specified $1.5 million for remodeling the Cotton Bowl. "If Clint would only be patient," Jonsson said, "we will build him a new stadium at Fair Park." The $1.5 million figure turned out to be $3.1 million, as the city did everything Murchison had originally requested. Meanwhile, Cowboy fans grumbled their way to the bond window, and construction began on the Irving stadium. "Not one old lady on Social Security is going to have her taxes raised because of *this* stadium," Murchison said. "What could be fairer? The people who like football games are putting up the money."

Now, less than four years after the first announcement, a capacity crowd which included owners of thirty thousand bonds jammed into the $25 million stadium. Fans in the lower deck walked *down* to their seats; those in the upper deck rode escalators. A vaulted roof covered everything except the playing field. In a rainstorm, the first three rows might get wet. All but thirty-six of the circle suites had been sold, and some of them were decorated with crystal chandeliers. LBJ and Lady Bird were guests in Murchison's suite.

The chairs in the press box were upholstered in glove-soft leather, and between each two seats a Sony TV was hooked into the network telecast for instant replays. Murchison strolled in to check them out for himself. He made a vague gesture toward the field and said, "It's a nice little place to play a ball game, wouldn't you say?"

On the fourth play of the game, Duane Thomas ran around right end, cut back to the left and went fifty-six yards for a touchdown. Blaine Nye flattened the cornerback, Rayfield Wright wiped out the linebacker, Lance Alworth cut down the safety and Bobby Hayes shielded off the last pursuit. It was no contest. Staubach hit Hayes for two touchdowns, ran two yards for another, and Clark kicked two short field goals. Dallas led 34-7 at the half and 44-21 at the finish. The Patriots' rookie quarterback, Jim Plunkett, hit seven of twelve in the first half, but Lilly and Pugh overwhelmed him the rest of the day. At the final gun I followed Niland over to say hello to Halvor Hagen. "I don't imagine he got much sleep last night," Niland said. "He used to hate to work out against Lilly." When Hagen saw Niland, he started grinning sheepishly and shaking his head. "It's not going to look good in the films," Hagen said.

"It was worse than practice, wasn't it?" Niland said.

"I got help from the center," Hagen said, "but you give that guy a crease"—he held his thumb and forefinger an inch apart—"and he's through."

The Cowboy locker room, a vast, paneled expanse in the decor of a country club, was disrupted by a visit from Lyndon Johnson making the circuit, saying, "Howdy" and "Nice game." His hair was long and silvery in the old Southern Senator style, and he wore a tan pancake makeup for photogenic effect. When he reached Staubach Johnson said, "You sure know how to break in a new stadium."

Staubach wasn't accepting much encouragement. "Nobody can be satisfied with this game," he said. "I'm eager about next week."

Later in the afternoon Washington lost at Kansas City, cutting the Redskins' lead over Dallas to one game.

At his Wednesday press conference, Landry announced that he would go with "the quarterback shuttle" against Chicago. "We are going with the shuttle," he said, "because of the many change-ups the Bears use on defense. This way we'll be able to combat that."

Landry had gone back nine years into Cowboy history to revive an invention of his he'd first used with Eddie LeBaron and Meredith. Morton would quarterback the first play of every series, Staubach the second, and they would alternate from there, with Landry calling all the plays. Landry had shuttled the tight ends, Ditka and Truax, in the New England game, and this was the "change" he had promised on the plane home from New Orleans. He explained once again that through his selection of plays from the sideline his assistant coaches in the press box—Ray Renfro, Jerry Tubbs and Ermal Allen—would be alerted. "We can watch the point of attack," Landry said, "see what the defense does and adjust accordingly."

"What do the players think about this?" said Frank Luksa.

"I didn't ask," Landry said.

"You told Morton and Staubach this yet?" Luksa said.

"Yes."

"What did they say?"

"They didn't say anything."

There was a bit of a pause here, and I asked Landry, "Did either one make a gesture—like putting his head in his hands?"

"Look," Landry said, "the players don't have to agree with everything I decide. That's not their job. It's what I'm here for. But they usually go along."

I called Morton and Staubach that night. Morton said, "There are some advantages to it."

"Which are outweighed by the disadvantages?"

"You said that. I didn't. All you can quote me is 'no comment.'"

Staubach was equally hesitant to go on the record. "He's right about one thing, though," Staubach said. "We have to go along with it."

If the Cowboys weren't talking, the Bears certainly were

when I checked in Chicago for reaction to the shuttle. "You've got to be kidding," said Ed O'Bradovich, the defensive end. "This has got to help us. We've had some quarterback trouble ourselves but [Jim] Dooley never played two of them at the same time. I don't see how they can get any confidence in themselves cutting it up that way."

Linebacker Doug Buffone said, "Landry must be cracking up. They'll probably get tired running on and off the field. . . . Hey! Maybe they'll even run into each other."

Gloster Richardson ran up the sideline to shout at Margene Adkins, the "up" man for the punt return, "Gene! You, Gene! Squeeze it, now! You squeeze it hard!" The kick went low over Adkins' head to the deep man, Cliff Harris, and Harris caught it on the dead run, sliced between two Bears, got hit by a third and fumbled. Chicago recovered and had the ball at the Cowboy thirty-nine with 1:40 to play and the score 23-19. I turned away in disgust and almost bumped into Murchison, who had also come down on the field for the closing minutes. He surprised me by grinning. "Well," he said, "just another given Sunday."

"You've had too damn many given Sundays," I said. "One more and you can forget about the playoffs."

The quarterback shuttle had worked beautifully everywhere but on the scoreboard. Morton and Staubach had hit twenty of thirty-three passes for 236 yards while alternating plays. With ten minutes left in the game and Chicago ahead by 23-12, Eddie LeBaron, now a CBS-TV commentator, told the audience back in Dallas, "Let's see if Coach Landry sticks with the quarterback shuttle now." LeBaron knew he couldn't. He went with Morton. Staubach had entered the game as the number-one passer in the National Conference and had hit seven of eleven attempts. Morton was number five, but Landry opted for his experience against a Bear defense which knew he would have to pass every down. Morton completed seven of fourteen, one a forty-five-yard touchdown to Richardson.

All the Chicago points had been set up by interceptions and fumbles, and finally Landry stood alone in the middle of the Soldier Field locker room shaking his head. "The field goals were the difference," he said. "They hit three and we missed three. Good gosh, if we'd only hit two of the three it would have been enough."

There was fine irony in that statistic. In 1967 the Cowboys conducted a "Kicking Karavan" search of the country for field-goal kickers—10,000 miles, twenty-nine cities, 1,300 kickers. And they'd found the best one in their own backyard. Mac Percival was a twenty-seven-year-old high-school basketball coach in a Dallas suburb. His wife entered his name for a Cowboy tryout. When the final cutdown came that summer, Landry traded Percival to Chicago and kept the lone Karavan survivor, Harold Deters, for the taxi squad. Deters retired to become a schoolteacher, and now Percival had kicked three out of four field goals to beat the Cowboys.

Clark had missed three of four, including chances from the twenty-five- and thirty-yard lines. "The last time we were in Chicago," Clark said, "I missed five. I don't know, maybe I was thinking about Percival too much."

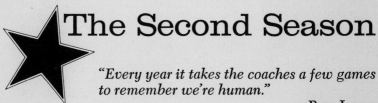

The Second Season

"Every year it takes the coaches a few games to remember we're human."

—Bob Lilly

The Cowboys were 4-3 to the Redskins' 6-1, two games behind with seven to play, and sure enough things got worse. Ralph Neely, on a motorcycle outing through the wilds of a nearby lakefront the day after the Bear game, stubbed his toe on a rock, trapping his foot between the rock and the pedal brace, dislocating the ankle and breaking the leg in three places. The accident also broke up what had become a traditional form of Monday relaxation for a dozen or more Cowboys.

"I didn't know anybody was riding motorcycles," Landry said, "but you can't have rules for everything. I'm not even going to have one now. If a guy is stupid enough to jeopardize his whole career that way, a new rule isn't going to protect him." The Neely injury was enough of a news bulletin for me to phone Landry at his home that night. It was so early in the week he hadn't made any hard decisions about his team's situation. "Maybe we aren't as hungry as we were last year," he said. "Teams that have been to the Super Bowl have a tendency to wait around for things to happen—and they happen all right, all of them usually bad."

"You think you will go with a number-one quarterback?" I said.

"We have to do *some* things," he said, "and going with one quarterback might be one of them."

I called Neely at his hospital room the next day, and his
first words were, "Know anybody wants to buy a motorcycle?
I got one for sale—cheap."

Landry kept his plans secret until the mid-week press
luncheon. As we were making our way through the buffet
line, Luksa said, "Who do you think it will be?"

"Morton," I said.

"Why do you say Morton?"

"When he had to go with one quarterback in the fourth
quarter at Chicago, he went with Morton, didn't he? Now
the whole season's a fourth quarter."

"Maybe you're right," Luksa said, "but I don't think so."

Landry bolted his food, stood up and announced that Mike
Clark had been waived out of the league and placed on the
taxi squad. Toni Fritsch had been activated. And Roger
Staubach would be the Cowboys' number-one quarterback
for the duration.

"If any part of the team is concerned that we don't have
an established number-one quarterback working for us, if
that upsets them at all—and I'm not sure it does, really—if
that's a possibility, then I must make a choice on the quarterback. It's a real shame to have to make a choice. Both quarterbacks have been outstanding. But I think it's Roger's time
to make his move, if he's going to make it. This is the way
we'll go—don't ask me if we'll go seven games this way. Who
knows? When you make a choice you expect it to go seven
games or you wouldn't make it. I'm not going to explain one
way or another why the choice was made. We will go with
Staubach and that's it."

But of course that wasn't *it,* and the story began filtering
out in bits and pieces. "Reeves was pushing for Staubach," a
player told me. Reeves didn't want to be quoted, and all he
would say off the record was, "The team needed a change.
Going with Craig wouldn't be a change."

The reactions of Morton and Staubach were predictable
enough. "It's fantastic!" Staubach said. I'd stopped him just
outside the locker-room door before practice. "This is the first
time I'm really the quarterback. If I make a few mistakes,

I'll still be in there. I won't be walking a tightrope any more.
This way I'll come through a winner. You know I always feel
like I'm going to walk off the field with a win, but that's
because of the people I have around me. I promised Mr.
Landry I wouldn't let him and the team down—but everything will have to be said in performance."

Staubach was clearly floating. He *ran* out to line up for
calisthenics. When I chatted with Morton after practice he
seemed careful not to appear depressed. "I'm behind Roger
and I'll do everything I can to help him," he said. "I'm going
to keep working hard because I just know, before this thing
is over, I'll have to play. It takes two quarterbacks to get you
there."

"If it only takes one," I said, "everybody will figure this is
it for you with the Cowboys."

Morton shook his head. "I'll talk about other situations
later. I'm not bitter. I've been throwing the ball better than
any time in my life. I know what I'm doing out there, and I
have confidence in my ability. I don't doubt it any more.
That's my strength. The whole team has got to realize now
we can't wait around for somebody else to help us. The other
guys have got to back up the starters. Whether I'm pleased
with it or not is immaterial."

The plane to St. Louis was full of hopeful conversation. "I
think eleven-three will win the division," Landry said, "but
I'm not sure how Washington is going to hold up."

"I talked with Charley Cowan this week," I said, naming
one of the Rams Allen had left behind him. "He said, 'If
George is working their tails the way he worked ours last
year, those old men are going to fold in the stretch.'"

Landry smiled and said, "I wouldn't know about that."
Circumspect as ever.

The players were harking back to memories of last season's
closing drive. I interrupted a conversation between Jordan
and Howley to ask them the odds on doing it again. "We're
a whole lot better team right now," Jordan said, "than we
were when we went up to Washington and beat them that
first game last year, something like forty-five to twenty-one."
He had it down pat; that *was* the score. "They gained three

hundred yards on us that day. Nobody's going to gain three hundred on this team."

Howley grinned his lopsided grin. "I don't see what's hard about winning seven in a row. We already won *nine* in a row once this year—but you guys don't count the exhibition games."

That night Ermal Allen and I resoundingly closed up the bar at the Bel Air East, as somewhere along the way I mentioned my surprise that Morton hadn't gotten the job. "Are you kidding me?" Allen said. "You have *got* to be kidding me. Staubach should have had the job when the season started."

"I thought they were even in the pre-season," I said.

"Roger was ahead in every department. Every way you could measure it he was clear-cut ahead."

"Why do you call him Staubach one time and Roger the next?"

"For effect," Allen said. "Like when I call you Perkins, it means I don't like you."

"Okay."

"Tom just wouldn't do that to Craig. He's a veteran, seventh year in the league, lah-dee-dah dee-dah. But there comes a time when you got to throw the sideline pass."

"He can't hum it no more, huh?"

"Craig's a good quarterback, and I tell you, he's done himself a lot of good, real good for the team the way he's acted this week. But Roger can be a great one. I mean, a Unitas. This guy is fantastic, wait and see."

I wondered why Allen had always been a little anti-Morton. When Jerry Rhome and Morton were backing up Meredith, Red Hickey was for Morton, and Allen was always boosting Rhome. But I didn't bring this up. Why ruin a pleasant evening?

For one moment in the third quarter the Cowboy season went down the drain. St. Louis led 10-6 and Jim Hart threw twenty-six yards for a touchdown to tight end Jackie Smith. A yellow flag wiped out the play, a holding penalty on rookie tackle Dan Dierdorf. The Cowboys then drove for their only touchdown, with Staubach throwing to Alworth or scrambling for a first down or sending Thomas around end. Herb

Adderley was out with a hip bruise, and rookie Ike Thomas was pressed into duty at left cornerback. Cardinal wide receivers John Gilliam and Dave Williams alternated in burning him deep. Williams got clear again for a thirty-seven-yard catch, and Jim Bakken kicked a tying field goal. Alworth, never a factor in a Dallas game until now, caught his sixth, seventh and eighth passes of the day, the last one reaching the nineteen-yard line, with 1:43 to play.

Toni Fritsch came in on fourth down to try for the winning points. Fritsch had kicked field goals of twenty-seven and fourteen yards, but he had also missed one from the forty-two. Cardinal linebacker Larry Stallings began yelling at Fritsch as the teams lined up: "Hey, you little shithead, you're gonna blow it! You're gonna choke, you midget bastard."

Dave Edwards, a blocking back on the field-goal unit, started laughing. "Save your breath, Stallings," Edwards said. "He can't understand a word of English."

Before the ball reached the uprights, Fritsch held his clinched fist high in the air and began jumping up and down. In the locker room a few moments later, the Cowboys gave him the Game Ball and a song: "Hurrah for Toni, hurrah at last/Hurrah for Toni, he's a horse's ass."

Fritsch had to give a translation to the press. "Horse's ass *ist pferde arsch*," he said, slapping himself on the rump. "The shoot for the winner is just twenty-six yards. It is no problem I must do it to win the game. The problem is the forty-two yards I miss. This *ist* my first game in two months. You cannot get this in practice. Once I get the feel of the game, I won't miss."

When the writers finally turned away, Fritsch grabbed my arm. "Why is this football?" he said.

"They're telling you you're the hero," I said. "You give it to Jack Eskridge, the equipment man, and he sends it off somewhere to get the score painted on and the date of the game. You put it on your mantle."

"Ah," Fritsch said, "the Man of the Match."

"You got it."

"I just wish they didn't have to lose a game before I got a chance to shoot."

"Did you hear Stallings yelling at you?"

"Yes. I hear. And I tell him something, too. I tell him, 'You got a big ass and nothing here.' " Fritsch tapped a finger at his temple.

In the center of the locker room Landry was saying to St. Louis writers, "Fritsch could be a catalyst, a guy to get you rolling. One guy can get in a hot streak and you never know what effect it will have on your team. It was great to come back for a win. This is the first game we've played since last year when everybody is hustling and fighting and wanting it. It takes more than one game to bring you back, but this is a starter."

"You have to be happy you went with one quarterback instead of two," said Rich Koster of the *Globe-Democrat*.

"A two-quarterback system is fine," Landry said, "but the public just won't identify with it. You divide the whole town if you have two quarterbacks, and there's so much talk about it, it's distracting."

Staubach completed twenty of thirty-one passes for 199 yards and the one touchdown, to Mike Ditka, and he ran seven times for sixty yards. "It takes a lot to satisfy *me*," Staubach said. "We're a lot more explosive team than we showed today. A lot of times I had to run, and that isn't one of Coach Landry's favorite plays. But Alworth added a lot for us—he did a great job getting open."

Alworth, dressing at the next locker, had to pry his way through the mob around Staubach to get to his clothes. "This is the first time I've felt like a member of the team," he said. "Now maybe we can get something going. You just got to have one quarterback. It's a matter of timing. A passer and receiver have to be tuned in. You remember that pass I dropped last Sunday, coming across the middle? When I made my cut I looked for the ball. I guess I didn't have it on my mind which quarterback was in there. I was thinking Roger when I turned for the ball, but it was Craig throwing. Their passes come in a shade different, and I was just off enough in my timing I had to grab for it by my shoulder. I should have caught it and I didn't."

On the plane home Luksa got Ray Renfro to talk about

that same subject. Renfro commutes to Dallas from Fort Worth, which makes him a faithful reader of the *Star-Telegram*. Even so, he's one of my favorite people in the organization, soft-voiced, gentle-natured, but hard-nosed on the subject of football. At training camp one year I asked him why a particularly flashy receiver had been cut. "Because he's a pussy," Renfro said, using a pro's one-word description of a player who doesn't like physical contact. He had come up through the harsh school of Paul Brown for twelve seasons beginning in 1952, the greatest long-distance threat the Browns have ever had, including Paul Warfield. Going over the Cleveland record book one day, I noticed he was in there for catching three touchdown passes in a game against Pittsburgh in 1959, and I asked him if he remembered it. "I'll never forget it," he had said. "Not because of the three I caught, but the one I dropped and what Brown said to me. We had messed up on an extra point, and Bobby Layne ran out the clock just right, so he could score and go ahead, twenty-one to twenty, and leave us only one play. I got open down the sideline and Milt Plum must have thrown the ball eighty yards in the air. It was almost perfect, but just a little long, and I guess I was about on the five when it came down. I stretched out for it and tried to bring it in, and my knee hit the ball and kicked it up in the end zone. That was the end of the game. Brown grabbed my arm and said, 'You're washed up, Renfro. You're through. You just can't make the clutch catch any more.'"

Now Renfro, with a lot more charity, was explaining why the quarterback decision went to Staubach. "It's like a championship golfer who goes into a long slump. He gets a new putter. Maybe he plays a different ball. He starts adjusting his swing. The point is, he has to make a change. Landry knows what Craig can do, how far he can take, you. With Roger, even though he's had his ups and downs, there's a feeling of not knowing what he can do. As for reading or handling defenses, naturally Craig has to be sharper. He should be sharper. He's experienced with our offensive sets. But he hasn't gotten us into the end zone like Roger has, although the fault hasn't been all quarterbacking. There's not enough difference in them other than that. You're betting Roger's strong arm and confidence will offset Craig's experience. I don't feel Craig has strong confidence in big games. It might be different if we'd won the Super Bowl and he'd had a decent day. He's a sensitive person. When he was booed this year, stuff like that really hurts him. Roger thinks he can throw the ball anywhere, and if he gets good protection and good pass routes, he's gonna throw completions. Still, Craig can handle the offense as well as anyone, in my opinion. With his ability, I think he's a championship quarterback. It all goes back to one thing—Roger has gotten us into the end zone more."

I drifted back to the players' section and bumped into Morton, standing at the stewardesses' galley just on the other side of the curtain. "Wait a minute," I said. "I know you. It's . . . uh . . . uh . . . Craig Morton!"

Morton grinned and shook his head. "You really know how to hurt a guy," he said.

Howley and Andrie were in the first row of seats on the left, and I said to Howley, "That's one down and six more in a row to go."

"I've revised the estimate upward," Howley said. "I overlooked a little thing the other day. It's going to be ten in a row altogether."

"Yeah," Andrie said. "You got to win in the playoffs, the games that count. Right now, it's like exhibition games."

"That's very good, George," I said, taking pen and paper out of my back pocket. "I got to get that down."

"I'm kidding, for God's sake, I'm kidding," Andrie said.

"I want to get back to New Orleans—for one reason," Howley said. "Aw, I mean we all want to go back and win the Super Bowl, but there's another reason I want to go back—that little bastard at Kolb's restaurant. Remember, George?"

"Yeah," Andrie said. "The busboy."

"This little guy starts riding us the night before the New Orleans game. How the Saints are going to whip our ass. How the Cowboys are overrated, all-time losers. It got so bad, the waiter had to chase him away."

"What are you going to do?" Andrie said. "You can't hit him. He weighs like a hundred pounds."

"I told the kid," Howley said, "I told him, 'I don't know how tomorrow's game's going to come out, but I'll make you a promise—I'll see you back here in January when we come for the Super Bowl.'"

"Yeah," Andrie said. "With our luck, the little bastard got fired since then."

Back up front Landry was discussing the upset of the day, Washington getting tied by Philadelphia. "That's the same as a loss," he said, "if we win all the rest of our games—but somebody else has got to beat 'em for us, too." In the NFL, tie games are thrown out, as if they were never played, and the division championship is decided on winning percentage. If Dallas (now 5-3) won all the rest of its games, that would include a win over the Redskins. Another Washington defeat would give them a 10-3-1 record for the year, to the Cowboys' 11-3.

One of the writers said to Landry, "I guess you go with Staubach next Sunday against Philadelphia."

"Yeah," Landry said, smiling. "That's one question you won't have to ask at Wednesday's press conference."

Duane Thomas had become a riddle wrapped in a mystery inside an enigma. He spoke to no one, including his teammates. When he came off the field after scoring the long touchdown against New England, Landry tried to shake his hand but succeeded in only grabbing his forearm as Thomas walked on past him. There were no racial overtones; he also ignored a handshake from Rayfield Wright. Once when he limped off the field and missed a series of plays, Jethro Pugh asked him, "How's the knee?" and Thomas said, "Why you want to know? You a doctor?"

Ever since the New Orleans trip he had adopted a yellow stocking cap for road games. He would plop himself in the middle seat of a row of three, pull the cap down around his ears and eyes and go to sleep. Stewardesses would ask him, "Are you ready to eat?" and he would shake his head negatively. They learned to stop asking. There was a team fine of $50 for not wearing a coat or tie on the plane. Thomas wore a waist-length jacket, unbuttoned, a sport shirt and an unknotted tie draped around his shoulders. At team meetings he would not answer roll call, explaining later to Landry that anybody could see he was there, so why answer?

During a game he had picked up another of hero Jim Brown's traits when he was tackled: getting up in slow motion, as if stunned or injured, then walking even more slowly back to the huddle. (The referee does not begin the thirty-second count between plays until all offensive players have returned to the line of scrimmage.) I knew, from the letters and phone calls I received at the paper, this tactic infuriated a large segment of Cowboy fans, the segment with latent or outright racial bias. Thomas had gained 101 yards against St. Louis, and his twenty-one-yard sweep was the longest gain of the touchdown drive, but his efforts had gone almost unnoticed in most reports on the game, including mine. A few days later I made my way around the locker room at the practice field, asking players for their reactions to Thomas.

Andrie said, "What he's doing between plays doesn't concern me. He's doing a helluva job, and I think that's the way all the guys feel."

Blaine Nye said, "I've always kind of liked the guy, and he's doing as well as he did last year. He's a little quieter than he was last year, but you know he never did talk much. He's not as outgoing with the players as some people, but so what?"

Herb Adderley said, "I'm glad to see him back there running the ball. He's got a good mental attitude for football and it shows. Coming back slow to the huddle, well, he should take any chance to relax, and that's his way. He is total concentration and one hundred percent athlete every time he goes on the field."

Staubach said, "I don't understand why he's like he is, but at this point we can't be concerned about that. One thing you know—when you give him the ball, he *goes*."

Bobby Hayes said, "Duane's going his own way. It must be a hard way, but he's going it. He's playing for the twenty-two thousand, I guess. I asked him why he won't talk to *you,* Steve, and he says if he talked to you, then everybody would be on him, and he doesn't want to open that deal again."

Landry said, "I've talked to Duane. He's got a good attitude."

What it all came down to, Thomas was buying his share of peace and quiet, one hundred yards at a time.

Lee Roy Jordan was working a hot comb through his stylish but medium-length hair. "Now," he said, "we got the biggie of the biggies."

Howley, facing the mirror next to Jordan, said, "This is the game we want. We like these stretch drives, so we can relax."

I said that must have been the problem all afternoon, with everybody looking ahead to Washington. "Well," Jordan said, "the offense had a little trouble in the line, and maybe they let up when we got ahead twenty to zip. I'd like to get the Redskins twenty to seven."

"What you're liable to get is Jurgensen," I said. "Think you can hold him to seven points?"

"Did he play today?" Howley said.

While Dallas was coasting past Philadelphia, 20-7, Washington was getting beat by Chicago—by one point. Bobby Douglass chased down a bad snap from center on an extra point and threw forty yards to Dick Butkus in the end zone. Jurgensen came in and completed four out of six passes to get within field-goal range, but kicker Curt Knight had missed it.

"I'd really like to see them start Jurgensen," Jordan said. "He can't be sharp after being out all this time, I don't care how good he is."

The Redskins' defeat cut their margin over Dallas to a half game, but the Cowboys had their own troubles. Don Talbert had taken Neely's place at left tackle against St. Louis and done a flawless job. In the first quarter of the Eagles game he limped off with a badly sprained ankle, Forrest Gregg subbed for him, and then Gregg hobbled to the sideline with a pulled hamstring muscle, the muscle along the back of the thigh. Rayfield Wright had to be shifted from right to left tackle, Blaine Nye moved from right guard to right tackle, and rookie center John Fitzgerald went into Nye's spot. In this mass confusion the pass blocking broke down and Staubach had to run for his life, six times for ninety yards. "I wish somebody would introduce me to my offensive line," said Jim Myers. "From what I can tell, we can't count on either Talbert or Gregg next Sunday. Nye and Fitzgerald handled themselves okay, what I could see from the sideline—but that's not the way you want to go into your big game of the year."

Landry, once again, had an idea. He called up a Dallas real-estate salesman, Tony Liscio, and talked him into returning to football. Liscio had been traded by San Diego to Miami just before the league season began, and, rather than move his school-age children cross-country again, Liscio retired.

Landry said, "Liscio might be the answer for us—he knows our system, and he never makes mistakes. He should be able to get through the Washington game okay. It's the one against the Rams on Thanksgiving I don't know about. That gives him only four days to recover."

I called Liscio at home. "I don't think I can do it," he said. "If I don't know Tom better, I'd have thought he was kidding me. You know, the night Neely broke his ankle I went to a team party and Dave Edwards told me I better start getting in shape. This is crazy. I haven't done anything except watch television for two months." But with the deal Landry had offered Liscio, he had to try it: a full year's salary and a full share of the playoff money.

George Allen had made believers of us all. "We are preparing," he said on the phone from Washington, "for the championship game with Dallas." He said it with a flavor of rich enjoyment.

I said, "Level with me, Coach. Did you really think last summer that nine games into the season you'd be a half game ahead of Dallas?"

"Certainly."

"Why? Just because you got all those old people from the Rams?"

"I had confidence in myself," Allen said, "and I believed in my program. Besides, this was the only way to go, with a thirty-seven-year-old quarterback. Those old guys from the Rams are leading this division in defense, by the way."

I tried to discuss the wild-card possibilities for the play-offs. Along with the three division champs, the second-place team with the best won-lost record gets a pass into the title games. "I was talking with Tom today," I said to Allen, "and he figures that either Dallas or Washington can get into the playoffs by winning four of their last five games."

"I never thought of it that way before," Allen said. "I don't think about finishing second."

There you have it. Was Allen conning me? Or himself? Was Landry more honest? Or did Allen have a superior winning attitude?

I stopped at the Braniff magazine stand and bought a *Sports Illustrated* to read on the way to Washington. Mike Clark was ahead of me at the cashier, a copy of *Reader's Digest* in his hand. Pro-football players are great readers of the *Reader's Digest*, the *National Enquirer* and the *Wall Street Journal*. I said, "Doesn't it feel like we just got off the plane from St. Louis?"

"Not to me," Clark said. "I didn't make it to St. Louis."

I had committed a gaffe. Toni Fritsch pulled a hamstring muscle in practice, and Clark was reactivated for this game. We walked down the concourse toward the charter gate. "Landry figures this one for a tight defensive game," I said, "probably decided by a field goal."

"I don't think so," Clark said. "I think we'll score so many points it won't matter. But if it takes a field goal, I'm ready. I feel like I've been born again."

"It was that rough?" I said for something to say. Clark's sincerity about football was very close to the surface. He has a strong down-home quality about him. You could see him as a great owner of bird dogs.

"The first couple days I was off the team were pretty bad,"

he said. "First time I'd experienced anything like it in nine years in the league, going to the taxi squad. I didn't have a very good attitude. I didn't know how the other guys felt about me. Then I just decided it wasn't the end of the world. I got back to my job, what your job is supposed to be when you're off the team—helping the other guys in the workouts all I could. Tom helped. He told me to stay proficient, that I never knew when I'd be needed. He was right about that."

"You think you went sour," I said, "because you had Fritsch right there?"

Clark nodded. "I guess I was thinking about him more than I should have been. I wasn't concentrating the way you have to do in this business. I thought about Fritsch in the Cleveland game—the one in the summer?—when I missed that easy field goal and it looked like it cost us the game. Everybody was saying if I hadn't kicked the second one, I would have been gone."

"You're wrong about that," I said. "You don't know Landry if you think that." I started to add, Landry will wait until you *really* goof up.

"Anyway, that's done and gone, and I got a new lease," Clark said. "I'm sitting on top of the world."

When we got on the team bus at the Washington airport, Reeves was a few rows in front of me, across the aisle. As he sat down he said, "Thanks a lot, Perkins. Now everybody in Dallas can hate Dan Reeves."

"It happened," I said.

"What's that all about?" Luksa asked me.

"I wrote a story how Fritsch hurt his leg. Reeves fumbled the snap and Fritsch tried to pull up, then he went ahead and kicked, and that did it."

Landry had said, "If we see Jurgensen, that means we'll have beaten Kilmer." With two minutes left in the third quarter, the Cowboys saw Jurgensen, and Cliff Harris cut across to intercept his first throw, deep to halfback Larry Brown. Dallas led, 10-0, on a twenty-nine-yard touchdown scramble by Staubach and a twenty-six-yard field goal by Clark. Clark missed his next two kicks, but with seven minutes left he made a forty-eight-yarder. It took off low over the line of scrimmage, like a Texas League single, and never fluttered.

The Cowboys showed their first real jubilation of the year, leaping and yelling on the way to the locker room. Jordan pretended he was still griped about having to chase Washington for two months. "I think they'll find out," he said, "that it's better to be in first place at the end of the season instead of the first eight weeks."

Lilly kept saying, "We shut the bastards out! Flat *out!* That's the beautiful part."

Kilmer had hit ten of sixteen passes when he was in there, but he had only one real shot at a touchdown, and that was batted out of Larry Brown's hands by Adderley. "Kilmer was throwing ante-up passes," Renfro said. "They nag at you but don't kill you." Renfro meant Kilmer specialized in the short tosses to the outside, laying off to his backs in the flat and quick tosses to his tight end over the middle.

"That kind of passing goes all right when you're running the ball," Landry was saying. He was ringed around by a gaggle of writers in a small cubicle off the locker room. Since he has been calling all the plays, Landry seems (likes to seem?) more weary after a game. His attitude reminded me of a comment he'd made after the New England game, "I tried to beat Kiner a couple of times, but he made two great plays." The operative word was "I."

"But we were stopping the run," Landry said. "Maybe if Brown and Harraway had been healthy, this one might have been like our last game." The two Washington running backs had played hurt, but Landry was merely being charitable for the foreign press. He *never* believes anybody should run on his defense. "That Staubach is a competitor—it was his run that kept the pressure off of us."

I went over and had Staubach explain for the tenth time how he'd done it. "It was a perfect pass play for a run," he said, grinning. "We had Hayes and Alworth out left in the flip formation. Hayes ran a post and Alworth went down-and-in under him, so the whole left side was cleared out. I ducked inside the end on that side and I didn't have anything in front of me. I guess it's okay for a quarterback to run sometimes, huh? No, I'm kidding. This is the kind of day when you're thankful for a defense."

I stopped by Clark's locker to shake his hand. "I used my driver on that last one," he said.

There's a special feeling about a team on top. I could sense it, for the first time this season, when I went into the players' section of the plane. Lilly and Andrie had taken over Neely's old spot at the dead end between the johns. Andrie looked a lot less happy than his buddy, I could tell. Young Pat Toomay had been subbing for him half the time in the last four or five games. I said, "This is your time of year, George."

"Yeah? How come?"

"Don't give me that, how come. From here on is when you come through—maybe it's a little early. You made MVP of the Pro Bowl in January. You picked up that TD off the ice in Green Bay, and last year you damned near made Johnny U. a hospital case."

Lilly said, "You know, he's right."

"Yeah," Andrie said. "Well, you can't make any big plays from the bench."

"Ernie is pacing you because you got a bad back," I said.

"Bull shit!" Andrie said, making it a definite two words. "Ain't nothing wrong with my back. I know what's happening."

"George," I said, "you're wrong. Landry is not going to trade you. Landry will hold onto you until you are old and gray and not worth a fifth-round draft choice. But he won't trade you."

"Yeah? We'll see."

"What's happened to this team?" I said. "Has the same damn thing happened that happened last year?"

Lilly said, "I think that's about it."

"Well, how did it happen this time?" I said.

Lilly thought a long moment, taking a pull at his beer. "The coaches," he said, "are perfectionists. Every year it takes 'em a few games to remember we're human. Then we can start playing football."

Lilly and I had been down this road before, and some of

it had gotten him in trouble, so I didn't press the subject. It said enough as it was.

Coming into the landing in Dallas, Landry said, "The Ram game Thursday is the key game."

"That's what you said about the Washington game," I said.

"Well, it was. But this is the super-key. If we lose this one, it'll be right back to a toss-up again. But if we can beat the Rams, we're in the driver's seat."

Tex Schramm, who has a weekly radio show during the season, scooped us all by disclosing that back in September when Thomas returned to the fold he was escorted by a new and secret adviser, Jim Brown. "I had a meeting with Brown on one evening and he brought Duane in the next," Schramm said. "Brown was in effect acting as his agent—he wasn't doing it for nothing. His only pitch to Duane was that he had no other alternative than to play, that he was under contract. It was Brown's idea that Duane come back and fulfill the contract—and do no more."

"You mean that's how the silent bit started?" I said.

"It seemed to me that was Brown's idea, but it was one that Duane could easily go along with."

"Whose idea was it to keep Brown's part a secret?"

"It was Duane's. He insisted on it. I don't know why. I thought it would make him look better if he could say he reported back with Jim Brown's help."

Schramm was slightly apologetic about breaking a news story on his own radio show. I asked him if his press card hadn't been picked up twenty-five years ago when he left the Austin *American* to become publicity man for the Rams. It was another case of Schramm's temper getting the better of him. Brown had just been quoted in a newspaper interview criticizing the Cowboys for being "cheap," and Schramm wanted to show that Brown was hardly an objective observer, since he acted as Thomas' "agent." But it was hard to conceive of the successful Brown taking any of Thomas' money as an agent's fee.

Lance Rentzel was standing near the fifty-yard line and gazing downfield where the Cowboys were going through pre-game warmups. He stood there a long while, staring at his former teammates, and I knew very well the sort of pangs he was feeling. The day before, when the Rams came into town for a workout on the stadium's strange Tartan Turf, Rentzel had said, "We have got to win every game the rest of the way, because we're going for the title—but, doggone, I sure will hate to see the Cowboys lose."

I never thought the Cowboys would lose. At certain parts of every season there is a *sense* of the team that is almost tangible, made up of bits and pieces, a gesture here, a word there, and now I had the feeling Dallas would not lose a game the rest of the way to the playoffs. For instance, Lee Roy Jordan discussed the reasons he hoped it wouldn't snow in Minnesota, the certain opponent for Dallas in the first round. It wasn't overconfidence; Jordan had merely looked past the Rams to the remaining league games against the Jets, the Giants and the Cardinals and saw nothing there to trouble him. It was clear that he also *knew* that the team which had just shut out the Redskins wouldn't be losing to the Rams. I shared his belief, and it was this curious certainty that kept the Ram game from seeming as exciting as it should have been.

Rookie Ike Thomas returned the opening kickoff eighty-nine yards for a touchdown, but before the quarter was over the Rams led 14-7. Roman Gabriel was having one of his great days and would complete twenty of thirty-five attempts. He completed several passes when Dallas defensive people were draped on him like Christmas-tree ornaments. "It's like trying to drag down another lineman," Andrie complained. He hit Rentzel for forty-one yards to set up the first Ram score, when Cliff Harris tried for an interception and missed. Renfro told me later he had chewed Harris out, including the rest of the Cowboy defense. "Damn! All you hear is 'Get yourself one, get yourself one,'" Renfro said. "To hell with that—break it up."

That was Rentzel's only catch of the day. Once he had Cornell Green beaten for a touchdown, wide open. But Green, covering him because he'd come out of a flip formation, recovered in time to tick the ball away.

The Rams' college coach, Tommy Prothro, had his usual

bag of surprises—an onside kick that worked, punting on third down and an extra offensive lineman in one formation that, in the confusion, turned tight end Bob Klein loose for a thirty-three-yard touchdown. Then Staubach hit Hayes for a fifty-one-yard bomb, and Howley intercepted a Gabriel overthrow, setting up a twenty-one-yard touchdown pass to Alworth, his first as a Cowboy. When Gabriel engineered a long drive in the third quarter to tie it again, 21-21, Staubach came back with another just like it—until he reinjured his bruised right shoulder on an eleven-yard run to the six-yard line. Morton came in and pitched out to Thomas sweeping left end for the winner.

"Well," Landry said, offering a rare opening remark to the post-game press, "nobody's happy in Washington today." It was his way of taking note of President Nixon's Tuesday visit to the Redskin practice field, an occasion for a Chief Executive pep talk. "I hate to go against the President, because he's my favorite," Landry added. "I hate to disappoint him, but if we don't flub it, we're in great shape."

Team depth—and the rightness of the Cowboy draft last winter—had been something of a savior this day. Jethro Pugh was hospitalized by an appendicitis attack, which the doctors hoped to fend off until late January. Rookie Bill Gregory, 6 feet 5 inches, 240 pounds and a third-round draft choice from Wisconsin, took his place and was in on nine tackles, more than any other defensive lineman. Right guard Blaine Nye was sidelined by injury, and first-year-man Rodney Wallace, 6 feet 5 inches, 260 pounds, a tenth-round choice from New Mexico, got his first start. Wallace's man, the great Merlin Olsen, never got to Staubach.

It was a laugher the rest of the way. Dallas rolled over Joe Namath and the Jets, 52-10; over Fran Tarkenton and the Giants, 42-14; and over the Cardinals, 31-12.

Everything had seemed to fall in place for the Cowboys all year. When Truax was hurt, Ditka was healthy. When Ditka went out, Truax had just recovered. Finally, they were both functioning for the stretch, as Landry used them for his messages to Staubach. When Alworth was nursing bruised ribs, Gloster Richardson caught touchdown passes. During Thomas' holdout, Calvin Hill was his old rookie self. Now, for the drive into the playoffs, Hill was back—and Garrison went to the bench.

During the Jets game, when Hill and Thomas were rolling up a total of 322 offensive yards between them, league publicist Jim Heffernan came over to me in the press box and asked, "What year was it that Calumet had Coaltown and Citation running out of the same stable?"

With the Super Bowl in sight, Garrison was no longer feeling like the illegitimate son of Buffalo Bill. "Did you notice," he said, "that the offense seemed to lack a little punch without me in there today?"

Staubach hit ten of fifteen against the Jets and turned the game over to Morton (who then hit four of six) in the third quarter. "I was disappointed," Morton joked. "I thought I had a good shot at starting the second half." The game had been billed as a showcase for Namath, who had returned to action only the previous Sunday. "I never saw a team get out in front so fast," Namath said. Weeb Ewbank yanked Namath when Dallas held a four-touchdown lead before the end of the first quarter. "It was the coach's decision," Namath said. "However, he didn't get any argument from me on it."

At New York the next week against the Giants, Thomas gained ninety-four, Hill eighty-nine, and Hill got another fifty receiving. Staubach connected with Hayes for a forty-six-yard touchdown and then truly an eighty-five-yard bomb. "Calvin," said Danny Reeves, "made fifteen yards on a sweep and not a soul has made a block yet."

Landry had a word of caution. "Neither Hill or Thomas can be stopped too easy by one man," he said, "but we are not catching teams that are up. We won't really know how strong we are in this setup until we get into the playoffs."

On the plane ride home from New York, Schramm and I were standing together in the aisle, and it occurred to me that he should answer the persistent charge against his organization: it was cold, computerized, producing an emotionless team. "And it's true," I said. "I've been around here eight years, and that's the way I read it." Schramm started to say something, but I still had the floor. "Leaving race out of it," I said. "Don Perkins pegged that department okay. He was through town a few weeks ago, and you know what he said? He said, 'There isn't any discrimination on the Cowboys. Management treats all players like they were black.'"

Schramm said, "Heh, heh. *Now* let Perkins try to make a comeback. Okay, the main subject, cold and clinical. I'm not going to tell you we're not. Every management group has its own character. It's set by the personalities of the people in authority. Our character, people say, is cold and clinical." Schramm paused for a long thought. "There's nothing more I'd rather do right now," he said, "than go back there"—a motion of his head indicated the curtain that separated our compartment—"and talk to some of the players. But I can't do it. I wouldn't know how to handle it, without causing a lot of complications, or maybe getting into some talk that wouldn't be good. I'm not an outgoing person.

"But being cool and clinical doesn't mean you can't get emotion from your team when you need it. If you go strictly for emotion, maybe you can win one championship that way, but that's not what you're aiming for. Our *clinical* operation has got us into the title playoffs the last five years—you might as well make it six and count this one—and no other team has done that."

Thomas ripped off a fifty-three-yard touchdown run, for openers, against the Cardinals and went on to score three more touchdowns in the final regular season game. Then he declined to appear for a post-game interview on the national telecast. I hadn't tried to talk to Thomas for a couple of months, and now when I did he said, "I'm tired, man." That was a friendly remark. When another reporter pressed him, he said, "Why don't you get the hell away and leave me alone?" and walked into the trainers' room to dress.

I turned and happened to catch Danny Reeves' eye at his locker across the aisle. "I wish," I said, "they'd put the bastard on waivers."

Reeves said, "You're getting tired of that shit, too?"

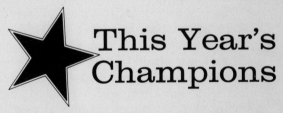

This Year's Champions

"Don't fuck around with me, man."
—DUANE THOMAS

The rest of the team was on the practice field loosening up and taking things light, trying to believe that Monday was Tuesday. Their bodies thought it was. The Cowboys had ended the season on Saturday, and they were drawn to play at Minnesota the following Saturday in the first playoff game, so Landry stepped the practice-week routine up by a day. Tony Liscio wasn't on the field, but I knew where to start looking for him—in the trainers' room, in an aluminum tub where the whirlpool waters flow.

"This is where I get my mail," Liscio said. "I have meals sent in. When Gardner gets through wrapping ankles, he comes over and we play checkers."

"Aren't you afraid of water rot?" I said. "If your skin gets any more puckered, you'll have fish scales."

"At least I'm alive, which is more than I thought I'd be after—how many games we played now?"

"Five for you. And Landry just told me, 'Liscio was the key to our season.'"

"Did he really say that?" Liscio said, honestly wide-eyed.

"What do you want me to do, repeat it? You didn't think you'd last a game. How did you make it? Or maybe you're all bunged up and not telling anybody."

"No, I feel great. I feel so great, it's scary. But I think I've got it figured out. You know how I've had back trouble for three years? And my knees always hurt? I think it was all the

pounding I took in training camp and the exhibition season—
and maybe I'm just not meant to play more than seven or
eight games at my age. I mean, at my body's age. I'm not an
old guy, you know."

"I know. When you get old, Annette's going to divorce you
and marry a handsome Italian."

Liscio's euphoria was contagious, and it emanated as well
from all the players. It was as if the team had negotiated all
the white water and was clear and into the quiet stream of
the river. The last seven days of the season settled all the
playoff pairings. Washington beat the Rams and clinched the
NFC wild-card spot which George Allen never thought
about. As the sun set on the final NFL game of the year in
San Francisco, Brodie guided the 49ers past Detroit to win
the West Division title. In the American Conference, Miami
was paired against Kansas City and wild-card Baltimore
against Cleveland. The Cowboy course was clearly charted—
beat Minnesota, beat the winner of the 49er-Redskins game
the following week in Dallas, then beat the AFC survivor
two weeks later in New Orleans.

"I think it'll be Kansas City," Jethro Pugh said, "either
them or Baltimore. I hope it's Baltimore. Everybody does.
It'd make it perfect to get another shot at those guys."

"You're not going to jinx yourself?" I said. "What about
Minnesota?"

"I'm thinking enough about Minnesota. We all know how
it goes in the playoffs, except the rookies, and they'll pick it
up from the rest of us. This is where we knew we'd be since
training camp. We just had to get the other stuff out of the
way to get here. Thing is, on the Cowboys, you just don't
have a successful season any more unless you *win* the Super
Bowl." The rest of the players were drifting in from the practice field. Calvin Hill had stopped to listen to Pugh.

"I want to get Washington down here," Hill said. "I'll
be pulling for 'em to beat San Francisco."

"Why do you want Washington?" Pugh said.

"So we can get 'em down to Texas Stadium and punish
'em," Hill said. "We were just beginning to be a football team
when we beat 'em the last time. And . . . if we're lucky, we
can get the President down here to watch it."

"I might have known it'd be something political," Pugh said.

Hill was grinning. "Well, Nixon is such a strong rooter, I don't see how he could desert his team if they got this far."

I moved on to carry a weather bulletin to Lee Roy Jordan: "It is twenty-three and cloudy today in beautiful Minneapolis."

"Let it snow," Jordan said. "Say, if it's going to get cold, I hope it gets real cold, like fifteen *below*. The Vikings never played in weather that cold, but we have. Who'd have the experience edge then? Hell, this team may be better equipped to play in cold weather than the Vikings. Do they have anybody running the ball like Calvin and Duane and Walt? The real reason I hate to play on the ice and snow is the crazy things that happen. A lot of football games are decided on funny bounces, anyway, but you hate to see something you've worked on for five months wiped out because somebody slipped on the ice."

Landry was not ready to agree that this Minnesota game was the crucial one of the playoffs, that Dallas would find the going comparatively easier through the Super Bowl if they could go up to the cold and come away still alive. But it seemed that way to everyone else—possibly because the Viking game was *now* and the other two games were in the hazy future. "When you get to this stage," Landry said at his press conference in mid-week, "they're all tough. I don't see any dominant team, but defense controls these games— just about every team in the playoffs, you can look and see that defense got them there."

That went doubly so for the Vikings, with their Purple People Eaters and a front four that was currently the most highly publicized defensive line in the league—Carl Eller, Gary Larsen, Alan Page and Jim Marshall.

"We'll have to create our own field position," Landry said. "You can't feel that you are going to hit big plays or have any consistency against a top defense. The thing to watch is you shouldn't get discouraged against this kind of team. You've got to wait for your breaks and take advantage of them when they come.

"We'll have to run the ball, because they limit you pass-wise—with their pass rush and with their zone defense which shuts off the deep pass. But our team is much more mature than it's ever been. My gosh, our guys have been through all the things you could possibly go through. They're tough mentally, and they're ready to play."

Dallas had finished the season with the top offense in the league, first in passing in the NFC, second in rushing. And the Cowboys had the second-best record on defense, first against the rush and ninth against the pass. The Vikings were best overall, third against the rush and second against the pass. But these were all yardage figures. On the scoreboard, that greatest of defensive barometers, it was no contest: Minnesota had given up 139 points, fewest in the NFL; Dallas had yielded 222.

The Vikings *had* to have the best defense; their offense ranked twelfth in the thirteen-team conference. Landry said, "They have won their division four years in a row, so what difference does it make where the offense ranks?" Their coach, Bud Grant, had never named a number-one quarterback. He had used Gary Cuozzo and Norm Snead and Bob Lee, a fellow whom everyone had regarded as a punting specialist. He still hadn't named one. He said he would do so on Friday, Christmas Eve, the day before the game.

"He'll probably use Cuozzo," Landry said, "but I'm just guessing. Not having a number-one quarterback is a problem that keeps tearing at you, but it doesn't seem to bother him."

After Landry had his question-answer session with the writers, he moved to an adjoining dining room to be interviewed for television and radio, and Ermal Allen took over to divulge a little bit of what his studies of the opponent's game films have shown. Allen came through the college coaching ranks on the staff of Bear Bryant at Kentucky, so his view of statistics is more pointed than most. "Minnesota," he said, "*survives* by giving the offense the ball on your thirty-yard line. The Purple Gang. Very terrifying. But, looka here! The Cowboys are not doing so bad their own selves. Quarterback traps—Dallas quarterbacks got trapped thirty-two times this season, and this is the best we've ever done, because we run such a fluid offense and use all type of pass protections. Minnesota uses the standard sets, three basic formations. Their quarterbacks got trapped twenty-eight times.

"Okay, look at traps the other way. The Cowboy defense got to the quarterback forty-three times, and this led the NFC. The great People Eaters, led by Mr. Eller and Mr. Page, trapped the opposing quarterback twenty-seven times.

"Now let's see what about turnovers, which is their specialty. The Cowboys lost twenty-one fumbles this season. Minnesota lost thirteen. Dallas had fourteen passes intercepted, the Vikings eighteen. Twenty-one and fourteen, that's a minus thirty-five for the Cowboys. The Vikings had a minus thirty-one.

"But . . . Dallas intercepted twenty-six passes and recovered another twenty-five fumbles, an all-time high for this club. That adds up to fifty-one and gives us an overall plus of sixteen. The Vikings intercepted twenty-seven passes and recovered eighteen fumbles. That gives them an overall plus of *fourteen.*"

My head was reeling from the figures, but Allen had made his point. I asked him about the Minnesota quarterbacks.

"Next to Hart at St. Louis and Lamonica at Oakland, these guys go deep more than any team in football. They do this because they know their offense can't generate a long drive—they might as well go for the bomb. Individually, you know what Snead can do. You've seen him with Philadelphia. He can't move around and he will still throw the ball up for grabs under pressure. Lee is more accurate than Cuozzo and he's a bigger boy and he'll roll out and run."

When the session broke up, I caught Allen outside the door. "Never mind the statistics," I said. "What do you really think about the game?"

"If we eliminate quarterback traps, fumbles and interceptions," Allen said, "I guarantee you there is no way we can lose."

Staubach and Hayes and several other Cowboys came out for the pre-game drills in short-sleeved jerseys. So much for the weather, thirty degrees and warming at kickoff, under cloudy skies. Quite a few Vikings wore sweatshirts under their numbers. "Cold is a state of mind," Bud Grant said at his press conference the day before. "The difference between us and Dallas in cold weather is that we *know* it's going to be cold and we're mentally prepared for it." It had been ten degrees then, and the forecast was snow.

Other Dallas expectations followed the rising thermometer. On Minnesota's first possession, Larry Cole hit Dave Osborn on a sweep and made him fumble to Pugh. Hayes ran straight at cornerback Ed Sharockman, then stopped and turned in front of him to take an eighteen-yard pass from Staubach—a fateful pattern—and Clark kicked a twenty-six-yard field goal.

The game was being played tighter than high-stakes stud poker, and two poor punts by Ron Widby were all Minnesota needed to get in position for a tying field goal from Fred Cox. The Viking quarterback was Bob Lee, who came in the league the same year Staubach did. Lee made the big offensive play of the first half, a roll-out pass for forty-nine yards to flanker Bob Grim at the Dallas thirty-nine, and then made the biggest mistake. Under a blitz by Jordan and Howley, Lee tried to lob the ball to Osborn. "The ball just sat up there like it was in slow motion," Howley said, "and I had time to think, 'Look what *I've* got!'" Howley ran twenty-six yards to the Viking thirty-seven, and Clark kicked a forty-four-yard field goal that limped over the bar. When Clint Jones returned the kickoff sixty-one yards, only a great one-on-one play by Renfro, the "safety" on the kicking team, saved a touchdown. Cox, who had kicked 69 percent of his field goals during the season, missed from the forty-two, and Dallas held a 6-3 lead at halftime.

The Cowboys had made only three first downs, none at all in the second quarter. The Vikings had moved for seven first downs—but only once had they been able to *start* a drive from the Dallas end of the field.

"I was concerned that we couldn't move the ball," Staubach said, "but I wasn't worried. Coach Landry drilled into us all week we'd have to sit tight and wait for our opportunities.

At least we scored on the two chances we had in the first half. We weren't beating the Viking defense, but the important thing was neither was their defense beating *us*."

At the start of the second half Lee tried to hit Grim deep again, on a stop-and-go move. When Grim stopped, Lee faked the throw, brought the ball back and then threw. "I've been looking for that pass since Monday," Cliff Harris said, "and I'd been waiting for it all day. It was my ball all the way." Harris drifted across in front of Grim like a center-fielder, made the interception and picked his way thirty yards downfield to the Viking thirteen-yard line. On first down from there, Duane Thomas cut back through the middle for a touchdown.

During the flight up from Dallas I had asked John Niland about his assignment, Alan Page. "I think I can handle him," he had said. "He's a great lineman, but he's not going to bowl me over. We're the same size, six-four and two-fifty. On passing plays, I've got to hit him before he gets rolling, make contact and just try to stay in front of him. Running plays— well, we've got some running plays where all I have to do is take him where he wants to go."

This Thomas run was one of them. Staubach faked a pitchout to Hill going left, then handed to Thomas, also moving left. Page followed the flow and Niland shielded him off, whereupon Thomas cut back to his right, through the gap in the middle. The middle linebacker had also taken the fake, and Dave Manders wiped him out of the play.

I was sitting two seats from Tex Schramm in the press box, and throughout the game he had kept up a muttering, suffering commentary. Now he stepped it up: "Come on, babies, pick one off. . . . Get the bastard! . . . . *Don't* let 'em do that!" Schramm was exhorting the defense, which I thought was a wasted effort. Minnesota's offense couldn't win this game unless the Cowboy offense lost it by giving up a big play to the Purple Gang.

After his interception, Lee had grown conservative, staying on the ground for five of the next six plays, folly against the Cowboys' rushing defense. Then a Lee punt soared fifty yards, outdistancing his punt coverage and giving Charley

Waters running room for a twenty-four-yard return to midfield. On third down, Landry sent in a play designed to victimize cornerback Sharockman, a variation on the eighteen-yarder Hayes had caught earlier. "Sharockman hates the turn-in-and-go," Alworth said, "He's scared to death of it because he doesn't have a lot of speed. This was something Ray Renfro worked out. I ran a turn-in in front of him, faked upfield, then turned and stopped again. Roger laid it right there. When I looked around, I couldn't even see Sharockman at first—he was flying deep." The pass went for thirty yards, and on third down from the nine, Staubach was chased out of the pocket to the left, scrambling, before he found Hayes in the back of the end zone for a touchdown. "You have to watch Roger and move to him," Hayes said. "I beat Sharockman to the inside, but when I saw Roger running I switched directions." Hayes and Sharockman passed each other along the end-zone line like two trains in the night.

Minnesota got a safety after a punt was downed on the Dallas three, but Jordan next intercepted a Gary Cuozzo pass, and the Vikings didn't score a touchdown until the two-minute mark. Final: Cowboys 20, Minnesota 12.

"Oh, God," Schramm sighed, "am I glad we got out of this icebox alive."

The locker room was quietly exultant. "We took their game away with the turnovers," Landry said. "If you throw Staubach against the Vikings, you can throw him against anybody." The remark seemed like a *non sequitur* until I realized Landry's mind had taken a quantum jump ahead. Staubach had run a flawless offense with no interceptions and no fumbles, and he'd been trapped only three times. Dallas had claimed the one Viking fumble and stolen four Viking passes.

Dave Edwards was telling Howley, "They didn't get any turnovers, and that's what they play for. They can't win without 'em."

"Yeah," said Howley, "and when we got our share, we made 'em count. We set 'em up, and the offense knocked 'em down."

The offensive linemen usually get as much star billing as

the spear carriers at the Met, but this day belonged to them, and to Rayfield Wright and Niland in particular. Their jobs on the two Minnesota game-breakers, Eller and Page, were the reasons Dallas didn't give the ball away. Wright beamed down at me from his 6-foot-7-inch height as I shook his hand. He flipped his hand up and grabbed mine in a soul-shake. "He got by me a couple of times," Wright said before I could ask. "He's going to do that. He's a good man. But I'm a good man, too."

Forrest Gregg, who had been in so many of these victorious locker rooms but who had not played at all in the game, was in the next locker. "They whipped them at their own game," Gregg said, nodding at Niland and Wright. "They whipped 'em inside, and whipped 'em good."

Niland was still covered with grime and sweat, still explaining to writers how the blocking went on Thomas' touchdown. The adhesive tape he wraps around his head to protect his brow from the helmet rim was curling at the edges. I said, "And Page never was a factor in the game."

Niland shrugged. "I never thought he would be," he said.

Hayes was at the opposite end of the room chanting, "Nobody's gonna stop us now, no nobody's gonna stop us from here on out. . . . I mean it. I don't want to downgrade everybody else in the playoffs, but this was really the team we had to beat."

He had a good argument. Minnesota and Dallas were the two teams in pro football who had won eleven games, and the Vikings had been three-point favorites to win this one, the only game of the season when the Cowboys were not on top of the betting line.

Staubach pretended to be dissatisfied with his day (ten for fourteen). "I thought we could go deep on them," he said, "but we never opened up." This was leaning perilously close to criticism of the Signal Caller on the Sidelines. But he *was* putting me on about the future. "This club," he said, shaking his head, "we're only good for two more games."

Schramm had a battery-powered TV in his lap, switching frantically from channel to channel to keep the Kansas City–

Miami game tuned in as the plane moved south. Stenerud missed a field goal, Yepremian didn't, and it was sudden-death defeat for the Chiefs.

"What did Stenerud miss?" Ernie Stautner asked me.

"A 'gimme' for him, from the thirty-two."

"Well, they never should have let the bums tie 'em," Stautner said.

"Didn't I notice you using Andrie a little more today?" I said.

"A little, but not much more. Next week is when I'm going to use him and two weeks from that."

"Why?"

"Because," Stautner said, making a palms-up gesture, "this is George's time of year."

Ermal Allen brushed by us in the aisle, stopped and announced that the playoffs were all straightened out when Kansas City lost. "That means a rematch in the Super Bowl," he said. "Baltimore's the class of that league."

The next day the 49ers came alive when Brodie hit a third-and-one seventy-eight-yard touchdown to Gene Washington, and they beat the Redskins 24-20. Baltimore demolished Cleveland 20-3, setting up a parlay of rematches: Nolan vs. Landry, and the Colts vs. Shula.

Pat Toomay had the headline and subhead from one of my stories pasted on the inside wall of his locker. "Landry Blames Upsets on Youth," it said, and "It's the Young People and Their Approaches to Life." The story wasn't there, just the headline. This had been after New England beat Miami, then came on and beat Baltimore, too. "We don't have the driving force in our young people that we had in the past," he had said. "We're living in a different era. It's part of our times. There is so much complacency. We're living in a very affluent age, and everything has come so easy to the young people we have playing football today. In athletics, you have to work hard for what you get, and if you don't, you get your head knocked off."

Toomay is the picture of youth, enlarged to 6 feet 5 inches

and 250 pounds, blond hair over his ears and down to his collar. He looks as though it would take him a month to go hippie. It would take longer than that; Toomay is a graduate of Vanderbilt, a member of the Southern Ivy League circuit.

"You didn't care for the story, but you loved the headline," I said.

"Just a little reminder," Toomay said.

"I was wondering how the Cowboys lost to New Orleans and Chicago."

"I've thought about it too," Toomay said, "and I decided it wasn't my youth. I wasn't in there long enough to make a difference one way or another."

"You chased down Osborn Saturday on a sweep away from you, just like Landry said in camp, like Dryer and like Deacon."

"You mean like Deacon used to. I've been waiting to hear about that play. I was probably out of position and very non-coordinated."

"What have you heard about *this* game?"

"I don't have to hear," Toomay said. "I figured it out. It's 'Get Brodie.' That's the whole deal. If we don't get to Brodie, he'll just stand back there and cut us up."

"You going to get him?"

"If I get a chance. If I could just get to *start* one of these games. Tell me, what's so great about age?"

Landry's press conference had moved uptown, to the press-room bar set up by the NFL in the Fairmont Hotel, where league publicist Jim Heffernan was in charge. "Time, gentlemen!" Heffernan cried when Landry went to a portable mike. Heffernan meant that the bar was closed. Cooper Rollow of the Chicago *Tribune* leaned over and said, "It's such a relief to talk to Landry after putting up with crap from the other coaches, like 'That's for me to know and you to find out.' Landry lays it all out for you."

"There are two significant things about the Forty-niners," Landry began. "One, they were in this championship game last year. Their attitude is bound to be a lot different this time, a lot more confident. The other thing is the improvement in personnel in two key offensive spots. Vic Washington, the rookie they got from Canada, gives them an outside attack they didn't have before. He's got great darting quickness. The other position is tight end—Ted Kwalick has come of age.

"Their passing game is our number-one concern, Brodie throwing to Gene Washington and Kwalick. Brodie's fifteen years of experience shows in the few times he's been trapped this season—eleven times. That means he's reading defenses very quickly and getting rid of the ball. No pass protection is that good. Your quarterback has to do that.

"Dick has got over the turnover part of this season. Brodie hasn't been throwing interceptions the last few games, and things have settled down for them. I expect a pretty good scoring game, but it depends on what your turnovers do for you. This thing really becomes close when you get down to the last four teams in the playoffs. Any one of the four is capable of going through to win the Super Bowl. It's whoever can put two games back to back without errors is going to make it."

The teacher-student story was with us again, and the fact that Landry and Nolan were the only two coaches in the NFL using the coordinated defense. "I'll have to make him think I'm going to change a whole lot," Landry said, smiling. "But I've *got* to change some."

After Landry was through, we had Nolan on a speakerphone hookup from San Francisco. "I know him like a book," Nolan said. "Sure, he'll have some changes . . . and I'll have some, too."

Luksa, whose history of needling Nolan goes back a long way, said, "What are you going to do, Nolan, when you keep losing these championship games?"

And Nolan said, "I guess I'll go to Fort Worth and take *your* job. They've got to be looking for somebody competent."

There was a little drama during the warmups that I missed, but Herb Adderley told me about it, dramatically. "I looked over at the Forty-niners and there was Brodie," Adderley said, "with his hands on his hips, staring at me. He nodded. You know what he was telling me? I knew. He was telling me, 'I'm coming at you.'"

"Why did you think he was coming at you?" I said.

"I knew it, man. Soft pickings is what he thought. He wasn't going to throw at Mel. He was coming to my side. Well, I nodded back, and he knew what *I* was telling *him:* 'You better be good, because I'm ready.'"

But Brodie wasn't capable of picking on anybody. The 49ers got one first down the whole first half, and when Brodie tried to throw a screen pass from his own fourteen-yard line, he threw it right into Andrie's gut. Andrie galumphed to the two, and Hill cracked over in two tries.

In the third quarter Brodie finally connected to Kwalick for a twenty-four-yard gain, and the 49ers got a field goal out of it. Cole and Lilly and Pugh were not giving him time to set up strong, and occasionally Green would come on a safety blitz. They were batting the ball down before it got out of the 49er backfield. "He throws sort of sidearm," Pugh said, "and we could see in the films he had a lot of passes tipped. All week Ernie's been drilling us to rush with our hands high."

Still, the game was sitting on dead center, and a 7-3 lead has never been safe against Brodie. Staubach broke it open with one of his own patented plays, wheeling out to the left, darting back to the right inside of 49er tackle Earl Edwards and outside of end Tommy Hart to throw to Danny Reeves along the right sideline. The seventeen-yard gain got Dallas out of a hole and started them on the game-winning drive. Then Staubach relied on Walt Garrison, a comer off the bench. Calvin Hill tore his knee cutting sharply in the second quarter, and Garrison had replaced him, with Thomas switching to halfback. Now Garrison bulled for four and seven and three and two, along the drive spiced by Staubach's passes to Mike Ditka. At the three-yard line, when Thomas tried to line up in the same position as Garrison and Garrison repositioned him, the play was a pitchout which Thomas carried around left end for the touchdown. With nine minutes left to play, the 49ers' fate was sealed.

"That drive," said Jordan, "used up seven and a half minutes and it had to take it out of them. From then on, they had to throw, and if they don't, we just love to see 'em run for five yards."

Jordan said the Cowboys came alive when Garrison produced. "You could feel the excitement on the sidelines when Walt started running."

Andrie was the bigger hero, explaining how he grabbed the pass from Brodie. "We had a blitz on," Andrie said, "so it was my job to head upfield and contain wide."

Dave Edwards said from an adjoining locker, "George, we didn't have a blitz on."

Andrie believed Edwards was kidding him. "Hey Chuck," he yelled at Howley, "didn't we have a blitz on?"

Howley solemnly shook his head no.

"Then what was I doing upfield?" Andrie said.

And Edwards said, "I guess, George, it was the pure instinct of a veteran pro."

Garrison was asked about the mixup on the second scoring play—Thomas still wasn't talking—and he said, "I guess I was in the wrong position, but Duane is such a tremendous athlete he was able to adjust and make the touchdown."

Staubach, in the next row of lockers, was busily contradicting him: "The formation was a green left and Duane lined up in the wrong spot."

I came back to Garrison and asked him why he was confused. He said, "Duane gets enough ridicule without me adding to it."

Jordan was reminded that this victory put Dallas in the Super Bowl again, and he said, "That one's not much bigger than the ones we've been playing."

Lyndon Johnson was again a visitor to the Cowboy locker room, and in the confusion I had missed Landry's post-game remarks. I stopped him on the way out. "The whole thing was Brodie, wasn't it?" I said.

"Yes," Landry said, "I'm afraid Dick is going to think Brodie let him down."

Landry was standing in the middle of the practice field, watching the players go through their warmup drills. He had given the squad two days off, resuming practice on Wednesday and setting a Sunday-afternoon departure for New Orleans. I asked him to analyze the mood of the team and explain, for instance, why there was such a lack of celebration in the locker room after the San Francisco victory. "No," he said, "I've never been in a locker room that took a big win like that so easy. But I've never been with a team that lost the Super Bowl the year before, either. They've felt all year that this is where they belonged. They'd be back playing for the championship. It was different after we beat the Forty-niners last year, because we'd never gotten past that game before. Right now, I imagine Miami is going through what we went through—the tremendous excitement."

Miami had beaten Baltimore in the AFC title game, 21-0, a result that surprised the Cowboys but didn't exactly fill them with awe. Dave Edwards and Chuck Howley, in the locker room a few minutes before practice, were discussing the Miami victory.

"I thought the Colts would take 'em easy," Edwards had said.

"Maybe they would have if Matte and Bulaich could have played," Howley said. "That makes all the difference when you got to go with two rookies—Nottingham and McCauley? —for your running attack."

"No matter how they did it, they did it," Edwards said, "and this gives 'em a lot of—what's that famous word? Begins with 'mo'? Oh, yes, the old momentum. They win sudden death and then they win by twenty-one to zip. I bet they got the whole thing figured out."

"I'll take our nine straight for momentum. Nine in a row, how strong is that?" Howley said.

Now I asked Landry about another angle of the game, the advantage Dallas had in Super Bowl experience. "We'll have an edge," he said. "I don't think it hurts that we were there last year. But Shula offsets that edge. He was in it before with the Colts, and he knows what it is."

After practice I walked off the field with Herb Adderley, and he had a different slant on the subject. "Shula can't explain it to them," he said. "The atmosphere of being down there the whole week, the pressure that keeps coming right up to game time. He can tell them about it, but you have to go through it. It's something you have to experience. It affected some of our people last year. It had to. It's impossible to go into a big game like that and not feel something inside." Adderley should know; this would be his fourth Super Bowl, a record. Since 1961, when Adderley first played in an NFL title game for Green Bay, his shares from playoffs, Super Bowls and College All-Star games amounted to $109,168.51, not counting the one coming up. He said, "There's a big difference around here this week, I can tell. The overall attitude of the entire squad going into this game is beautiful. This is the way we went into 'em when I was with the Pack. You have fun, but be serious in practice. We don't want to be the first team to lose two Super Bowls."

Staubach was dressing to get out and go home, but he was willing to stop and talk more football. I told him what Landry had said and what Adderley had said. "This is like no other game you ever play," Staubach said. "The first thing— maybe the worst thing that throws you off—is that the game isn't *this* Sunday. We're all creatures of habit, and we have a set routine through the season—play a game, have a day off, practice for five days and then you're back in another game. Now suddenly we have that extra week thrown in. It's great for making something special about the Super Bowl, but it's really tough on your nerves if you haven't been through it before. *I* even felt it last year, and I knew there wasn't much chance I'd get to play.

"The other thing is all the attention you get and the strange surroundings. During the season, no matter whether we're playing a road game that week or playing at home, we practice right out of this locker room, and when we're through we go home to our families or our apartments. For a road game, you spend one night in a hotel, so maybe it doesn't matter that the air conditioning is strange or the bed doesn't feel right. But when you go to the Super Bowl, all that's changed and you're at a road game for a whole week."

Miami got some unexpected strategic help when President Nixon called Don Shula to wish him luck. Shula said the President told him, "The down-and-in pass to Warfield ought to work against Dallas." The Associated Press wirephoto transmitted a diagram of the President's play: Warfield going straight for ten yards, then slanting sharply toward the middle of the field, inside the cornerback and between the middle linebacker and free safety.

I phoned Landry at his office and asked him if he was going to vote Democratic in the next election. "You're not going to get me to comment on this thing," he said, laughing. "The President is quite a fan, and he spends a lot of time around Miami. He's entitled to pull for his own team. I'll have to say he's picked a pretty good play. Miami has been hitting it all year. Heck, it was a good play when Warfield was with Cleveland."

Thursday night, or Super Sunday minus nine, a New Orleans television sportscaster named Buddy Diliberto called me to check an interesting story—that Duane Thomas, on the advice of Jim Brown, had decided not to play in the Super Bowl. It seemed that a friend of Diliberto's had been having a beer in Houston with former Cowboy safety Obert Logan and a Houston Oiler assistant coach, George Dickson. Logan told them he had it on good authority from a friend of Brown's in Los Angeles that Thomas was going to quit the Dallas squad.

I relayed this word to Schramm at his home and drew a long silence. "It doesn't make sense," he said. "Even if it was a crazy thing to get more money, I couldn't give him any money or a new contract at this stage of the season. It's against the league rules."

"Just give me your assurance," I said, "that there's absolutely no basis for the story."

"I can't do that," Schramm said. "Let me make a couple of phone calls and I'll get back to you."

Two hours later I found out why Schramm was giving no assurances. "Thomas wasn't at practice today," he said. "We sent a guy to his house just now and nobody's home. We have another man looking all over town for him. But I still can't believe there's anything to the story. A stunt like that would have everybody in the country down on him—and Brown, too. Battling the organization is one thing, but letting down your teammates is another."

The next morning Thomas reported for the 9:30 meeting at 9:29. He was in the front door and into the meeting room as if he were cutting off tackle. "Duane!" I said. "I've got to talk to you." I followed him halfway across the room, picking a way around the chairs of other players. "Duane!" I said. "This is important." He was heading for a seat against the far wall, but then he stopped and, without quite looking at me, said, "Don't fuck around with me, man." Reeves was at the lectern, ready to start calling the roll, and I was out of bounds, so I left. It was either that or start a one-way shouting match with Thomas.

At the break-up of the first session, Thomas went into Landry's cubicle and stayed there for forty minutes. Lee Roy Caffey passed me in the hall outside Landry's door. He was grinning. "That's okay, Steve," he said. "The rest of us will still talk to you." After all these months the players were weary of being asked for their reactions to Thomas, but I wondered how many of them had been aware the day before that he was AWOL. Hayes said he never noticed, but when I asked Garrison he almost exploded. "Goddamit, why do you want to get me involved in this thing?" he said. "Course I knew he wasn't there. I'd be pretty damned dumb if I didn't notice he wasn't lined up alongside me."

"You could have thought he was in the trainer's room, or jogging in sweats," I said.

"Where Thomas is concerned, I don't think, one way or another," Garrison said.

Thomas came out and ducked around the corner into the john, and I went into Landry's room. "I don't know that I can shed much light on this," he said. "He didn't say much of anything. I guess I did most of the talking. He had no excuse for missing practice. All he would tell me was 'Personal reasons.' I asked him about the Jim Brown thing, and he just wouldn't comment at all. He's got his own ideas. He doesn't think anything that happens away from football has anything to do with him playing football."

"Did you ask him if he *is* going to play in the Super Bowl?"

"He's here, he's ready to practice. I have to assume he's going to play in the game. He'll be fined for missing practice. The size of the fine is up to me, according to the importance of the practice. I have to think that a practice when you're preparing for the championship game is pretty important."

Just before we boarded the plane late Sunday afternoon, Landry was handed a telegram. He showed it to me: "My prayers and my presence will be with you in New Orleans, although have no plans to send in any plays—Lyndon B. Johnson."

"That was very thoughtful of him," Landry said. "How many of our games did he see?"

"Three," I said. "New England, St. Louis and San Francisco."

"At least," Landry said, "we have one President on our side."

One year makes a tradition in the NFL, and the last time the Super Bowl was played in New Orleans AFL champion Kansas City stayed at the Hilton Inn near the airport, a half hour's drive from town, and NFL champion Minnesota stayed at the Fontainebleau Hotel, ten minutes from the French Quarter. To even things out, the lodgings were reversed this time—Dallas at the Hilton, which was chosen because it is only five minutes from the New Orleans Saints' practice field, and Miami at the Fontainebleau, the closest major hotel near the Dolphins' practice site, Sugar Bowl Stadium.

The difference between the Hilton and the Fontainebleau could be more than incidental over a long week. The Hilton is a motel, a two-story structure sprawled in a U-shape over an area the size of a good city block. At the open end of the U there is a tiny lobby, and separate from that are a coffee shop–restaurant and a cocktail lounge. When you step out of your room, you are either in an open-air walkway or on a balcony. At the six-story Fontainebleau, where the Cowboys stayed when they came down to play the Saints, the players can leave their doors open and wander through the halls from room to room, in their underwear if they have that entire wing booked up. The Fontainebleau's larger lobby and cozier patio even then were packed with fans and autograph seekers. It figured to be bedlam for the Dolphins. Only a truly dedicated autograph hound would make the half-hour drive out the Airline Highway to reach the Cowboys, and when they got there it would be difficult to get a handle on the players.

As the players milled around the luggage truck, trying to sort out hanger bags and suitcases, Danny Reeves said to Jerry Tubbs, "Did you notice this place is right in the landing pattern?"

"I noticed," Tubbs said. Tubbs is perpetually nervous about every phase of air travel.

"Well, don't stay in the south wing," Reeves said. "A seven-oh-seven landed right smack in the middle of it a few years back, woke everybody up and killed fourteen people."

"I'm glad you told me," Tubbs said. "Now I won't feel good in the *north* wing."

The players were in a hectic hurry to get their bags put away, because the night was theirs, courtesy of Tom Landry. Also Monday and Tuesday nights. Curfew would be midnight Wednesday through Friday and then drop back to the customary 11:00 the eve of the game.

I ran into Landry as he was crossing the vast courtyard patio and asked him why he was so lenient on the hours. "That'll give them three nights to get the French Quarter out of their system," he said. "In fact, by Wednesday I hope they'll be sick of it."

That night, on my way into the French Quarter, I stopped by the lobby to check for messages, and I saw Staubach scanning the church directory posted on the wall. "Going to Mass this week, Roger?" I said.

"I'm thinking about it," he said. "Which one do you think is closest?"

"Our Lady of Perpetual Help," I said. "It's between here and the practice field, less than five minutes."

"That's a good church for Super Bowl week," Staubach said.

"Are you going to pray for a win?" I said.

"I never pray for a *win*. I just pray for general things."

"Me, too," I said. "but not this time. This time I'm praying for a win. Enough is enough."

Charlie Waters set the mood of the Cowboys' photo session Monday morning. He came out of the Saints' locker room with one arm tucked inside his jersey and an empty sleeve blowing in the wind. Bob Hayes stuck a middle finger in Waters' face and said, "Say a few words for the radio audience, Charlie."

"I thought I had a pretty good year at free safety," Waters said, "considering my handicap."

Then Hayes amused himself, and John Niland, on the half basketball court by demonstrating his dunk shot with a football from a flat-footed stance under the goal. Hayes is 6 feet 1 inch. Danny Reeves said, "That's what we need—for Hayes to break a wrist on the rim."

The players sat on slat-wood bleachers behind the end zone until called out for interviews, and soon a half-dozen film crews had interviews going on the bright green Astro-Turf. I strolled from group to group, eavesdropping.

Mel Renfro: "Sure, I remember Paul Warfield very well. I covered him in a couple fiascos we had with Cleveland. . . ."

Tom Landry: "The team started winning because it had its back to the wall. . . ."

Cornell Green: "I don't have to get 'up' for a game. I don't like anybody very much except my wife, and some days I don't speak to *her*. . . ."

I went over to the stands and sat next to Reeves, because it occurred to me this might be his last game as a Cowboy player. "You're right," he said, "unless they can figure out some plays I can run from a wheelchair. The only good thing about my knees is that after five operations there's nothing left inside can go wrong."

Thomas and Garrison and Hill, if the knee Hill hurt against San Francisco recovered by game time, figured to be the primary backs against Miami, but Landry had a way of using Reeves on pure passing downs, and Reeves had a way of producing. "That's because Calvin and Duane are young players," Reeves said, leaning back with his elbows on the bleacher row behind him, "and you have to make adjustments running a pass route. These are always big downs, so if we connect, it's usually an important play."

"Give me a for-instance," I said, "so I can write it down simple in the paper."

"If you write it," Reeves said, "I'm sure it will be simple. Okay—we have a sixty-two-wing sideline play. It's a pass going to the flankerback, what we call the wing, on the sideline. Well, suppose I see the cornerback is covering the wing short and the safety on that side is taking him deep. I've got to move to the cornerback to draw him off. If the cornerback comes to me, the wing is open. If the cornerback doesn't pay any attention to me, I stop and take the pass.

"Now suppose they're in a safety zone, which is what we call it when the safety covers the short area and the cornerback takes the wide receiver deep. I go at the safety to force the same decision.

"Again, say they're in what we call a twenty-defense, which has Sarah—the strong-side linebacker—covering the sideline area. When Sarah moves to the sideline he has to turn his back on me and *run* out there. Now, I know Meg, the middle linebacker, is moving to that side, too, as fast as he can. I've got to run right at Sarah and split the difference, getting between him and Meg, then hooking back to take the pass."

"It sounds easy," I said. "All you have to do is recognize one of fifteen defenses within two-point-five seconds and have a clock in your head telling you when the quarterback has to throw."

"There's that," Reeves agreed. "It's a feeling, mostly. It helps when you've played a few years."

Someone had produced an oversize golf cart covered by a five-foot-high Cowboy helmet, and Hayes and Green commandeered it to scoot back and forth, delighting the movie men. A battery of radio people were crowded around Staubach, no doubt asking him about his scrambling tendencies, but there was only one writer talking to Craig Morton, Den-

nie Freeman of the AP Dallas bureau. I walked out to where
they were standing, passing Landry on the way. Landry was
saying, "Buoniconti is the key to their defense, the quick-
est middle linebacker we've seen all year. He makes tackles
sideline to sideline. To beat their defense, you first have to
figure a way to deal with Buoniconti."

"Where do you figure you'll be next season?" I asked
Morton.

"Where do you think I ought to go?" he said. "Which club
do you think would be my best shot?"

"How about Philadelphia?" Freeman said. "They need a
quarterback."

"Philadelphia!" Morton said. "And fight that weather? Can
you imagine what it would be like playing all season in Green
Bay? No thanks. If I had to play someplace like that, I believe I would get out and go to work for a living."

"How do you feel now about what's happened to you on
the Cowboys this season?" I said.

"How do I feel? It's according to how you mean. I'm much
wiser now. I think it's made me a better person. I'm not bitter, but I'd be lying if I didn't say I was disappointed the
way things turned out. But I'm sure this isn't the toughest
thing I'll face in my life. If it is, I'll have an easy life."

"I had an inside tip," I said, "supposed to be from a friend
of yours, that you'd love to stay here next year and be number two, because you can't get hurt if you're not playing.
I figure you only want to be number one . . . somewhere."

"There are things I hear about myself you wouldn't believe," Morton said.

"Oh, yes, I would," I said. "I got another hot tip you tried
to commit suicide one night at the Losers' Club."

"With a gun or a knife?" Morton said. "There are reports
to the Cowboy office about me every week, things I'm supposed to have done I simply don't understand. Do you think
it's something about Dallas?"

"No," I said. "It's pro football and you're a quarterback.
You'd get the same crap all over the league."

"What about being number one next season with Dallas?"
Freeman said.

"I could get the job back if something happened to Roger,"

Morton said. "Otherwise, I feel it would be very . . . hard
. . . to do." We talked of other things for a few moments and
then Morton, who was facing the bleachers, said, "Hey, look
at that. Isn't that ridiculous?"

The tableau in the bleachers did look a bit ridiculous, and
it seemed more so as I drew closer. Duane Thomas was
sprawled comfortably across three rows, ringed around en-
tirely by writers. Thomas was staring stonily out into space,
and nobody was saying a word. I whispered to John Crittenden of the Miami *News* to show me his notes. At the top of
his pad he'd written, "Duane:" and below that was an empty
sheet of paper. "How'd this get started?" I said.

"Will Grimsley," Crittenden said, naming the AP man out
of New York, "came over to talk to Thomas and when everybody saw Thomas' lips move they came running. Me too."

"When they moved, what did they say?"

"They said, 'I don't feel like talking.' "

At that moment Thomas spoke again, thusly: "What time
is it?"

Grimsley looked at his watch and said, "Twelve thirty-
four."

That was it. Jerry Green of Detroit sat facing Thomas,
notebook also poised, staring into his face. The Sounds of
Silence prevailed. Gene Roswell of the New York *Post*, standing on the edge of the crowd with me, said, "This is sick, and
we're sick for pressing him. I'm getting a little ashamed of
ourselves." The other writers drifted away, and Thomas
climbed down and went into the locker room.

The interview sessions for Tuesday, Wednesday and Thursday are staggered so that it's possible to catch the Dolphins
at the Fontainebleau, then hustle back to the Hilton for
Landry and the Cowboys. The sessions are handled differently. Miami's interview room is on the ground floor in a
small night club that has been abandoned to private parties.
A lectern with a microphone is against one wall at the edge
of a dance floor. The coach and the players handle questions,
en masse, from there. Don Shula led off for the Dolphins and
was immediately asked to compare them with the Baltimore
team he brought to the Super Bowl three years before. "That

Colt team had a lot of veteran ballplayers," Shula said, "people who had won world championship football games. When I came to Miami two years ago there were only a few players who had been on *winning* teams. Baltimore that year won fifteen of its sixteen games coming into the Super Bowl. It could have gone down in history as one of the great teams of all time—if we'd beaten the Jets." There was a wistful note in Shula's voice when he made that latter statement. A former defensive back at Cleveland, Baltimore and Washington, the forty-one-year-old Shula has become something of a phenomenon as a coach. In seven years at Baltimore his teams were 71-23-4, the highest winning percentage for that span in the NFL. Miami was 3-10-1 the year before Joe Robbie enticed Shula away with an offer of a piece of the club, and he instantly turned in 10-4 records back to back. The name of his home town had been used as a symbol for his approach to football: Painesville, Ohio. (Landry's was also apt: Mission, Texas.) Cameron Snyder, the Baltimore writer, asked him now if he was still as hard-nosed as ever.

"I'm the same nice guy I always was," Shula said. "How can you chart a coach over the years? I couldn't even chart myself. But the principle hasn't changed. I don't care if the players say I'm tough as long as they say I'm fair."

Shula was asked to comment generally on the Cowboys, and he gave a lengthy, stem-to-stern analysis, emphasizing two points over and over: "Their multiple offense presents a problem for a young defense like ours. They give you a lot of window dressing, and then they come at you with basic football. I don't want our aggressiveness taken away by indecision. Aggressiveness is the way we've made up for a lack of experience, and we're working this week to make sure we keep it. . . . You look at the Dallas defense, and you have to start with Lilly. I don't know what anybody can do with him. The more you study him in game films, the more you realize how great he is. He and Alan Page are the two greatest defensive linemen in pro football. It doesn't help all that much to direct your attack to the other side. If you go away from him, you better make damn sure you've got somebody to cut him off."

Quarterback Bob Griese, who led the AFC in passing the

same as Staubach led the NFC, followed Shula to the mike
and covered the same ground except when he was asked
about Super Bowl pressure: "There are so many people
around, and so much emphasis on the game, you *could* let
it bother you"; and when he was asked about Lilly: "You
better talk to the offensive linemen. I did notice our left
guard is being awful nice to our center this week." This drew
a laugh, because it is the center who drops off and helps the
guard double-team Lilly every game he plays. It was Griese's
only lighthearted remark of the interview. He seemed a no-
nonsense, even dour, personality. Too much so for a twenty-
six-year-old who had just been named All-NFL quarterback.
Even when he made the crack about Lilly, his plain but
regular features had remained unmoved. I followed him out
of the room and into the patio for a private word. When the
New Orleans *Item* folded under me in 1958, I put in two hard
years with an Evansville, Indiana paper at the same time
Griese was there beginning to play high-school football. I
stopped him and told him this, expecting to cut up a few
do-you-remember touches, but Griese said, "Yeah? Well, I
live in Miami now. Excuse me, will you?" And he walked off.

Whatever public charisma Griese lacked was more than
made up by the tandem appearance of his two running backs,
Larry Csonka and Jim Kiick. Aside from leading the Dolphins
to the best rushing record in the NFL, their personal styles—
and their handlebar mustaches—had earned them a tag as
"Butch Cassidy and the Sundance Kid." Csonka was Cassidy
and Kiick the Kid. They worked the mike back and forth
between them with almost show-biz aplomb:

CSONKA: "The front four of Dallas is impressive. There's
Jethro and then there's the fellow on the other side . . ."

KIICK: "The fellow on the other side?"

CSONKA: "Thought I'd get a little dig in there, but on second thought maybe we better not mess with him."

KIICK: "Neither one of us is the swivel-hip outside type. We
just dig it out."

CSONKA: "We take a one-point lead and we're happy as
hell."

KIICK: "The AstroTurf never bothers us because Larry and

I can't make ninety-degree turns. In fact, I don't think we move fast enough to slip."

CSONKA: "The guy I didn't know about isn't the only reason Dallas has a great defense. They play great as a team and the linebackers are fantastic together."

KIICK: "Yeah, when Howley burps—"

CSONKA: "Jordan says, 'Pardon me.'"

Then somebody asked Csonka what rushing strategy Miami would use against the Dallas defense, which was the best in the NFL against the run. Csonka said, "Is there a Dallas writer here?"

I said, "Yeah."

"Okay," Csonka said, "how would you advise us to attack Dallas on the ground?"

"Throw the ball," I said.

"Thanks," Csonka said. "You are very encouraging."

"If it'd make you feel any better," said Cameron Snyder, "Gerry Philbin of the Jets said you were the hardest runner in the league to bring down."

"I'd feel a lot better if Lilly said it instead of Philbin," Csonka said.

The NFL's Cowboy setup for the press at the Hilton was in a 100-foot-by-50-foot banquet room back of the cocktail lounge, and it included a luncheon buffet followed by answers from Landry: "Whichever team can run on the other one has a better chance. We're very confident of winning the game." There were more than one hundred writers taking notes at the long tables. Jerry Magee of San Diego said, "Most of us have been listening to Miami talk about Lilly. Is there anyone on the Miami defense that Dallas respects that much?"

Landry said, "We respect Buoniconti, their middle linebacker, very much. He's their defensive leader. He sets the tempo. He has great pursuit and a lot of freedom. He's not guessing out there, because he has eleven years' experience and he knows where to be because he studies the other team's sets. Buoniconti sets the tone Shula wants, all-out aggressiveness, and he makes up for some of their inexperience. But the poise that Miami showed against two great teams, Kansas City and Baltimore, that indicates experience might not be much of a factor in this game."

After Landry's remarks ended, the writers moved to still another huge convention room, where groups of straight-backed chairs were sorted in clusters, and the Cowboy players entered in relays of four and five, one per cluster. It reminded me of the arrangement the year before at the Galt Ocean Mile. It also reminded Lee Roy Jordan. "This is a big part of this whole deal," Jordan said to five of us huddled around him. "You guys asking the same questions day after day. Not you, individually. Other people come right behind you and ask what you asked. If you're not anticipating it, that can wear on your nerves. Last year we didn't know what to expect from these press conferences. It can bother the concentration of some people a good deal. This time we knew what it was going to be, all the chairs all over, one player to a group—it feels sort of familiar."

"How many times were you asked last Super Bowl about Dallas losing the big ones?" I said.

"Oh, about ten thousand times."

"How many times you've been asked that this time?"

"Not once," Jordan said. "Yeah, I think we laid that dog to rest."

Staubach, of course, was surrounded by the biggest mob, and one writer after another took him over the jumps about Landry calling his plays. Staubach refused to scramble. "There's some inner conflict about Coach Landry sending in every play," he said. "I want to use plays that depend on my own ability—like on third-and-five, I'll want to throw a turn-in, or maybe a deep pass. Coach Landry will send in a deceptive play, a draw or a screen. He has really called some great deceptive plays this season. But I want to be a complete quarterback, and a quarterback has to call his own plays if he's going to take over and be in control. That's in the future. I'm certainly not going to worry about it this week."

They took him back through his Navy career and where it ended and blended into professional football. Then Staubach said something that was news to me. "If you want to know the *real* turning point in me becoming a pro," he said, "it was when I took a two-week leave in 1968 to go to the Cowboy training camp. I set that time aside to find out whether I should leave the Navy or not. If I learned I wasn't in good enough shape, or that I couldn't cut the competition after being away from it for three years, I would have stayed in. I liked the Navy. My wife, Marianne, liked it. We had a lot of good friends, and it wouldn't have been a difficult decision to make it a career. But, really, I never had any doubt how I'd do. I felt great, and I felt like I could still move and throw. I had a good scrimmage against the Ram rookies and I think Coach Landry was impressed. Those two weeks turned out to be more important than I thought. If Landry hadn't been impressed, I don't think he would have traded off Jerry Rhome the next summer, leaving it open for me to be number two as a rookie."

"What kind of an officer were you," said Dick Young of the New York *News*, "in the eyes of the enlisted men you had under you in Vietnam?"

"I had about a hundred and forty men under me," Staubach said, "and I imagine there will be more than a few pulling for Miami on Sunday."

Calvin Hill had edged up to the outer circle, borrowed my paper and pen, and he was standing there making faces at Staubach, pretending to take notes. Without blinking Staubach said, "Uh, Calvin, if you don't mind, this interview is for the *white* writers."

The pool-patio and courtyard at the Hilton was as quiet and deserted all week long as a monastery during vespers, because the thermometer had dipped. In New Orleans, where you can dig down two feet and strike water, anything below forty degrees is bone-chilling. So the players stayed in their rooms, unless they were en route to town for dinner. I found Lilly alone in his, sprawled across the bed and raised on one elbow to pore over a computer chart of Miami's offensive tendencies.

"The last two days at the Fontainebleau," I said, "everybody's been talking about you."

"Yeah?" Lilly said. "What are they saying?"

"They're saying the guard may have to have help from the center."

Lilly made a great show of searching through a book on a night stand before coming up with the names. "The two Bobs," he said. "Kuechenberg and DeMarco. The way I feel this week, I may kill 'em both. They might have to haul 'em away in a meat wagon." In the past two years, Lilly had at last lost the callow-youth appearance he brought with him out of Throckmorton, Texas. His straw-blond hair, which used to blow in the wind, was now trimmed biweekly by a stylist, and there were character lines in his face. Bob Lilly would grow old handsomely.

"I've been meaning to tell you," Lilly said. "I appreciate what you did, not writing about my marriage." Lilly had separated from his college sweetheart almost a year before. They have three children.

"That doesn't have much to do with football," I said.

"I know, but you could have worked some way to mention it. I appreciate you didn't. It was really rough last spring. I think that's why I worked so hard on the training program. I'd just go out to the field and work my ass off and get my mind on football. You know I got down to two-forty?"

"I heard."

"And I think maybe I had the best year I've ever had. That's funny, isn't it? I guess you compensate."

"What about Sunday?"

"It's kinda scary," Lilly said. "I don't see how we can lose. Don't you see it like that?"

"No. I used to feel that way about this team, but I got over it. Would you flesh out the details a little? Then maybe I'll believe it."

"They're not going to run on us," Lilly said. "Csonka and Kiick aren't that much a threat except inside, and nobody runs inside on us. The thing about Csonka is you got to hit him early before he gets rolling. He doesn't get off too fast, either."

"You make me wonder how he gained a thousand yards."

"He didn't play Dallas every week," Lilly said. "And I don't see why we can't run on them." He looked at some figures in the back of his playbook. "They give up four-point-one yards a carry. Anything over three-five, you're in trouble."

"That leaves Griese-to-Warfield," I said.

"You mean it leaves Griese. When we've stopped the run, and he has to throw on third-and-seven every time, we can begin to tee off on him. He's a good quarterback, quick feet, and he throws on timing with his receivers so it's hard to get to him. But we will eventually."

"After you've maimed Keuchenberg."

"Is that his name?" Lilly said.

Offensive line coach Jim Myers parked his car by the front door of the Hilton press room Thursday afternoon and hurried in to pop a can of Fresca. "How's their attitude?" I asked him as he hurried out again. Practice sessions were off limits to the press in Super Bowl week, and though I went to few practices anytime during the season, the ruling made me feel I was being denied vital information.

"I don't know," Myers said, "but they seem too damned quiet and relaxed to me. If somebody doesn't start getting excited tomorrow, I'm going to start worrying. Check with me then."

A press-room guest at the moment was Commander Paul Borden, USN (ret.), who had been the legal officer at Annapolis when Staubach graduated and who had handled all of his contracts with the Cowboys. He was an endless font of information on Staubach, including his baseball and basketball careers at the Academy.

"Did it ever occur to you, Commander," I said, "that this is really Staubach's first Super Bowl, he's only a third-year pro, and if any Cowboy is going to feel pressure, it's him?"

The commander shook his gray head. Negative. "This game is a big one," he said, "but I'm not sure how much bigger it is, in comparison, than the Army-Navy games when Roger was so much younger. Every midshipman, every officer—why, every admiral in the fleet—they were all on Roger's shoulders. But he thrives on pressure. He seems to respond to it perfectly."

"Well, maybe attending daily Mass will help, too," I said.
"Roger always attends daily Mass," the commander said.
"For four years at the Naval Academy he was the altar boy
at daily Mass. When he graduated, his classmates gave him a
rosary of pearl and gold."

Pete Rozelle and his men in the NFL office have everything figured out. The grand soiree, the pre-game party
blowout, is staged two nights before the game to give everybody time to weather their hangovers on Saturday and show
fresh for the kickoff Sunday. The previous year's party had
been held in a former 747 hangar in the Americana Hotel on
Miami Beach, with alternating bands and floor shows across
the wide divide from one another. The Roosevelt Hotel in
New Orleans, official NFL headquarters, had nothing so
grand to offer for the occasion. What it did have was five
invited guests for every one seat in the buffet hall. The solution was to stay in the stand-up area amid the eight open
bars and mingle with all the pretty people. Lamar and Norma
Hunt happened by, nondrinking, and I asked him how, as
president of the American Conference, could he be rooting
Sunday for Dallas.

"That's against league rules," Hunt said, "but I'm not going
to wear myself out pulling the other way. The Cowboys are
just too much the better team. I think they'll win easy, by
three touchdowns."

Everybody in the place seemed to think the same. Or
maybe I had that impression because of my affiliation. Who
is going to buttonhole a Dallas writer and predict the
Dolphins would win by three? Maybe a Tex Maule, but
there were no Tex Maules on the side of Miami. The *Sports
Illustrated* expert walked up and said, "Stephen, you're in,
or at least the Cowboys are in. I would bet my house and lot
on it. In fact, I think I already have."

The first "enemy" face I saw was unmistakable by its great
and scimitar-shaped nose. Danny Thomas had been one of
the original Dolphin partners and perhaps still was. I introduced myself and told him about Staubach's intention not to
pray for a Dallas win but that I had no such intention.

Thomas drew himself up and moved his forearms to his waist, in the gesture of a fighter tugging at his trunks. "You *know,* of course," he said, "that all I have to do is go to St. Jude and you're dead."

"I know," I said. This was why I brought it up.

"I'm afraid for you and the Dallas Cowboys if I so much as let St. Jude cross my mind," Thomas said. And in two beats he was saying, "Okay. Oklahoma is on a forty-umpteen-game winning streak, hasn't lost a game since Bud Wilkinson was a teenager, and Notre Dame comes down to play 'em. *My* Notre Dame. Notre Dame is like eighteen-point underdogs. I turn the situation over to St. Jude, and the day of the game, a national telecast, I am piled up in bed, all relaxed for a good afternoon. Notre Dame gets the kickoff and fumbles inside the twenty. They stop 'em, get the ball back, run one play and fumble—inside the twenty. We have a statue of St. Jude in our backyard. I get out of bed, go over to the window and throw back the curtain. 'St. Jude,' I said, 'are you going to put up with this shit?' Notre Dame won the game, seven to nothing."

I had been hoping to bump into Dave Manders for the past three days, and now, in the waning hours of Saturday afternoon when I had finished writing everything for the paper, I did. I could have gone to his room, but what I wanted to talk about was not right for that kind of formality.

"Sorry, no interviews," Manders said, making a mock try to get by me on the patio. "Not on the eve of the big game. I'm too uptight." He was about as uptight as a glob of whipped cream.

"I'm written out, *kaput.* No more stories. So tell me what you're going to do about Buoniconti."

"Buoniconti is going to spend Sunday afternoon on his ass," Manders said.

"But how?" I said. "The guy is a whirling buzz saw for a whole year, and Dallas is going to put him on his ass. How?"

"Buoniconti goes for the ball," Manders said. "He's five-ten and two hundred and ten. What we call a reject in the Cowboy system."

"The program says five-eleven and two-twenty."

"He's five-ten. Gil Brandt measured him. But he's quick, right? All over the damn place. So we show him the ball going one way, and then we have it coming back the other. Buoniconti goes with the flow, and this gives us the angle to cut him off."

"Counter plays."

"Not only counter plays. Every running play we call, the back will be looking to cut back against the grain."

"Like the play Duane scored on at Minnesota," I said, "where Niland took Page the way he was going and you cut off Warwick."

"Right."

"But there has to be more to it," I said. "I figured special blocking assignments, a whole lot of X's and O's. What makes it special?"

"Landry makes it special," Manders said. "He just emphasizes it. That's all you hear—Buoniconti, Buoniconti. Anytime Tom wants to get one thing done that bad, it gets done."

A New Orleans writer, Hap Glaudi, had described pro football in the Sugar Bowl: "Mardi Gras every Sunday." On a Super Bowl Sunday it holds the frenzy of three Mardi Gras, in a pre-game show of fifteen college bands, two hundred dancing girls with cheeks of tan and white, soaring balloons, flying pigeons and Al Hirt blowing his brains out. But I was tuned out of all this. All I cared about was seeing how the players performed in the warmups. Garo Yepremian, the Cypriot tie salesman, was missing his field goals. Roger Staubach was throwing strikes. Y.A. Tittle once told me he could tell how a quarterback was going to do in a game by watching his accuracy in the pre-game drills. Omen one. Finally, a flight wing of the Blue Angels in their "missing man" formation blasted directly over the stadium at the moment when eighty thousand people were singing, ". . . o'er the land of the free," and Miami took the kickoff.

Six minutes into the game, Csonka took a hand-off from Griese and fumbled it away to Howley. Csonka had never fumbled all season, in 256 carries, but this time he came in too low—trying for a little bit extra?—and Griese laid the ball on his forearm. Staubach used Garrison on counter plays up the middle for eight and ten yards, then hit Hayes over the middle for twenty-one. But inside the ten, Miami's young line stopped first Thomas, then Garrison at the two, and Clark kicked a nine-yard field goal.

One Dallas score on one Miami error, and Griese soon made another, dodging away from a quickly free Lilly and into the path of Larry Cole coming from the other side, then dodging this way and that, always back, as Lilly and Cole crisscrossed after him. Lilly finally dropped him at the Miami eight for a thirty-yard loss.

But Dallas was making its own mistakes. Staubach threw to the wrong side of Hayes when he was open for a touchdown. Ditka dropped a third-down pass, wide open. Griese hit his flankerback, Howard Twilley, for thirty yards, completing the one long pass somebody always completes on Adderley. Csonka, however, was being stopped cold, and Kiick could not get first downs.

Six minutes before halftime the Cowboys began to roll, apparently using the formula Manders told me about. Now and then I saw Manders flatten Buoniconti, and once Nye shielded him out of the play. I even saw Rayfield Wright blocking on him. But I can't watch a game that way; I have to follow the ball—and the ball was moving to the Miami goal. Landry lifted Garrison and inserted Hill, shifting Thomas to fullback, and Hill went through center for fourteen, through right tackle for seven, crossed from a shallow position into left tackle for five more—to the Miami seven. That was all Buoniconti territory. Then Staubach threw a ball as hard as he can throw it, to Alworth at the front corner of the end zone. Alworth trampled the goal-line flag as he scored, and Dallas led, 10-0.

Landry took out Andrie and put in D.D. Lewis for a three-man rush and a "prevent" defense, because Miami had to race the last seventy-five seconds on the clock. The "prevent" prevented a touchdown, but Warfield caught a twenty-three-yard pass to set up a thirty-one-yard field goal by Yepremian.

Those were a vital three points, sending Miami into the locker room only a touchdown behind.

In the first eight plays of the second half the Cowboys won the Super Bowl. They did it going wide instead of up the middle. Garrison took a pitchout at left end, Thomas another pitch around the right, Staubach threw to Hill (subbed especially to catch the pass) for twelve. And then Thomas was rolling on a power sweep at right end, the short side of the field which Landry always loves, and rolling again that way the next play for twenty-three yards to the Miami twenty-three. On first down from there, Hayes flew on an end-around to the same side for seventeen more yards, behind blocks by Manders and Nye, and two plays later Thomas took a pitchout around left end for the touchdown. It was a 17-3 lead, and I stopped keeping my own play-by-play. There was no way Miami could make up fourteen points on the Dallas defense. Howley and Edwards were helping Renfro shut off "the Nixon Play" to Warfield. When Warfield went in motion toward the flanker, he was covered by the Cowboys' "third cornerback," strong safety Cornell Green. Csonka and Kiick were held to forty yards each, and no team had ever stopped Csonka before. The Dallas offense had as much to do with that as the Dallas defense. The Cowboys controlled the football for sixty-seven plays to Miami's forty.

Miami never came close to scoring, and when Howley intercepted a pass for Kiick and ran it back forty-one yards to the Miami nine in the fourth quarter, Staubach applied the clincher with a seven-yard touchdown pass to Ditka: 24-3.

When the final gun went off, Rayfield Wright and Mike Ditka jerked Landry into the air to ride him on their shoulders, and for some reason the picture that flashed before me was Henry Jordan and Willie Davis doing the same to Vince Lombardi when Green Bay beat Dallas in the Cowboys' first NFL title game in 1966. That damn Lombardi rode those shoulders as if he'd known all along the Packers would win the game, and now Landry was taking the same—no, a greater—ride. When they put Landry down, Shula was by his side, hugging his neck. No handshakes for Shula. I wondered if there was a photographer among the mob who got a picture of the sweet and genuine gesture.

The Cowboy locker room was jammed tighter than sixteen college boys in a Volkswagen. TV men with cameras strapped on their shoulders tried to clean their lenses from the steam of body heat. Danny Reeves elected himself in charge of throwing Dallas executives into the shower. Pat Summerall and Tom Brookshier manned an elevated platform, above jock-strap level, for the CBS post-game interviews. And the writers were wrestling each other to get within earshot of a player, any player.

I sought out Lilly, and then I didn't know what to say to him. He had a big cigar stuck in his face, and he was grinning contentedly around it. He rested one elbow on the shelf of his locker. "I told you how it was going to be," Lilly said. "But I didn't really believe it." Lilly took a deep drag on the cigar and blew smoke at the ceiling. "Oh, goddam! Isn't it great! You know when I really started believing it? When the offense crammed the ball down their throats in the third quarter. On their butts! They just knocked everybody on their butts."

"Do you think Griese panicked when you ran him down?"

"Me and Cole? Yeah. No. He wanted to dump the ball, but he never had a chance. We ran him down like sheep dogs, huh? But did you see Tom's face? Did you see it there at the end? I'm happy for me, I'm happy for all of us, but what I feel for Landry winning this thing—I can't tell you how big it is."

Landry was near the CBS platform with a phone pressed to one ear and a hand pressed against the other. The word was passed along: At last, the President was calling a winner. Landry said, "Yes, Mr. President . . ." And then there was a stunned look on his face, and he said, "Oh." He laughed and pointed the phone at Summerall. "Pat! It's for you." Eventually, they were to get Summerall's fan off the phone and put through the call from the White House.

I fought off six other guys and got within range of Staubach's voice. He had just learned he'd been voted MVP of the game. "That's the way it is in this business," Staubach said. "When the team does good, the quarterback gets the credit. I'll take it, I'm not turning it down, but there are an awful lot of guys who ought to be in for a share."

Staubach went over and over the intricacies of the game— Miami used a zone defense that double-covered both wide receivers and he should have been throwing to the tight end; the touchdown pass to Alworth resulted from the flanker-back's tip that his man was covering him to the inside, leaving the out-route open; the pitchout to Thomas for the score that gave Dallas a 17-3 lead was *his* call, made at the line of scrimmage when he saw the Dolphins were in a defense that would stop the play Landry had sent in.

"There's only one thing that won this game," Staubach said. "When the Cowboys run the football, everything else works. What did we get, two-fifty-two rushing? Somebody said that's a Super Bowl record. When you're running like that, the passing has to open up. You really want to know what I'm thinking now? I'm thinking I just want to repay the good Lord."

And in the midst of all the struggling humanity there was Clint Murchison, dropping a cool line on me. "I think it's a successful end to our twelve-year plan," he said.

I tried to assess the mood and the atmosphere of the Cowboys in their World Championship aftermath and decided it was nothing I could have imagined. They had reached the far shore, but they weren't so damned happy about the trip. There was an undertone of anger, or at least fatalism, in their reception of the "ultimate" victory, except it wasn't as ultimate as all that, as Duane Thomas had pointed out the year before. Mel Renfro was telling the people around him: "I think we deserved everything we got today. We worked long and hard for it. Hard, man, I can't tell you, but you know how long. I remember running sixty-five kickoffs back in 'sixty-four, set a record, which tells you how much they were scoring on us. And this week I got sick and tired of hearing about Warfield, Paul Warfield. He never caught a pass on me all day. We doubled him most of the time, and we were cutting him with a linebacker at the line, but I had him four, five times alone, and he never caught a pass on me."

This was a time to visit my favorite people, and I went to them one by one. Dave Edwards, the unheralded linebacker, provided the "key" (Landry phrase) to the shutoff of the Miami offense. "They're a young team," he said. "So we knew they had to keep on doing the same things in this game they did in the season. They weren't versatile enough to put a new wrinkle here or there. From the flip formation we knew what they were going to run, who was going to come where with the ball. They give the ball to Csonka with a guard pulling— zap, baby, you know they're coming around end. And we played it. You know how the defense was today? We weren't going to take chances on our offensive team. We were going to keep them from scoring, period."

"Nobody ever shut the other team down from a touchdown in the Super Bowl," I said.

"Yeah," Edwards said, "and you know what? If we don't let Minnesota get that cheap-ass touchdown at the end of the game, we go through the whole playoffs without letting anybody cross our goal."

A sudden, inexplicable hush had fallen on the whole scene. Duane Thomas was on the CBS platform with Jim Brown by his side. I pushed up close to hear the deathless words.

Brookshier seemed nonplused by Thomas' appearance, and he stammered his first question, which was really more of a remark than a query: "You have a lot of speed for such a big man."

Thomas said, "Evidently."

Brookshier, completely flummoxed now, said, "How is it you weigh two-oh-five for some games, then two-fifteen for others?"

Thomas said, "I weigh what I have to weigh."

Then Brown grabbed the mike. "It's obvious," he said. "Duane is one of the most gifted runners in football today. The reason for his silence was because he wanted to show America how good a football player he was—and it was because of his silence that he was able to do this."

Thomas didn't even say "Amen."

When Brown climbed down from the platform, Dick Young asked him, "Do you think Thomas was MVP today?"

"If he wasn't," Brown said, "he was awfully close to it. But Roger Staubach did a great job."

Reeves had gotten to Schramm, and the club president looked like a wet Persian cat and just as unhappy emerging from the shower. But his joyous arrogance managed to overcome. "We'll be back," Schramm was telling us all, in a quiet niche at the coaches' end of the locker room. "This was only a start. They can't say we don't win the big one any more. I don't know which big one is left. We're going to be like the Yankees and the Celtics—a dynasty."

Landry would hang around till the last dog died this day. Only a few of us were with him in the coaches' quarters when he reanalyzed the game, as if he'd be willing to go over it and over it, hours on end. "We would slide the tackle through, or the guard or the fullback to get to Buoniconti," he was saying. "We did something different on pass defense. We doubled both wide receivers and covered the tight end with a linebacker, not because it was Marv Fleming [the Miami tight end] but just because we were playing the percentages. Miami doesn't throw to its tight end. We were hard to beat after that third-quarter drive. I went outside because I knew they'd change their defense at the half. They stacked people into the holes we were hitting in the first half."

"So what did the President say?" I said.

"It was a bad connection," Landry said, "but he said the offensive line did a great job."

"Did he say anything about the down-and-in?"

"No," Landry said, allowing himself a small smile. "When your down-and-ins aren't working, you don't mention 'em."

I went down to the Roosevelt Hotel to write my story, and my friends from Miami filled me in on the Dolphins' reaction. Shula said he knew their number was up when Dallas rammed in the third-quarter touchdown. Csonka said, "Anyone that plays in the Super Bowl has to feel the pressure. We didn't think it would affect us, but it's there. You can't hide from it. But that's part of it all. If you want to be a champion you have to handle it."

Jim Kiick was asked if he felt that he and Csonka had met the same fate as Cassidy and Sundance. "No," Kiick sad. "Those guys ended up dead and didn't know it. We're alive and got to live with it six months."

I got back to the Hilton Inn at midnight, and the Cowboy victory party had ended—ended, I learned the next morning, more or less with a whimper.

I sat next to Tom and Alicia at the counter in the coffee shop, just before noon on Monday, and when Alicia left to complete her packing, I took my first long look at Landry in a long time. I was struck by how much he'd aged, suddenly, it seemed. I said, "You said yesterday it would take some time to sink in. Has it sunk in yet?"

"A little bit," Landry said. "When I woke up this morning, I had to remind myself twice that we'd won the game, that we weren't going out to play it again."

"Is it as great as you'd thought it would be?"

"In a way," Landry said.

"It's not for me," I said. "You-all wore me out. It's an anticlimax."

"Well," he said, "it's really only sweet if you win it the first or second time you go up for it. If we'd won back then, you'd feel it more, and I would, too. But this is good enough. I'll take it."

Staubach was awarded the keys to a new car on Monday, to go along with his MVP award. It was a hyped-up sports model, and he asked them if he could swap it for a station wagon. And then he stated his basic creed: "I enjoy my Christian ideals. I believe there's something greater than what we're here for."

Dave Anderson of the New York *Times* asked him, "Do you think there are zone defenses up there?"

And Staubach said, "From what I understand, every pass is a touchdown up there."

"If you're a defensive back," said Dick Young, "every pass wouldn't be a touchdown."

And Staubach said: "They don't have any defensive backs up there."

THE 1971 SEASON
AT A GLANCE

Cowboys 49, Bills 37

At Buffalo, September 19

Dallas	7	21	7	14 — 49
Buffalo	14	10	6	7 — 37

Cowboys—Hill 2 run (Clark kick)
Bills—Moses 73 pass from Shaw (Guthrie kick)
Bills—Simpson 6 run (Guthrie kick)
Cowboys—Hayes 76 pass from Morton (Clark kick)
Cowboys—Garrison 3 run (Clark kick)
Bills—Guthrie 40 field goal
Bills—Briscoe 75 pass from Shaw (Guthrie kick)
Cowboys—Hill 3 run (Clark kick)
Bills—Briscoe 23 pass from Shaw (kick blocked)
Cowboys—Rucker 19 pass from Morton (Clark kick)
Cowboys—Hill 1 run (Clark kick)
Cowboys—Hill 1 run (Clark kick)
Bills—I. Hill 26 pass from Shaw (Guthrie kick)
Attendance—46,206

TEAM STATISTICS

	Cowboys	Bills
First Downs	19	18
Net Yards Gained	371	401
Net Yards Rushing	160	66
Net Yards Passing	211	335
Passes	10–14	18–30
Passes Intercepted By	3	0
Punts, Average	6–40.2	3–33.7
Fumbles, Fumbles Lost	2–1	1–1
Penalties, Yards	13–129	8–95

RUSHING

Cowboys—Hill, 22 for 84, 4 touchdowns; Garrison, 16 for 78, 1 touchdown; Reeves, 1 for 7; Ditka, 1 for minus 9.

Bills—Simpson, 14 for 25, 1 touchdown; Patrick, 7 for 30; Shaw, 1 for 11.

PASSING

Cowboys—Morton, 10 of 14 for 221 yards, 2 touchdowns.

Bills—Shaw, 18 of 30 for 353 yards, 4 touchdowns, 3 interceptions.

RECEIVING

Cowboys—Hill, 4 for 43; Hayes, 2 for 91, 1 touchdown; Ditka, 2 for 35; Garrison, 1 for 33; Rucker, 1 for 19.

Bills—Jones, 5 for 58; Brisco, 3 for 113, 2 touchdowns; White, 3 for 52; R. Chandler, 2 for 16; Patrick, 2 for 11; Moses, 1 for 73, 1 touchdown; I. Hill, 1 for 26, 1 touchdown; Simpson, 1 for 4.

Cowboys 42, Eagles 7

At Philadelphia, September 26

Dallas	0	21	7	14 — 42
Philadelphia	0	0	0	7 — 7

Cowboys—Hill 1 run (Clark kick)
Cowboys—Lilly 7 fumble return (Clark kick)
Cowboys—Garrison 4 pass from Morton (Clark kick)
Cowboys—Richardson, 16 pass from Morton (Clark kick)
Cowboys—Morton 2 run (Clark kick)
Cowboys—Welch 2 run (Clark kick)
Eagles—Nelson 101 FG return (Feller kick)
Attendance—65,358

TEAM STATISTICS

	Cowboys	Eagles
First Downs	23	12
Net Yards Gained	369	170
Net Yards Rushing	150	32
Net Yards Passing	219	138
Passes	19–29	14–36
Passes Intercepted By	7	3
Punts, Average	2–42.5	4–41.3
Fumbles, Fumbles Lost	1–1	1–1
Penalties, Yards	11–120	8–73

RUSHING

Cowboys—Hill, 21 for 80, 1 touchdown; Welch, 5 for 27, 1 touchdown; Williams, 8 for 26; Garrison, 8 for 15; Morton, 1 for 2, 1 touchdown.

Eagles—Bull, 5 for 8; Bouggess, 9 for 7; Bailey, 3 for 7; Arrington, 1 for 6; Hawkins, 1 for 4.

PASSING

Cowboys—Morton, 15 of 22 for 188 yards, 2 touchdowns, 2 interceptions; Reeves, 2 of 3 for 24 yards; Staubach, 2 of 4 for 23 yards, 1 interception.

Eagles—Liske, 11 of 29 for 132 yards, 6 interceptions; Arrington, 3 of 7 for 28 yards, 1 interception.

RECEIVING

Cowboys—Garrison, 7 for 56, 1 touchdown; Richardson, 3 for 43, 1 touchdown; Hill, 3 for 38; Ditka, 3 for 34; Hayes, 2 for 50; Williams, 1 for 14.

Eagles—Bouggess, 4 for 42; Jackson, 4 for 31; Ballman, 2 for 35; Hawkins, 2 for 30; Bull, 1 for 11; Carmichael, 1 for 11.

Cowboys 16, Redskins 20

At Dallas, October 3

Dallas	0	9	0	7 —	16
Washington	7	7	3	3 —	20

Redskins—Harraway 57 run (Knight kick)
Cowboys—Clark 22 field goal
Redskins—Jefferson 50 pass from Kilmer (Knight kick)
Cowboys—Clark 9 field goal
Cowboys—Clark 27 field goal
Redskins—Knight 25 field goal
Redskins—Knight 32 field goal
Cowboys—Hill 1 run (Clark kick)
Attendance—72,000

TEAM STATISTICS

	Cowboys	Redskins
First Downs	20	14
Net Yards Gained	267	285
Net Yards Rushing	82	200
Net Yards Passing	185	85
Passes	17–35	5–10
Passes Intercepted By	1	0
Punts, Average	5–42.6	3–51.0
Fumbles, Fumbles Lost	1–1	3–2
Penalties, Yards	5–35	3–15

RUSHING

Cowboys—Hill, 19 for 65, 1 touchdown; Garrison, 5 for 13; Hayes, 2 for 7; Morton, 2 for 3; Alworth, 1 for minus 6.
Redskins—Harraway, 18 for 111, 1 touchdown; Brown, 21 for 81; Mason, 1 for 6; Kilmer, 1 for 2.

PASSING

Cowboys—Morton, 11 of 26 for 124 yards; Staubach, 6 of 9 for 103 yards.
Redskins—Kilmer, 5 of 10 for 94 yards, 1 touchdown, 1 interception.

RECEIVING

Cowboys—Garrison, 5 for 44; Ditka, 4 for 45; Hayes, 3 for 69; Hill, 3 for 29; Alworth, 1 for 24; Richardson, 1 for 16.
Redskins—Jefferson, 2 for 67, 1 touchdown; Taylor, 2 for 17; Smith, 1 for 10.

Cowboys 20, Giants 13

At Dallas, October 11

Dallas	3	10	7	0 — 20
New York	3	3	0	7 — 13

Cowboys—Clark 42 field goal
Giants—Gogolak 35 field goal
Cowboys—Clark 41 field goal
Giants—Gogolak 20 field goal
Cowboys—Truax 4 pass from Staubach (Clark kick)
Cowboys—Hayes 48 pass from Morton (Clark kick)
Giants—McNeil 24 pass from Tarkenton (Gogolak kick)
Attendance—68,378

TEAM STATISTICS

	Cowboys	Giants
First Downs	21	18
Net Yards Gained	393	332
Net Yards Rushing	214	67
Net Yards Passing	179	265
Passes	11–23	26–46
Passes Intercepted By	0	1
Punts, Average	2–47.0	5–42.8
Fumbles, Fumbles Lost	7–5	5–5
Penalties, Yards	6–80	5–33

RUSHING

Cowboys—Thomas, 9 for 60; Reeves, 8 for 58; Hill, 12 for 48; Staubach, 6 for 23; Garrison, 6 for 19; Morton, 1 for 4; Williams, 3 for 2.

Giants—Duhon, 11 for 28; Morrison, 7 for 27; Tarkenton, 1 for 10; Coffey, 2 for 2.

PASSING

Cowboys—Staubach, 8 of 17 for 106 yards, 1 touchdown; Morton, 3 of 5 for 79 yards, 1 touchdown; Reeves, 0 of 1, 1 interception.

Giants—Tarkenton, 26 of 46 for 294 yards, 1 touchdown.

RECEIVING

Cowboys—Truax, 5 for 76, 1 touchdown; Hayes, 4 for 99, 1 touchdown; Thomas, 1 for 11; Garrison, 1 for minus 1.

Giants—Duhon, 9 for 111; McNeil, 5 for 69, 1 touchdown; Tucker, 5 for 54; Morrison, 3 for 18; Houston, 2 for 41; Coffey, 2 for 1.

Cowboys 14, Saints 24

At New Orleans, October 17

Dallas	0	0	7	7 — 14
New Orleans	7	10	0	7 — 24

Saints—Baker 29 pass from Manning (Durkee kick)
Saints—Durkee 36 field goal
Saints—Manning 13 run (Durkee kick)
Cowboys—Richardson 41 pass from Staubach (Clark kick)
Cowboys—Hayes 16 pass from Staubach (Clark kick)
Saints—Manning 2 run (Durkee kick)
Attendance—83,088

TEAM STATISTICS

	Cowboys	Saints
First Downs	20	10
Net Yards Gained	300	157
Net Yards Rushing	96	108
Net Yards Passing	204	49
Passes	17–34	6–15
Passes Intercepted By	1	3
Punts, Average	5–49.2	7–41.6
Fumbles, Fumbles Lost	3–3	1–1
Penalties, Yards	5–58	7–63

RUSHING

Cowboys—Thomas, 16 for 58; Garrison, 11 for 19; Staubach, 2 for 12; Reeves, 1 for 4; Welch, 1 for 3.
Saints—Manning, 7 for 52, 2 touchdowns; Baker, 12 for 35; Ford, 10 for 19; Granger, 2 for 2.

PASSING

Cowboys—Morton, 10 of 24 for 113 yards, 2 interceptions; Staubach, 7 of 10 for 117 yards, 2 touchdowns, 1 interception.
Saints—Manning, 6 of 15 for 83 yards, 1 touchdown, 1 interception.

RECEIVING

Cowboys—Alworth, 5 for 46; Garrison, 3 for 54; Hayes, 3 for 30, 1 touchdown; Truax, 2 for 38; Ditka, 2 for 23; Richardson, 1 for 41, 1 touchdown; Thomas, 1 for minus 2.
Saints—Dodd, 2 for 28; Abramowicz, 2 for 26; Baker, 1 for 29, 1 touchdown; Granger, 1 for 0.

Cowboys 44, Patriots 21

At Dallas, October 24

Dallas	10	24	0	10 —	44
New England	7	0	0	14 —	21

Cowboys—Thomas 56 run (Clark kick)
Cowboys—Clark 16 field goal
Patriots—Nance 1 run (Gogolak kick)
Cowboys—Staubach 2 run (Clark kick)
Cowboys—Clark 17 field goal
Cowboys—Hayes 35 pass from Staubach (Clark kick)
Cowboys—Hayes 28 pass from Staubach (Clark kick)
Cowboys—Clark 12 field goal
Patriots—Vataha 33 pass from Plunkett (Gogolak kick)
Cowboys—Williams 2 run (Clark kick)
Patriots—Beer 31 pass from Plunkett (Gogolak kick)
Attendance—65,708

TEAM STATISTICS

	Cowboys	Patriots
First Downs	20	17
Net Yards Gained	406	259
Net Yards Rushing	168	76
Net Yards Passing	238	183
Passes	16–25	16–29
Passes Intercepted By	1	0
Punts, Average	3–47.0	6–41.5
Fumbles, Fumbles Lost	2–0	2–2
Penalties, Yards	5–58	4–59

RUSHING

Cowboys—Garrison, 15 for 70; Thomas, 7 for 61, 1 touchdown; Staubach, 2 for 15, 1 touchdown; Welch, 2 for 12; Reeves, 4 for 7; Williams, 3 for 7, 1 touchdown; Alworth, 1 for minus 4.

Patriots—Nance, 9 for 27, 1 touchdown; Garrett, 7 for 22; Plunkett, 2 for 15; Maitland, 4 for 11; Gladieux, 2 for 1.

PASSING

Cowboys—Staubach, 13 of 21 for 197 yards, 2 touchdowns; Morton, 3 of 4 for 44 yards.

Patriots—Plunkett, 16 of 29 for 228 yards, 2 touchdowns, 1 interception.

RECEIVING

Cowboys—Hayes, 3 for 83, 2 touchdowns; Williams, 2 for 45; Alworth, 2 for 38; Adkins, 2 for 24; Ditka, 2 for 20; Garrison, 2 for 1; Truax, 1 for 19; Thomas, 1 for 12; Welch, 1 for minus 1.

Patriots—Vataha, 7 for 107, 1 touchdown; Moss, 2 for 24; Beer, 1 for 31, 1 touchdown; Gladieux, 1 for 25; Sykes, 1 for 15; Sellers, 1 for 12; Bryant, 1 for 11; Garrett, 1 for 6; Nance, 1 for minus 3.

Cowboys 19, Bears 23

At Chicago, October 31

Dallas	7	2	3	7 —	19
Chicago	10	3	3	7 —	23

Cowboys—Thomas 3 run (Clark kick)
Bears—Douglass 9 run (Percival kick)
Bears—Percival 44 field goal.
Bears—Percival 38 field goal
Cowboys—Safety Green tackled in end zone by Welch
Bears—Percival 35 field goal
Cowboys—Clark 10 field goal
Bears—Gordon 28 pass from Douglass (Douglass run)
Cowboys—Richardson 45 pass from Morton (Clark kick)
Attendance—55,049

TEAM STATISTICS

	Cowboys	Bears
First Downs	26	7
Net Yards Gained	481	194
Net Yards Rushing	139	76
Net Yards Passing	342	118
Passes	27–47	7–19
Passes Intercepted By	1	4
Punts, Average	3–48.3	6–37.8
Fumbles, Fumbles Lost	4–3	2–1
Penalties, Yards	7–80	2–10

RUSHING

Cowboys—Thomas, 18 for 65, 1 touchdown; Garrison, 12 for 50; Staubach, 4 for 24.

Bears—Shy, 23 for 62; Grabowski, 3 for 7; Pinder, 1 for 5; Douglass, 5 for 3, 1 touchdown; Tucker, 1 for minus 1.

PASSING

Cowboys—Morton, 20 of 36 for 257 yards, 1 touchdown, 3 interceptions; Staubach, 7 of 11 for 87 yards, 1 interception.

Bears—Douglass, 7 of 19 for 140 yards, 1 touchdown, 1 interception.

RECEIVING

Cowboys—Alworth, 5 for 67; Garrtison, 5 for 29; Hayes, 4 for 62; Ditka, 4 for 52; Thomas, 3 for 19; Adkins, 2 for 29; Reeves, 2 for 22; Richardson, 1 for 45, 1 touchdown; Truax, 1 for 19.

Bears—Gordon, 3 for 58, 1 touchdown; Farmer, 2 for 59; Shy, 1 for 16; Tucker, 1 for 7.

Cowboys 16, Cardinals 13

At St. Louis, November 7

Dallas	3	0	3	10 —	16
St. Louis	0	10	0	3 —	13

Cowboys—Fritsch 27 field goal
Cardinals—Bakken 41 field goal
Cardinals—Williams 11 pass from Hart (Bakken kick)
Cowboys—Fritsch 14 field goal
Cowboys—Ditka 4 pass from Staubach (Reeves run)
Cardinals—Bakken 36 field goal
Cowboys—Fritsch 26 field goal
Attendance—50,486

TEAM STATISTICS

	Cowboys	Cardinals
First Downs	20	11
Net Yards Gained	372	228
Net Yards Rushing	173	36
Net Yards Passing	199	192
Passes	20–31	12–23
Passes Intercepted By	0	0
Punts, Average	4–38.5	4–39.2
Fumbles, Fumbles Lost	0–0	2–1
Penalties, Yards	8–98	5–53

RUSHING

Cowboys—Thomas, 26 for 101; Staubach, 7 for 60, Garrison, 5 for 12.
Cardinals—Roland, 6 for 17; Lane, 4 for 10; Edwards, 4 for 5; Shivers, 2 for 4.

PASSING

Cowboys—Staubach, 20 of 31 for 199 yards, 1 touchdown.
Cardinals—Hart, 12 of 23 for 227 yards, 1 touchdown,

RECEIVING

Cowboys—Alworth, 8 for 89; Garrison, 5 for 49; Ditka, 3 for 13, 1 touchdown; Richardson, 2 for 25; Truax, 2 for 23.
Cardinals—Gilliam, 3 for 67; Lane, 3 for 61; Williams, 2 for 48, 1 touchdown; Smith, 2 for 37; Roland, 2 for 14.

Cowboys 20, Eagles 7

At Dallas, November 14

Dallas	3	7	7	3 — 20
Philadelphia	0	0	0	7 — 7

Cowboys—Fritsch 23 field goal
Cowboys—Thomas 1 run (Fritsch kick)
Cowboys—Thomas 13 run (Fritsch kick)
Cowboys—Fritsch 46 field goal
Eagles—Liske 1 run (Feller kick)
Attendance—60,178

TEAM STATISTICS

	Cowboys	Eagles
First Downs	21	14
Net Yards Gained	308	286
Net Yards Rushing	179	44
Net Yards Passing	129	242
Passes	14–29	23–39
Passes Intercepted By	2	0
Punts, Average	6–45.8	5–41.6
Fumbles, Fumbles Lost	1–1	3–3
Penalties, Yards	10–115	7–104

RUSHING

Cowboys—Staubach, 6 for 90; Thomas, 17 for 57, 2 touchdowns; Garrison, 15 for 32; Reeves, 2 for 0.
Eagles—Arrington, 2 for 14; Baker, 5 for 12; Woodeshick, 3 for 6; Bailey, 1 for 4; Davis, 1 for 3; Hawkins, 1 for 3; Bull, 4 for 1; Liske, 1 for 1, 1 touchdown.

PASSING

Cowboys—Staubach, 14 of 28 for 176 yards; Thomas, 0 of 1.
Eagles—Liske, 13 of 21 for 167 yards, 1 interception; Arrington, 10 of 18 for 91 yards, 1 interception.

RECEIVING

Cowboys—Alworth, 4 for 59; Hayes, 3 for 46; Garrison, 3 for 7; Ditka, 2 for 28; Truax, 1 for 22; Thomas, 1 for 14.
Eagles—Jackson, 8 for 81; Carmichael, 4 for 74; Howkins, 4 for 61; Baker, 3 for 22; Bull, 2 for 8; Kramer, 1 for 10; Davis, 1 for 2.

Cowboys 13, Redskins 0

At Washington, November 21

Dallas	7	0	3	3 — 13
Washington	0	0	0	0 — 0

Cowboys—Staubach 29 run (Clark kick)
Cowboys—Clark 26 field goal
Cowboys—Clark 48 field goal
Attendance—53,041

TEAM STATISTICS

	Cowboys	Redskins
First Downs	16	15
Net Yards Gained	279	232
Net Yards Rushing	146	65
Net Yards Passing	133	167
Passes	11–21	19–32
Passes Intercepted By	2	0
Punts, Average	4–38.0	4–43.2
Fumbles, Fumbles Lost	2–1	1–0
Penalties, Yards	6–30	3–50

RUSHING

Cowboys—Thomas, 20 for 53; Staubach, 5 for 49, 1 touchdown; Garrison, 10 for 38; Hill, 2 for 6.
Redskins—Brown, 11 for 27; Harraway, 9 for 27; Jurgensen, 1 for 11.

PASSING

Cowboys—Staubach, 11 of 21 for 151 yards.
Redskins—Kilmer, 10 of 16 for 118 yards; Jurgensen, 9 of 16 for 76 yards.

RECEIVING

Cowboys—Garrison, 4 for 48; Hayes, 2 for 40; Truax, 2 for 27; Alworth, 1 for 25; Ditka, 1 for 8; Reeves, 1 for 3.
Redskins—Dowler, 5 for 52; Harraway, 4 for 16; Jefferson, 3 for 51; Brown, 3 for 41; Mason, 3 for 30; McNeill, 1 for 4.

Cowboys 28, Rams 21

At Dallas, November 25

Dallas	7	7	7	7 —	28
Los Angeles	14	0	7	0 —	21

Cowboys—I. Thomas 89 kickoff return (Clark kick)
Rams—Smith 1 run (Ray kick)
Rams—Klein 33 pass from Gabriel (Ray kick)
Cowboys—Hayes 51 pass from Staubach (Clark kick)
Cowboys—Alworth 21 pass from Staubach (Clark kick)
Rams—Curran 2 pass from Gabriel (Ray kick)
Cowboys—D. Thomas 5 run (Clark kick)
Attendance—66,595

TEAM STATISTICS

	Cowboys	Rams
First Downs	15	21
Net Yards Gained	278	301
Net Yards Rushing	112	74
Net Yards Passing	166	227
Passes	8–14	20–35
Passes Intercepted By	1	0
Punts, Average	6–40.1	4–51.0
Fumbles, Fumbles Lost	1–0	5–2
Penalties, Yards	4–25	3–35

RUSHING

Cowboys—Thomas, 14 for 49, 1 touchdown; Staubach, 6 for 33; Garrison, 13 for 30.
Rams—Ellison, 13 for 30; Smith, 7 for 25, 1 touchdown; Josephson, 7 for 16; Gabriel, 4 for 4; Rentzel, 2 for minus 1.

PASSING

Cowboys—Staubach, 8 of 14 for 176 yards, 2 touchdowns.
Rams—Gabriel, 20 of 35 for 234 yards, 2 touchdowns, 1 interception; Rhome, 0 of 1.

RECEIVING

Cowboys—Garrison, 3 for 71; Alworth, 2 for 34, 1 touchdown; Thomas, 2 for 20; Hayes, 1 for 51, 1 touchdown.
Rams—Snow, 5 for 77; Josephson, 5 for 35; L. Smith, 4 for 32; Klein, 3 for 50, 1 touchdown; Rentzel, 1 for 41; Curran, 1 for 2, 1 touchdown; Ellison, 1 for minus 3.

Cowboys 52, Jets 10

At Dallas, December 4

Dallas	28	10	7	7 — 52
New York	0	3	7	0 — 10

Cowboys—I. Thomas 101 kickoff return (Clark kick)
Cowboys—Hill 27 pass from Staubach (Clark kick)
Cowboys—Hill 27 pass from Staubach (Clark kick)
Cowboys—D. Thomas 3 run (Clark kick)
Cowboys—Hill 9 run (Clark kick)
Jets—Howfield 35 field goal
Cowboys—Clark 45 field goal
Cowboys—D. Thomas 18 pass from Staubach (Clark kick)
Jets—Nock 1 pass from Davis (Howfield kick)
Cowboys—Alworth 20 pass from Morton (Clark kick)
Attendance—66,689

TEAM STATISTICS

	Cowboys	Jets
First Downs	26	12
Net Yards Gained	439	149
Net Yards Rushing	218	130
Net Yards Passing	221	19
Passes	14–21	6–20
Passes Intercepted By	3	0
Punts, Average	2–23.0	3–41.3
Fumbles, Fumbles Lost	1–1	4–3
Penalties, Yards	3–34	2–20

RUSHING

Cowboys—Thomas, 14 for 112, 1 touchdown; Hill, 11 for 62, 1 touchdown; Williams, 7 for 32; Welch, 4 for 9; Staubach, 1 for 3.

Jets—Davis, 3 for 37; Riggins, 13 for 36; Harkey, 9 for 31; Boozer, 2 for 12; Nock, 2 for 8; McClain, 1 for 6.

PASSING

Cowboys—Staubach, 10 of 15 for 168 yards, 3 touchdowns; Morton, 4 of 6 for 75 yards, 1 touchdown.

Jets—Davis, 5 of 15 for 7 yards, 1 touchdown, 2 interceptions; Namath, 1 of 5 for 20 yards, 1 interception.

RECEIVING

Cowboys—Hill, 4 for 80, 2 touchdowns; Ditka, 4 for 64; Alworth, 3 for 54, 1 touchdown; Hayes, 1 for 19; Thomas, 1 for 18, 1 touchdown; Truax, 1 for 8.

Jets—Riggins, 3 for 2; Maynard, 1 for 20; Caster, 1 for 4; Nock, 1 for 1, 1 touchdown.

Cowboys 42, Giants 14

At New York, December 12

Dallas	14	14	14	0 —	42
New York	0	7	0	7 —	14

Cowboys—Hayes 46 pass from Staubach (Clark kick)
Cowboys—Thomas 3 run (Clark kick)
Cowboys—Hill 10 pass from Staubach (Clark kick)
Cowboys—Hayes 85 pass from Staubach (Clark kick)
Giants—Hermann 6 pass from Tarkenton (Gogolak kick)
Cowboys—Thomas 7 run (Clark kick)
Cowboys—Hill 4 run (Clark kick)
Giants—Athas 37 interception return (Gogolak kick)
Attendance—62,815

TEAM STATISTICS

	Cowboys	Giants
First Downs	23	17
Net Yards Gained	439	247
Net Yards Rushing	197	64
Net Yards Passing	242	183
Passes	12–22	25–43
Passes Intercepted By	2	2
Punts, Average	4–35.5	6–41.5
Fumbles, Fumbles Lost	1–1	5–2
Penalties, Yards	3–25	2–12

RUSHING

Cowboys—Thomas, 16 for 94, 2 touchdowns; Hill, 13 for 89, 1 touchdown; Hayes, 1 for 11; Reeves, 1 for 3; Welch, 2 for 0.

Giants—Thompson, 8 for 35; Coffey, 5 for 16; Johnson, 1 for 10; Morrison, 2 for 3; Frederickson, 2 for 0.

PASSING

Cowboys—Staubach, 10 of 14 for 232 yards, 3 touchdowns; Morton, 2 of 6 for 30 yards, 1 interception, Hill, 0 of 1, 1 interception; Reeves, 0 of 1.

Giants—Tarkenton, 17 of 29 for 151 yards, 1 touchdown, 2 interceptions; Johnson, 8 of 14 for 74 yards.

RECEIVING

Cowboys—Hayes, 4 for 154, 2 touchdowns; Hill, 4 for 50, 1 touchdown; Ditka, 2 for 32; Alworth, 2 for 26.

Giants—Hermann, 7 for 91, 1 touchdown; Thompson, 6 for 37; Tucker, 5 for 54; Morrison, 5 for 35; Coffey, 2 for 8.

Cowboys 31, Cardinals 12

At Dallas, December 18

Dallas	7	14	0	10 —	31
St. Louis	0	6	6	0 —	12

Cowboys—Thomas 53 run (Clark kick)
Cowboys—Thomas 3 run (Clark kick)
Cardinals—Bakken 33 field goal
Cowboys—Thomas 34 pass from Staubach (Clark kick)
Cardinals—Bakken 29 field goal
Cardinals—Bakken 23 field foal
Cardinals—Bakken 35 field goal
Cowboys—Clark 24 field goal
Cowboys—Thomas 3 run (Clark kick)
Attendance—66,672

TEAM STATISTICS

	Cowboys	Cardinals
First Downs	18	14
Net Yards Gained	323	215
Net Yards Rushing	205	88
Net Yards Passing	118	127
Passes	10–16	12–43
Passes Intercepted By	1	1
Punts, Average	4–38.5	5–36.4
Fumbles, Fumbles Lost	4–3	5–1
Penalties, Yards	8–60	2–20

RUSHING

Cowboys—Thomas, 18 for 83, 3 touchdowns; Garrison, 11 for 53; Hill, 6 for 34; Staubach, 2 for 24; Ditka, 1 for 11.
Cardinals—Edwards, 20 for 65; Gilliam, 1 for 12, Roland, 5 for 11.

PASSING

Cowboys—Staubach, 10 of 16 for 147 yards, 1 touchdown, 1 interception.
Cardinals—Hart, 11 of 36 for 141 yards, 1 interception; Beathard, 1 of 7 for 2 yards.

RECEIVING

Cowboys—Thomas, 3 for 61, 1 touchdown; Hayes, 3 for 46; Alworth, 1 for 25; Ditka, 1 for 6; Garrison, 1 for 5; Hill, 1 for 4.
Cardinals—Gilliam, 4 for 49; Gray, 2 for 49; Hyatt, 2 for 24; Roland, 2 for 11; Edwards, 2 for 10.

NATIONAL CONFERENCE
PLAYOFF GAME

Cowboys 20, Vikings 12

At Bloomington, Minnesota, December 25

Dallas	3	3	14	0 —	20
Minnesota	0	3	0	9 —	12

Cowboys—Clark 26 field goal
Vikings—Cox 27 field goal
Cowboys—Clark 44 field goal
Cowboys—D. Thomas 13 run (Clark kick)
Cowboys—Hayes 9 pass from Staubach (Clark kick)
Vikings—Safety (Staubach tackled by Page in end zone)
Vikings—Voigt 6 pass from Cuozzo (Cox kick)

TEAM STATISTICS

	Cowboys	Vikings
First Downs	10	17
Net Yards Gained	183	311
Net Yards Rushing	98	101
Net Yards Passing	85	210
Passes	10–14	19–38
Passes Intercepted By	4	0
Punts, Average	7–37.0	4–43.5
Fumbles, Fumbles Lost	0–0	1–1
Penalties, Yards	2–10	2–18

RUSHING

Cowboys—D. Thomas, 21 for 66, 1 touchdown; Hill, 14 for 28; Staubach, 2 for 2; Garrison, 2 for 2.

Vikings—Jones, 15 for 52; Osborn, 6 for 13; Lee, 3 for 28; Grim, 1 for 2; Lindsey, 1 for 6.

PASSING

Cowboys—Staubach, 10 of 14 for 99 yards, 1 touchdown.

Vikings—Lee, 7 of 16 for 86 yards, 2 interceptions; Cuozzo, 12 of 22 for 124 yards, 1 touchdown, 2 interceptions.

RECEIVING

Cowboys—Hayes, 3 for 31, 1 touchdown; Alworth, 2 for 33; I. Thomas, 1 for 3; Hill, 2 for 14; Ditka, 2 for 18.

Vikings—Washington, 5 for 70; Grim, 4 for 74; Reed, 4 for minus 3; Voigt, 4 for 46, 1 touchdown; White, 1 for minus 2; Lindsey, 1 for 25.

NATIONAL CONFERENCE
CHAMPIONSHIP GAME

Cowboys 14, 49ers 3

At Dallas, January 2

San Francisco	0	0	3	0 —	3
Dallas	0	7	0	7 —	14

Cowboys—Hill 1 run (Clark kick)
49ers—Gossett 28 field goal
Cowboys—D. Thomas 2 run (Clark kick)

TEAM STATISTICS

	Cowboys	49ers
First Downs	16	9
Net Yards Gained	244	239
Net Yards Rushing	172	61
Net Yards Passing	72	178
Passes	9–18	14–30
Passes Intercepted By	3	0
Punts, Average	6–45.0	6–38.1
Fumbles, Fumbles Lost	2–1	0–0
Penalties, Yards	2–30	1–12

RUSHING

Cowboys—D. Thomas, 15 for 44, 1 touchdown; Hill, 9 for 21, 1 touchdown; Staubach, 8 for 58; Garrison, 14 for 52.
49ers—V. Washington, 10 for 58; Willard, 6 for 3.

PASSING

Cowboys—Staubach, 9 of 18 for 103 yards.
49ers—Brodie, 14 of 30 for 184 yards, 3 interceptions.

RECEIVING

Cowboys—Hayes, 2 for 22; Truax, 2 for 43; Alworth, 1 for 17; Ditka, 1 for 5; Thomas, 1 for 7; Garrison, 1 for minus 8; Reeves, 1 for 17.
49ers—G. Washington, 4 for 88; Kwalick, 4 for 52; V. Washington, 3 for 28; Witcher, 1 for 6; Willard, 1 for 6; Cunningham, 1 for 4.

NATIONAL FOOTBALL LEAGUE
CHAMPIONSHIP GAME

Cowboys 24, Dolphins 3

At New Orleans, January 16

Dallas	3	7	7	7 — 24
Miami	0	3	0	0 — 3

Cowboys—Clark 9 field goal
Cowboys—Alworth 7 pass from Staubach (Clark kick)
Dolphins—Yepremian 31 field goal
Cowboys—D. Thomas 3 run (Clark kick)
Cowboys—Ditka 7 pass from Staubach (Clark kick)

TEAM STATISTICS

	Cowboys	Dolphins
First Downs	23	10
Net Yards Gained	352	185
Net Yards Rushing	252	80
Net Yards Passing	100	105
Passes	12–19	12–23
Passes Intercepted By	1	0
Punts, Average	5–37.2	5–40.0
Fumbles, Fumbles Lost	1–1	2–2
Penalties, Yards	3–15	0–0

RUSHING

Cowboys—D. Thomas, 19 for 95, 1 touchdown; Garrison, 14 for 74; Staubach, 5 for 18; Hill, 7 for 25; Hayes, 1 for 16; Reeves, 1 for 7; Ditka, 1 for 17.
Dolphins—Kiick, 7 for 40; Csonka, 9 for 40; Griese, 1 for 0.

PASSING

Cowboys—Staubach, 12 of 19 for 119 yards, 2 touchdowns.
Dolphins—Griese, 12 of 23 for 134 yards.

RECEIVING

Cowboys—D. Thomas, 3 for 17; Hayes, 2 for 23; Alworth, 2 for 28, 1 touchdown; Garrison, 2 for 11; Ditka, 2 for 28, 1 touchdown; Hill, 1 for 12.
Dolphins—Warfield, 4 for 39; Kiick, 3 for 21; Hill, 2 for 18; Twilley, 1 for 20; Fleming, 1 for 27; Mandich, 1 for 9; Csonka, 2 for 18.

THE CHAMPIONSHIP SQUAD

Name	Pos.	Ht.	Wt.	Age	Yr.	College	Games in 1971
Adderley, Herb	CB	6-1	200	33	12	Michigan State	12
Adkins, Margene	WR	5-10	183	24	2	Henderson JC	3
Alworth, Lance	WR	6-0	180	32	11	Arkansas	12
Andrie, George	DE	6-6	250	32	11	Marquette	14
Asher, Bob (1)	T	6-5	250	24	2	Vanderbilt	0
Caffey, Lee Roy	LB	6-3	240	31	10	Texas A&M	6
Clark, Mike	K	6-1	205	31	10	Texas A&M	12
Cole, Larry	DE	6-4	250	26	5	Hawaii	14
Ditka, Mike	TE	6-3	213	32	12	Pittsburgh	14
Edwards, Dave	LB	6-1	225	32	10	Auburn	14
Fitzgerald, John	C	6-5	250	24	2	Boston College	14
Flowers, Richmond	S	6-0	180	25	4	Tennessee	4
Fritsch, Toni	K	5-7	185	27	2	None	2
Garrison, Walt	RB	6-0	205	28	7	Oklahoma State	13
Green, Cornell	S	6-3	208	32	11	Utah State	14
Gregg, Forrest	OT	6-4	250	37	15	SMU	4
Gregory, Bill	DT	6-5	255	22	2	Wisconsin	14
Harris, Cliff	S	6-0	184	23	3	Ouachita	14
Hayes, Bob	WR	5-11	185	29	8	Florida A&M	14
Hill, Calvin	RB	6-4	227	25	4	Yale	8
Howley, Chuck	LB	6-2	225	36	14	West Virginia	14
Jordan, Lee Roy	LB	6-1	221	31	10	Alabama	14
Lewis, D. D.	LB	6-1	225	26	4	Mississippi State	14
Lilly, Bob	DT	6-5	260	33	12	TCU	14
Liscio, Tony	T	6-5	255	32	9	Tulsa	5
Manders, Dave	C	6-2	250	31	8	Michigan State	14
Morton, Craig	QB	6-4	214	29	8	California	10
Neely, Ralph	T	6-6	265	28	8	Oklahoma	7
Niland, John	G	6-3	245	28	7	Iowa	14
Nye, Blaine	G	6-4	251	26	5	Stanford	14
Pugh, Jethro	DT	6-6	260	28	8	Elizabeth City	12
Reeves, Dan	RB	6-1	200	28	8	South Carolina	14
Renfro, Mel	CB	6-0	190	30	9	Oregon	14
Richardson, Gloster	WR	6-2	200	30	6	Jackson State	11
Rucker, Reggie	WR	6-2	190	24	2	Boston U.	4
Smith, Tody	DE	6-5	245	23	2	So. California	7
Staubach, Roger	QB	6-3	197	30	4	Navy	13
Stincic, Tom	LB	6-4	230	25	4	Michigan	7
Talbert, Don	T	6-5	255	32	9	Texas	9
Thomas, Duane	RB	6-1	205	25	3	W. Texas State	11
Thomas, Isaac	CB	6-2	193	24	2	Bishop	7
Toomay, Pat	DE	6-5	244	24	3	Vanderbilt	14
Truax, Billy	TE	6-5	240	29	9	LSU	12
Wallace, Rodney	G	6-5	255	23	2	New Mexico	11
Washington, Mark	CB	5-10	188	24	3	Morgan State	2
Waters, Charlie	S	6-1	193	23	2	Clemson	14
Welch, Claxton	RB	5-11	203	25	4	Oregon	14
Widby, Ron	P	6-4	210	27	5	Tennessee	14
Williams, Joe	RB	6-0	193	25	2	Wyoming	12
Wright, Rayfield	T	6-6	255	27	6	Ft. Valley State	14

(1) Missed entire 1971 season because of injury